YORK HANDB

GENERAL EDITOR:
Professor A.N. Jeffares
(University of Stirling)

AN A·B·C OF SHAKESPEARE

His Plays, Theatre, Life and Times

P. C. Bayley

MA (OXFORD)
Professor Emeritus of the University of St Andrews

LONGMAN
YORK PRESS

The illustration of 'A conjectural reconstruction of the Globe' (PLATE 3)
is from *The Globe Restored in Theatre: A Way of Seeing* by C. Walter
Hodges, published by Oxford University Press. © Oxford University Press

PLATE 1, 2 and 4: The Mansell Collection

YORK PRESS
Immeuble Esseily, Place Riad Solh, Beirut.

LONGMAN GROUP UK LIMITED
Longman House, Burnt Mill, Harlow,
Essex CM20 2JE, England
Associated companies, branches and representatives
throughout the world

© Librairie du Liban 1985

All rights reserved; no part of this publication may be
reproduced, stored in a retrieval system, or transmitted
in any form or by any means, electronic, mechanical,
photocopying, recording, or otherwise, without
the prior written permission of the copyright owner.

First published 1985
Fourth impression 1991

ISBN 0-582-02250-9

Produced by Longman Group (FE) Ltd.
Printed in Hong Kong

Contents

PLATES

For Nicholas, Rosalind and Clare

Preface

This book is intended for students, teachers, readers and theatre-goers. There has always been a need for a compact reference book in which could be found reliable and up-to-date information on Shakespeare, his plays, his theatre, his life, his times: about the editing and the publishing of the plays, and about the playhouses in which they were presented; about his reading; about the influences on him – the earlier English drama, mystery cycles, moralities and interludes; Roman comedy, Senecan tragedy, romances, pastoral, *commedia dell'arte*, masques, homilies, the Bible; about his times and about his contemporaries and what they thought, for example, about Jews, Moors, ghosts, order, kingship, the Wars of the Roses. I have tried to meet all these needs and others in this *ABC of Shakespeare*. In addition I give complete and detailed summaries of all the plays act by act, with information about their texts, probable date and chief sources.

I have cross-referenced generously to make the book easier to consult (although it has meant some repetition of material at times), using the symbol □ as a signal. This indicates that the word or words it follows has a separate entry elsewhere. Since Shakespeare's name and play titles are very frequently mentioned, however, the symbol has been omitted in these cases.

Where I quote it is from the Arden Shakespeare editions of the separate plays, in one case (*All's Well That Ends Well*) modernising the spelling of two names.

Of course there are the magisterial *Shakespeare Encyclopaedia* edited by O. J. Campbell and E. G. Quinn (see Select Bibliography) and F. E. Halliday's *A Shakespeare Companion 1550–1950*, Duckworth, London, 1952, which I have often consulted, but both are large volumes and my emphases are rather different. They will be found invaluable, especially the former, by those seeking more information and scholarly detail, especially about Shakespeare's contemporaries and on historical fact.

I am grateful to the General Editor, Professor A. N. Jeffares, for his generous encouragement and support and to Mrs Patricia Richardson for much typing and for helpful comments.

St. Andrews   P. C. BAYLEY
April 1984

MR. WILLIAM

SHAKESPEARES

COMEDIES,
HISTORIES, &
TRAGEDIES.

Publiſhed according to the True Originall Copies.

LONDON
Printed by Iſaac Iaggard, and Ed. Blount. 1623.

PLATE 1: The title page from a copy of the First Folio, with the engraving of Shakespeare by Martin Droeshout.

A

Act and scene division. The practice of dividing a play into acts and scenes derived from the Greek drama and was known to sixteenth-century England from the plays of the dramatist Seneca□ (*c*.4BC–AD65), whose work was well known because it was studied in grammar schools and seen in translations in the Elizabethan theatre. But it is believed that in the Elizabethan theatre there were no breaks in the performance of a play and the Quartos□ of Shakespeare's plays have no divisions except a few markings in three of the 'bad' quartos. However, in the First Folio□ (1623) the majority are divided into acts and scenes. Shakespeare seems to have been conscious of 'five-act structure' because there are five appearances of the Chorus□ in *Henry V*, and of Gower,□ a chorus-figure, in *Pericles*, and they have the effect of dividing those plays into five acts. The early play *Gorboduc*□ (1562) was in five acts and had a sort of classical Chorus, of old men. Most modern editions of Shakespeare follow the scene divisions of the eighteenth-century editors, Nicholas Rowe and Alexander Pope.

Acting. Until the building of the covered theatres (see Playhouses□) Elizabethan actors□ appeared in the open air in daylight, and had little help from scenery and none from lighting, and they played to large audiences.□ To begin with, acting was stylised with elaborate conventional gestures, the actor being more concerned to represent actions by mime, movement and gesture than to interpret character. Early plays in any case did not demand much in the way of characterisation. Hamlet's advice to the players (III.2.20 ff.) suggests that Shakespeare expected greater naturalness, and it is difficult to believe that the subtlety of his characterisation and poetry did not produce subtle, sensitive and 'natural' acting which held 'the mirror up to nature'. Actors – all male – were very well trained from youth, being apprenticed for several years. The wonderful female roles, all played by boys or young men, must have required that; and the scores of parts of great variety, complexity and emotional depth created by Shakespeare would not have been written if there had not been extremely well-trained and skilled professionals to portray them.

Actors. The development of acting as a full-time organised profession was rapid, taking place virtually during the reign of Queen Elizabeth□ (1558–1603). Drama had developed over about two centuries from occasional amateur activity by members of trade-guilds in some towns (notably York, Chester, Wakefield and Coventry) performing annually the mystery cycles□ of short plays which covered the chief incidents of the Bible from the Creation of the world to the Ascension of Christ. There had been travelling players, some of whom had gradually been taken under the patronage of nobles. This last became necessary because 'Common players in interludes□ . . . not belonging to any Baron of this realm' were classed as 'rogues and vagabonds'. Authorities in big cities, and in London especially, were hostile towards theatrical performances because they attracted crowds which might cause disturbances. In 1574 the City of London authorities drew up regulations to control theatrical activity, and despite occasional attempts on the part of the authorities to prohibit actors from acting or else to prohibit people ('servants, apprentices, journeymen, or children') from attending, the profession quickly established and organised itself. It was greatly helped by the fact that, some time between the granting of the first royal patent (or authority, permission) in 1574 to the Earl of Leicester's Men and 1597, the monarch, through the Lord Chamberlain and the Master of the Revels□ (who were distinguished officials of the Royal Household) took over complete control of theatrical activity in the capital.

By 1597 the four original companies had been added to by the Queen's Men, the Admiral's Men, Lord Strange's Men and in 1594 the Lord Chamberlain's Men,□ of which Shakespeare was a member. There were children's companies, the best known being the Children of the Chapel and the Children of Paul's (St Paul's Cathedral Choir-school) which had both grown out of choir-schools which had occasionally performed plays and now did so regularly. The children's companies performed in roofed indoor theatres.

Actors' companies. Companies of boy actors from the Chapel Royal, St Paul's Cathedral and some of the London schools were active in the world of the drama in the early days of Elizabeth's reign. Well-trained in music and speech and well-educated, they performed before the Court, the Inns of Court□ and in general for educated upper-class audiences. They performed rather academic learned plays or sophisticated comedies such as those John Lyly□ wrote for them. Eventually they played in their own theatres. After the building of the first proper theatres in 1576 (The Theatre, the Curtain), the adult companies began to dominate and the popular drama to flourish. The Queen's Men, under Elizabeth's patronage, were formed in 1583, the Lord Chamberlain's Men□ in 1594, Shakespeare and Richard Burbage□ being members of it, until in 1603 the company came under the patronage of the new king, James I, and was known as the King's Men.

The organisation of theatres and companies was not uniform. Some theatres were owned and run fairly despotically, for example, the Fortune Theatre controlled by Philip Henslowe□ and Edward Alleyn,□ the other great Elizabethan actor and rival of Burbage. But members of Shakespeare's company, including the great dramatist, were not only 'sharers'□ in the company but 'housekeepers'□ of the theatre. Burbage and his brother owned half of the shares, and five members of the company (Shakespeare, Heminge□, Will Kempe the comedian and two others) owned the other half. The seven 'house-keepers' shared proportionately in the cost of rent and maintenance, and received proportionate shares of the receipts, as well as being paid as players. In fact they also enjoyed some emoluments as 'Grooms of the Chamber' at court under the Lord Chamberlain, receiving livery (uniform) for ceremonial duties as well as for more ordinary use. No records of the Lord Chamberlain's Men survive, but records of Henslowe's company, the Admiral's Men, show a very large repertory of about thirty plays performed in six months, there being altogether 150 performances of them in that time. Alleyn, their chief actor, played seventy different parts in a three-year period. The best companies were engaged to play at court from time to time, especially during the Christmas festivities and when foreign dignitaries visited London, and Shakespeare's company was summoned to perform twice as often as any other company. The London companies (as distinct from travell-ing companies which for economy seldom numbered more than six to eight players) had a nucleus of between eight and twelve players, plus stagekeepers and hands, musicians and costume-keepers. Many plays needed twenty or more actors, made up by temporarily hired men. During the season a repertory of plays was performed six days a week.

Alleyn, Edward (1566-1626). The two great Elizabethan/Jacobean actors were Alleyn and Richard Burbage,□ who served respectively the two greatest acting companies, the Lord Chamberlain's Men,□ later the King's, and the Admiral's Men. Alleyn's company, the Admiral's, played in Henslowe's□ theatre, The Rose, and later in The Fortune. Their principal and most famous writer was Christopher Marlowe,□ but they also had plays by Peele and Greene□ among others. They also toured extensively. Philip Henslowe was the chief shareholder/owner, and his *Diary* (ed. W. W. Greg, 1904–8) gives the fullest details we have of the work of an acting company of the time. Alleyn's chief parts were Dr Faustus, Tamburlaine and Barabas. He retired from acting in 1605 and founded what became known as Dulwich College, south of London; the school still has in its library Alleyn's and Henslowe's papers. Alleyn is recorded as 'stalking and roaring' in the great parts by Marlowe that he created; his rival, Burbage, was a more restrained and naturalistic actor – but Marlowe's plays demanded more of the former, and Shakespeare's more of the latter.

All's Well That Ends Well. One of the 'middle' comedies, dating probably from about 1602–3.

Act I: Bertram, who on the recent death of his father has become Count of Rousillon, is made the ward of the King of France and sum-moned to the Court in Paris. (That the King becomes his guardian means that Bertram is less than twenty-one years old, and his youthfulness and immaturity are important in the play.) The King is ill, and apparently dying. Helena, the orphaned daughter of a great physician and healer, has been cared for by Bertram's mother, the Countess of Rousillon, in her household. After Bertram has left for Paris, accompanied by Lafeu, an elderly lord, and by Parolles, the young Count's lying, bragging, wastrel companion, we learn that Helena is secretly in love with Bertram but has always felt that her rank in society is too low for her love to be returned. The Countess discovers from Helena that she loves her son, and is glad of it. Helena has already decided to go to the court in an attempt to heal the King, and she has a remedy for his illness among the prescriptions left by her doctor father. The relationship between the Countess and Helena is charmingly affectionate, and the former encourages her in her journeying to Paris and wishes her success – by implication not only in healing the King but in winning the love of her son.

Act II: At the court in Paris young noblemen are leaving to take part in the Florentine wars, but the ailing King has refused Bertram permission to go because he is too young. The Lord Lafeu asks the King to see Helena, who has just arrived. She persuades the King to let her try to cure him, with God's help and her late father's remedy. If successful, she asks as reward to be allowed to choose a husband from among the unmarried courtiers. She is successful in healing the King, and he gratefully offers her the choice among the bachelors of the court. She of course chooses Bertram, who scornfully objects, complaining of Helena's lowly rank. Seeing the young Count's sullen unwillingness, she is prepared to give up, saying that she is content that at least the King's health is restored; but the King insists on Bertram's acceptance of her, and they are married. Bertram, encouraged by Parolles, decides to abandon her and go off to the wars in Tuscany. Lafeu briefly warns Bertram of Parolles ('There can be no kernel in this light nut'), the young Count abruptly leaves Helena before the wedding night, ordering her to return home, and sets off for Florence with his worthless companion Parolles.

Act III: Helena returns sadly to Rousillon. She receives a letter from Bertram stating that he will never be her husband *in fact* until she can get hold of a ring which he always wears and have a child by him. (This is the 'impossible task', as in folk-tales and fairy-stories, the achieving of which will resolve the plot.) The Countess, now her mother-in-law, is angry at Bertram's selfish and cruel behaviour, but Helena, anxious only because he has put himself at risk in going to the wars because of being forced to marry her, decides to leave Rousillon. Disguised as a pilgrim she goes to Florence. She meets an old widow with whom she lodges, and learns from her that Parolles has attempted to procure her virtuous daughter Diana for Bertram. She also hears that Bertram has abandoned his unwanted wife. Bertram is now persuaded by two other French lords that Parolles is a coward and liar, and the three decide to play a trick upon him. A second trick is being arranged: Helena convinces the widow that she is the rejected wife of Bertram, and persuades her to tell her daughter Diana to seem to agree to Bertram's lustful proposals, to ask for the ring he wears as payment, and then to make an appointment with him at which she will give in to him, but Helena will take her place in bed.

Act IV: Parolles is encouraged to set out to regain a drum seized by the enemy. His comrades lie in wait, and, as they anticipate, find that the cowardly fellow is only going to pretend to have tried to regain the drum. They seize and blindfold him, speaking in an absurd pretended foreign language, and Parolles is soon exposed as a coward and is lured into slandering Bertram before they reveal themselves. Meanwhile, the other 'trick' has been played: Diana had secured Bertram's ring and made an appointment for midnight, and we learn soon that Helena has taken her place unrecognised, received the ring, slept with him and given him a ring. Helena now tells the widow that Bertram has been told of her (Helena's) death and is on his way home.

Act V: Helena goes to Marseilles, where she has heard the King is, but learns that he has left for Rousillon. Here all believe Helena to be dead, and all mourn, but also forgive Bertram, led by the King. Lafeu's daughter is to be the repentant Bertram's second wife, and Bertram gives the old lord a ring for her. It is immediately recognised as Helena's – given to her by the King. Bertram lies about the ring (which Helena had given to Bertram the night she slept with him when he supposed her to be Diana), saying it had been thrown to him from a window by a Florentine lady. This leads the King to suspect that Bertram has killed Helena, and so he is arrested. At this point, Diana arrives with her mother and accuses Bertram of having seduced her, promised to marry her and then abandoned her. Enraged with this, Bertram denies it, slanders Diana, and there follows a riddling scene in which Diana shows as proof the ring Bertram had given her and offers to give it back in return for the one he had been given at night supposedly by her but in fact by Helena. She manages to evade questions from the King about how she came by it, which angers the King, who orders her to be imprisoned. She declares that Bertram had defiled her bed, without 'harming' her, and at that same time got his own wife with child. Here Helena enters and the mystery is cleared up. A swiftly repentant Bertram – 'I'll love her dearly, ever, ever dearly' – is immediately forgiven by Helena.

SOURCES The main plot of Bertram and Helena is from Boccaccio's☐ (1313–75) *Decameron* (about 1350), the ninth *novella* of the third day, the story of Beltramo de Rossiglione and Giglietta de Narbone; but Shakespeare almost certainly used a later version, either the English translation by William Painter☐ (?1540–94) in his *Palace of Pleasure* (1566) or a French version (published 1545) by Antoine le Maçon, or both. Much remains of the basic medieval narratives which long antedated Boccaccio. There is the story of morality or virtue, in which a woman's love and constancy survive the scorn or neglect of a lover or husband and bring the reward of acceptance and happiness; the story of an 'impossible task', common in folk-tales and fairy-stories; and the story of the 'clever wench' who is able to fulfil impossible conditions imposed by a husband before he will consummate the marriage. The 'bed-trick', another popular medieval plot, cleverly brings all these together.

Shakespeare, as always, made changes from his source material, chiefly in compressing the time the story occupies and in inventing characters: the Countess and her Clown, Lord Lafeu, and Parolles. He also invented the comic sub-plot of the exposure of Parolles as coward and liar.

TEXT   The play appears only in the First Folio☐ (1623), there being no earlier printed version.

Anti-masque. A part of a masque,☐ often humorous or grotesque, making a contrast to the main action or argument and providing a relief, often light relief, to it.

Antony and Cleopatra. A late tragedy on the historical love-story of Mark Antony and the Egyptian queen Cleopatra. It dates from 1607 or early 1608.

Act I: Antony, a great soldier and one of the three triumvirs (that is, the three men, Octavius Caesar, Antony and Lepidus, who ruled the Roman empire), is neglecting his duty in Alexandria, besotted like a young lover with Cleopatra. When he learns of gathering trouble in Rome and then of his wife Fulvia's death, his conscience is stirred and he resolves to return to Rome ('These strong Egyptian fetters I must break,/or lose myself in dotage.'). His friend and favoured officer Enobarbus tells Antony that his departure will destroy Cleopatra, but he determines to go. Cleopatra theatrically taunts and reviles him but finally wishes him victory and success.

Act II: In Rome, Lepidus acts as peace-maker as Octavius Caesar charges Antony with ignoring his messages as well as with general disregard of his duties. The general, Agrippa, proposes a marriage between Antony and Caesar's sister Octavia, to which Antony agrees. They discuss the threat posed by Pompey briefly before going off to meet Octavia and then to arm. Enobarbus describes to Agrippa and to Maecenas, another officer, life in Egypt and, above all, the wonder and fascination of Cleopatra ('Age cannot wither her, nor custom stale,/ Her infinite variety.'). After a brief scene of amity with Caesar and Octavia, Antony is visited by an Egyptian soothsayer, and we hear him longing for Cleopatra, and saying 'Though I make this marriage for my peace,/ I' the east my pleasure lies.' In Alexandria, Cleopatra, longing for Antony, learns of his re-marriage. In rage she strikes and threatens the messenger. Meanwhile in Rome Pompey makes peace with the triumvirate, and a celebratory feast is arranged, but Enobarbus is convinced that Antony will leave Octavia (who 'is of a holy, cold, and still conversation') for 'his Egyptian dish again'. At the feast in the middle of the revelry, one of Pompey's officers, Menas, suggests to his master that he can now become master of the world by ordering the murder of the triumvirs, but Pompey replies: 'Ah, this thou shouldst have done,/ And not have spoke on't!'

Act III: This act has thirteen scenes and ranges over much of the Mediterranean world. Antony and Octavia leave Rome for Athens. In Alexandria Cleopatra asks the Roman messenger to describe Octavia and is relieved to hear that she is, as Cleopatra summarises his replies, 'dull of tongue, and dwarfish!' Antony and Octavia arrive in Athens and hear that Octavius has broken the precarious peace by making war on Pompey, and has spoken slightingly of Antony. It is arranged that Octavia will return to Rome and try to heal the new division. Then we learn, from a conversation between Enobarbus and another officer, Eros, that Octavius has imprisoned Lepidus and that Pompey is dead. In Rome, Octavius reports that Antony has returned to Egypt, been 'enthroned' with Cleopatra and has divided the eastern provinces of the empire between her and her children and himself. Octavia arrives in Rome and learns of Antony's betrayal of her, and Caesar swiftly moves his fleet to near Actium in Greece. Enobarbus fails to persuade Cleopatra not to go into battle with Antony for fear she will distract and over-influence him. Antony decides to fight at sea despite Octavius's naval superiority. In the battle, the Egyptian fleet turns tail and flees, and Scarus, one of Antony's officers, declaims against Cleopatra for her cowardice and against Antony – 'the noble ruin of her magic' – for following her 'like a doting mallard'. Canidius, one of Antony's generals, decides to desert to Octavius as others have done, but Enobarbus resolves against his own reason that he will 'yet follow the wounded chance of Antony'. In Alexandria Antony reviles himself, tells his friends to divide his gold between them and make their peace with Octavius, and bitterly reproaches Cleopatra; but the scene ends with their reconciliation. Octavius, in Egypt, rejects Antony's offered submission and sends Thyreus to detach Cleopatra from Antony by any means.

In the final scene, Antony sends a challenge to Octavius to single combat, which Enobarbus sees as a further sign of his lost judgement;

Thyreus comes with friendly overtures which Cleopatra receives cordially; Antony berates Cleopatra when he finds Thyreus kissing her hand, and calls her a whore, but she wins him round again and he resolves wildly to fight again, calling for one more 'gaudy night' of feasting, at which Enobarbus, dismayed at his folly and boastful wildness, decides to 'seek some way to leave him'.

Act IV: This again has many scenes. Octavius, scorning Antony's challenge, decides to fight the next day. In the streets of Alexandria a strange music is heard at night, interpreted as the sound of the god Hercules 'whom Antony lov'd' now leaving him. Antony learns that Enobarbus has left him, leaving behind his chests and treasures; he orders them to be sent after him with kind messages – 'O, my fortunes have/ Corrupted honest men.' Octavius orders battle to begin, and the deserters from Antony to be put in the front line, and while Enobarbus is commenting on this dastardly act, a soldier tells him of Antony's contrasting generosity of spirit. Bitterly remorseful, Enobarbus decides to seek 'some ditch, wherein to die'. At first the battle seems to go well for Antony, and he joyfully and in triumph greets Cleopatra that night. Enobarbus dies, broken-hearted. Antony sees to his horror the Egyptian fleet surrender, and bitterly reviles Cleopatra for it. She, fearful at his anger, takes refuge in her Monument, telling her attendants to report that she has died. This false news fills Antony with grief and remorse, and he resolves to die, to 'overtake' Cleopatra, envisaging their future happy reunion after death, and calls on his follower Eros to fulfil an earlier promise and kill him. Eros begs to be excused; his master insists; and Eros, asking him to turn away, uses his sword on himself. Antony then deliberately falls on his own sword, and is discovered by a messenger from Cleopatra sent to tell him she is not dead. Antony is taken to the Monument and hauled up to be briefly re-united with her, before dying. The queen expresses her passionate grief ('O withered is the garland of the war . . .') and resolves on death.

Act V: Octavius is moved by Antony's death ('the breaking of so great a thing should make/ A greater crack'). He sends Proculeius to allay any fears Cleopatra may have; he is anxious to prevent her killing herself as he wants to take her to Rome as part of his triumph. Proculeius again asserts Octavius's kindly intentions, yet at that moment other Roman soldiers break in. Cleopatra is prevented from stabbing herself with a dagger. Another of Octavius's men, Dolabella, enters to take charge, and to him Cleopatra delivers one of her great poetic celebrations of the dead Antony. Octavius comes, and remains conciliatory despite the exposure of Cleopatra's attempt to cheat him over an inventory of her possessions. But Dolabella tells her Octavius intends to take her in triumph to Rome. Cleopatra is resolved to forestall this by death, sends for her most splendid garments, and receives from a countryman she has summoned a basket of figs concealing small poisonous snakes. Attired by her ladies in her finest robes, she applies one asp to her breast and another to her arm and dies peacefully 'As sweet as balm, as soft as air, as gentle'. Charmian does likewise, Iras having already died, and the play ends on this exalted but tranquil note with Octavius Caesar paying generous tribute to this 'pair so famous'.

SOURCES   The source was the Elizabethan translation (1579) by Sir Thomas North□ of a French translation by Jacques Amyot of the life of Antony by Plutarch,□ a first-century Greek biographer and philosopher, whose *Parallel Lives* are biographies of Greek and Roman notables presented in pairs with brief 'comparisons'. Antony was paired with Demetrius; a character of this name appears in the first scene but has only five lines. Many lines and phrases, notably Enobarbus's description of Cleopatra in her state barge, are closely imitated from North. Shakespeare's chief innovation was the creation of the character of Enobarbus.

TEXT   The play appears only in the First Folio,□ (1623). It is one of the longest of the plays (over 3000 lines), too long to have been an actual acting text. This supports the view that in the Folio it was printed from a manuscript of Shakespeare's own, either from his 'foul papers'□ or rough copy or from his 'fair copy'.

Apocrypha, the Shakespeare. 'Apocrypha' means that which is hidden; the name comes from the 'apocryphal' books of the Bible and is used for plays thought originally to be by Shakespeare. They include *Pericles* (now again accepted as largely by Shakespeare), *The London Prodigal, Thomas Lord Cromwell, Sir John Oldcastle, A Yorkshire Tragedy, The Puritan,* and *Locrine.* They were printed in the Third Folio of Shakespeare, 1663, having all previously appeared as quartos.□ Other plays were attributed to Shakespeare in the seventeenth and eighteenth centuries, notably *The Merry Devil of Edmonton* and *Arden of Feversham,* nearly fifty in all.

Apron (apron-stage). The part of the stage which projects into the audience.

Arcadia. A pastoral romance or 'heroic poesy' (C. S. Lewis) in prose by Sir Philip Sidney (1554–86). It combined elements of two early kinds, pastoral (see Pastoralism□) and romance,□ which both have their origins in Greek literature. Sidney's first *Arcadia* was fairly straightforward; it was not published until this century, whereas a later, richer and more complicated version, *The Countess of Pembroke's Arcadia,* which was never finished, was published in 1590 and with three further books in 1593. The popularity of *Arcadia* and of Edmund Spenser's□

(?1554–99) *The Faerie Queene* (1590–6) almost certainly influenced Shakespeare, who shows his fascination with romance throughout his career, from early plays like *Two Gentlemen of Verona* to the late romances (especially *The Winter's Tale*). The story of the blind king of Paphlagonia clearly suggested the Gloucester sub-plot in *King Lear*.

Arden, Forest of. This used to cover a large part of Warwickshire, at least from Hampton-in-Arden in the north to Henley-in-Arden to the south of the county. It was not dense 'forest' in the European or American sense but originally natural woodland, chiefly oak, preserved and developed with many glades and open places in the interests of hunting. It was later useful for timber for building, and for burning for power in early industry. Considerable stretches of its oakwoods and spinneys can still be seen. The Forest of Arden in *As You Like It* is meant to be in Northern France and means the Ardennes (now partly also in Belgium), but Shakespeare certainly also had his own native woods in mind – even though, like the Ardennes, they do not contain lions.

Arden, Mary. Shakespeare's mother, the daughter of a substantial yeoman-farmer but related to grander Ardens in the Midlands, of Wilmcote, three miles north-east of Stratford, where the beautiful large timbered farmhouse may still be visited.

As You Like It. A comedy, dating from 1599 or early 1600.

Act I: Orlando, youngest of three brothers, is treated like a farm servant by his oldest brother Oliver, despite the injunctions of their late father, Sir Rowland de Boys. The local ruler, Duke Senior, has been banished by his younger brother, Duke Frederick, and gone into exile in the Forest of Arden with three or four lords, where 'they live like the old Robin Hood of England' and 'fleet the time carelessly, as they did in the golden world'. The banished duke's daughter Rosalind has not been banished, because of the intercession of her cousin Celia, the usurping duke's daughter. Orlando demands of Oliver either to be treated properly as a gentleman's son or to be given his small inheritance; they come to blows and Orlando resolves to go. Charles, the Duke's wrestler, reports that Orlando intends to wrestle with him in disguise, and fears to hurt him, but the wicked Oliver vilifies his younger brother and says he would be as glad to have Charles 'break his neck as his finger'.

In Scene 2 Rosalind and Celia are introduced, and also the court fool, Touchstone. The wrestler is about to wrestle with his challengers at that very place, and the princesses see with interest and then anxiety young Orlando making ready. They try to persuade him not to wrestle, but he does, and overthrows Charles, earning both their admiration and a chain which Rosalind takes from her neck to give him. She has fallen in love with him – 'Sir, you have wrestled well, and overthrown/ More than your enemies' -- and when she has left the stage we learn that she has indeed 'overthrown' him too. But he is persuaded to leave the court, for the usurping Duke had been an enemy of Orlando's father. Orlando learns that the Duke has 'ta'en displeasure 'gainst his gentle niece' Rosalind. Rosalind and Celia discuss Orlando and Rosalind's love for him. Suddenly Rosalind is banished by her uncle the usurping Duke, and Celia decides to accompany her loved cousin into exile, to the Forest of Arden to Rosalind's banished father. Rosalind (who is 'more than common tall') will go in disguise as a young man, and they decide to take the court fool Touchstone with them.

Act II: The scene moves to the forest, introducing Duke Senior and some of his 'court'. Duke Frederick learns to his anger of the flight of his daughter and niece. Adam, an aged servant of the de Boys family, has warned Orlando that his brother Oliver plans to get rid of Orlando by setting fire to his lodging, and he offers Orlando his life-savings and asks to go with him. A tired Rosalind (as the young man Ganymede), Celia (as Aliena) and Touchstone have just arrived at the Forest of Arden. They observe and overhear a young shepherd, Silvius, telling an old one, Corin, of his love for a shepherdess, Phebe. This prompts Rosalind to another brief declaration of her own love (for Orlando) and Touchstone into claiming with comic exaggeration that he also has been in love. In another part of the wood the 'melancholy' Jaques describes to Duke Senior and others a chance encounter with Touchstone ('I met a fool i' th' forest') and claims a role – of critical comment about life and human behaviour — related to that of a licensed fool or jester, before Orlando bursts in upon them demanding food for Adam and himself. He is kindly received by the Duke, and while he goes off to fetch old Adam, Jaques launches into his famous speech about the seven ages of man.

Act III: Duke Frederick requires Oliver to bring him Orlando dead or alive, or to lose all his own land and belongings. In the Forest of Arden Orlando hangs sheets of his love-poems on trees, and Touchstone talks with Corin, comically mocking and devaluing the shepherd's life as if he were himself a courtier, while the old shepherd speaks of the pastoral life with dignity: 'I earn that I eat, get that I wear – owe no man hate, envy no man's happiness – glad of other men's good, content with my harm'. Rosalind finds Orlando's tree-hung verses, and Celia tells her she knows who has written them – Orlando. Rosalind's immediate response is 'Alas the day, what shall I do with my doublet and hose?' While they are talking of this, Orlando comes in with Jaques, sparring wittily together. Jaques leaves, and a delightful scene of love-raillery follows; Rosalind/ Ganymede tells him how 'time travels in divers paces, with divers persons' and declares that Orlando cannot be in love for he has none

of the marks of a lover – 'a lean cheek . . . a beard neglected . . . hose
. . . ungartered . . . shoe untied', etc. Orlando admits that he is in love
with Rosalind and she tells him how he may be cured: he is to imagine
that he (Rosalind/Ganymede) is his beloved, and he/she will 'set him
every day to woo' and will make him realise how 'changeable, proud,
fantastical . . . shallow, inconstant, full of tears, full of smiles' a lover
is; this will cure him. Orlando agrees to play this game and to come
every day. Meanwhile Touchstone has cynically pursued and won a
simple country girl, Audrey, and arranges for them to be married by
Sir Oliver Mar-Text, a country clergyman. Corin comes and takes
Rosalind and Celia to see another 'love'-affair, that of Silvius and the
proud and disdainful shepherdess Phebe. Ganymede chides her for
her cruelty to Silvius but Phebe instantly falls in love with 'him': 'I
had rather hear you chide, than this man woo'.

Act IV: Nearly an hour late, Orlando comes for his appointment with
Ganymede, whom he finds talking to Jaques and deriding him for his
self-regarding disillusioned melancholy. There follows a charming
scene of great delicacy and humour in which Ganymede gets Orlando
to say what he would do if he were actually wooing his real Rosalind,
and gets Celia to act the priest and 'marry' them. When Orlando has
to leave, to dine with the banished Duke, Ganymede says that she
cannot 'lack' him 'for two hours', and when he has gone, says that
Celia cannot know 'how many fathom deep I am in love!' The lords in
another part of the forest celebrate in song the killing of a deer, before
Rosalind and Celia are shown, Rosalind impatiently waiting for
Orlando's return. To them comes the shepherd Silvius, bearing a
letter to 'Ganymede' from Phebe declaring her love for Ganymede.
There now re-enters the plot Orlando's brother Oliver, now contrite
and gentle. We discover why Orlando was late, for Oliver gives
Ganymede/Rosalind a bloody cloth and tells how Orlando, in
rescuing him from a famished lioness, had been hurt in the encounter.
The brothers were of course reconciled and Oliver forgiven; the
bloody cloth has been sent by Orlando to explain his failure to come
to Ganymede, who faints on receiving it.

Act V: begins with a drop into the absurd, as Touchstone with comic
rhetoric, as a grand court figure, disposes of Audrey's rustic suitor,
William. Oliver tells Orlando that he and Celia/Aliena have fallen in
love; he asks Orlando's approval and offers him their father's house
and estate, as he intends to stay in the country and 'live and die a
shepherd'. He goes off to make the wedding arrangements with
'Aliena', and Ganymede enters; Orlando tells 'him' that the others
are to be married on the following day, and speaks of his heavy heart
that he cannot also be marrying. When Ganymede asks 'Why then,
tomorrow I cannot serve your turn for Rosalind?', he replies 'I can

live no longer by thinking'; whereupon Ganymede tells him 'he' knows a magician who will enable him to marry Rosalind, if he so wishes. At this point there enter Silvius and Phebe, 'a lover of mine, and a lover of hers' as Ganymede says, and in a teasing sort of 'round' 'he' calls on them all to meet tomorrow and the love complications will be unravelled. In the final scene all is resolved in the presence of Duke Senior and his greenwood court. Rosalind appears in her girl's attire, is re-united with her loving father the Duke and revealed to Orlando as not Ganymede but Rosalind; the god of marriage, Hymen, joins Rosalind and Orlando, Celia and Oliver, Touchstone and Audrey and Phebe and Silvius in marriage. Finally the middle brother, Jaques de Boys, appears for the first time and reports the sudden change in the usurping Duke Frederick, who had come with an army to the forest to seize Duke Senior but after discussion with an old hermit had been converted, and, penitent, now forsook the world and bequeathed the crown and lands to his banished brother. On hearing this, the melancholy Jaques decides to join the penitent Duke Frederick and withdraw from the world.

SOURCE The play is closely based on an Elizabethan novel by Thomas Lodge,□ *Rosalynde* (published 1590), a wandering pastoral romance in which most of the characters appear, although most of them, except Rosalind and Phebe, have different names. Shakespeare concentrated the plot, introduced Touchstone with his comic mockery of the pastoral life and the colder cynicism of Jaques, made the story infinitely more playful and delightful, and above all irradiated it with the vivacity and tenderness of his portrayal of Rosalind, to many people the most glorious of all Shakespeare's comic heroines.

TEXT The play appears only in the First Folio□ (1623). It is a good text which seems to have been printed from the theatre's prompt-book.□

Audience. Shakespeare's audience in the public theatre included almost all ranks of society, except the lowest and poorest, from nobles, courtiers and professional men down to ordinary citizens – shop-keepers, tradesmen, housewives, artisans, apprentices. Foreigners were surprised to find ladies and respectable women at the theatre. The audiences were large; it is thought that the Globe,□ for example, could hold over three thousand people. The private theatres catered for better-off people; admission cost six times as much as for the cheapest tickets at the public theatres. It seems clear that the London audience was an alert and intelligent audience, and one that became increasingly so, if we may take as evidence Shakespeare's increasing subtlety and complexity, and the cruder but still complex and often learned plays of his Jacobean contemporaries and successors.

B

Bad quarto. The term was first used of the quarto□ editions of Shakespeare's plays which the editors of the First Folio□ (1623), Heminge□ and Condell,□ called 'divers stolen and surreptitious copies maimed and deformed by frauds and stealths' – the 1st Quarto separate editions of *Romeo and Juliet, Henry V, The Merry Wives of Windsor* and *Hamlet*. They are called 'bad' because of their omissions, garbled speeches which often seem more like paraphrases (and often are), lines and sometimes scenes misplaced, prose printed as verse and *vice versa*, when compared with later quartos or the Folio versions. They were thought to have been put together from inadequate short-hand notes made during performances, but now are generally thought to be 'memorial reconstructions'□ by actors setting down or dictating what they could remember of plays they had acted in for unauthorised printing. A characteristic feature is that some parts are nearly perfect, indicating that it was the actor who had played that part or those parts that did the job. Two plays, for long thought to be sources for *Henry VI Parts 2 and 3*, and known as the 'contention plays' (the 'contention' or struggle between the ducal families of Lancaster and York) are now accepted as bad quartos of the original Shakespeare plays.

Bandello, Matteo (1480–1562). An Italian writer whose *Novelle* (novels) (1554–73) or prose romances similar to those of Boccaccio's□ *Decameron* were translated into French by Belleforest□ and thence into English by Sir Geoffrey Fenton (1539–1608) as *Certain Tragicall Discourses* (1567). A number of the original tales, of which there were 214, were also told by William Painter□ in his *The Palace of Pleasure* (1565–7). Through translations Shakespeare owed to Bandello the story of *Romeo and Juliet*, which he got from Arthur Brooke's□ English version, the idea of the Orsino – Viola story for *Twelfth Night* and the Hero story of *Much Ado About Nothing*.

Belleforest, François de (1530–83). A French writer who took over the translation of Bandello□ begun by him and another, and in the end added to the original collection. The seven volumes were published 1559–82 and were translated into English by Sir Geoffrey Fenton (1539–1608) as *Certain Tragicall Discourses etc.*, yielding material to Shakespeare for *Romeo and Juliet, Much Ado About Nothing, Twelfth Night* and *Hamlet* (the version by Saxo Grammaticus of the legendary story of Hamlet.)

Berners, John Bourchier, 2nd Baron Berners (1469–1533). He translated the *Chronicles* by Sir John Froissart□ to which Shakespeare was indebted for details in *Richard II*.

Bible. Shakespeare rarely refers to the Holy Bible in his works but there is hardly a page of his writings without some reference, allusion or quotation and it is clear that the Bible was intimately known to him and was a strong influence on his mental make-up and outlook. Protestant England, far from forbidding the vernacular Bible, encouraged – indeed required – familiarity with it. Shakespeare's use of Biblical references and phrases, greater than that of his contemporaries in the theatre, while never obtrusive and rarely didactic, means that his plays live naturally within a Christian dimension. It has been found that there are quotations from or references to forty-two of the books of the Bible (eighteen each from the Old Testament and the New and six from the *Apocrypha*).

Blackfriars (theatre). Part of the upper half (the *frater* or refectory, dining-hall) of the original Dominican priory suppressed in 1538 was leased to The Children of the Chapel from 1576 to 1584 for the boys to perform plays in public before their presentation at Court. This was the 'first Blackfriars' theatre. It returned to private occupation until in 1596 Richard Burbage□ tried to make and run a theatre there again, but was frustrated by neighbours. It was not until 1609 that he was able to use it for his professional adult company, the King's Men, in addition to the Globe.□ Shakespeare, Heminge,□ and Condell□ who later edited the First Folio□ were with Burbage among the seven 'housekeepers'□ or partners jointly owning and running the theatre. The theatre was 66 feet (about 20 metres) long by 46 feet (about 14 metres) wide with the stage almost certainly at one end. It was the first indoor rectangular public theatre. See also Playhouses.□

Blank verse. Unrhymed verse in a five-stress (ten-syllable) line, first used by the Earl of Surrey (1517–47) in his translation of part of Virgil's *Aeneid* (1557). It was first used in drama in *Gorboduc*□ (1561). At first stiff and with little variation, in basically iambic measure (two-syllabled with the first stressed) with end-stopped lines complete in themselves, Marlowe loosened it and Shakespeare freed it. Shakespeare ran the sense on into sometimes very long sentences, even paragraphs, varying the *caesura* or stop when he liked, added to the line's length with 'feminine' endings (final unstressed syllables) and varied the measure from the iambic. He made it a wonderfully flexible, lively and versatile form for dramatic speech.

Boccaccio, Giovanni (1313–75). Italian writer best known for his *Decameron* (1353) (meaning 'ten days'), a hundred tales supposedly told by three gentlemen and seven ladies taking refuge outside Florence in time of plague. They are mostly tales of intrigue with a light comic tone, but there are also sad and tragic tales. Shakespeare was indebted indirectly through translations – but also probably directly, for he almost certainly knew Italian – especially for the casket plot in *The Merchant of Venice*, the plot of *All's Well That Ends Well* and the wager plot in *Cymbeline*.

Book-keeper (or book-holder). The member of the acting company responsible for preparing the theatre-copy or acting-copy of the play, making clear in it the entrances and exits and other stage-directions. He had also to submit it for approval to the Master of the Revels.□ He also probably 'kept' the book and acted as prompter during performances. The book became the property of the company, not the writer.

Book of Martyrs, The. Popular name of *Actes and Monuments of These Latter and Perilous Days* (1563) by John Foxe (1516–87). It was a collection of accounts of the martyrdom of Protestants, first published when Foxe was in exile in Strasbourg during Queen Mary's reign (1553–8). Originally in Latin, Foxe turned it into English and extended it when he returned to England and entered the new (Protestant) English church. Powerful, terse writing accompanied vivid woodcut illustrations. Its Protestantism was also strongly national: England, by its faithfulness to the scriptures and emphasis on the importance of the Bible, and by its break with Rome, was specially favoured of God. Copies were placed in most churches and it was exceptionally widely known and influential. Shakespeare was indebted to it for elements in *King John* and *Henry VI, Part 2*, and for details of the conspiracy against Cranmer (later a martyr) in *Henry VIII*.

Boy actors. There were no actresses on the English stage before the Restoration (of King Charles II in 1660), female parts being played by boys and young men. Each company had two or three. They were highly trained, serving an apprenticeship of several years. There were also of course the boy-actors (who were school-boys or choirboys and not originally professional players) of the children's companies who played all parts, male and female, young and old. See also Actors□ and Actors' companies.□

Brooke, Arthur (?–1563). His long poem in rhyming couplets, *The Tragicall History of Romeus and Juliet* (1562), based on a tale in *Histoires Tragiques* of Belleforest□ and his early collaborator Boiastuau, was the source for Shakespeare's early love-tragedy. Brooke's additions to the source, including a comic nurse, and his emphasis on the power of Fortune in causing the tragedy, were adopted by Shakespeare.

Burbage, Richard (1568–1619). One of the two leading Elizabethan/ Jacobean actors, the other being Alleyn.□ He was the son of James Burbage (1530–97), a member of Leicester's Company, who, with John Brayne, built The Theatre, the first public theatre, in 1576, and in 1596 acquired the Blackfriars. Richard Burbage was in the Lord Chamberlain's Men,□ later the King's Men, with Shakespeare, and almost certainly created most of the great tragic roles, including Richard III, Hamlet, Othello and King Lear. Richard and his manager-brother Cuthbert (1566–1636) built the Globe□ in 1598/9 which then became the company's theatre until the Blackfriars was added to their theatrical empire in 1609. As an actor he was 'lively' (life-like) and it is recorded that in *Hamlet* he would 'leap into the Grave/suiting the person . . . with so true an Eye/that there I would have sworn, he meant to die'. His rival Alleyn was more given to 'stalking and roaring', but he was acting in Marlowe's plays, not Shakespeare's.

C

Canon, the Shakespearian. The thirty-six plays of the First Folio□ plus *Pericles*; those plays that are confidently accepted by all or most authorities as being by Shakespeare. Sometimes attempts have been made to add to the canon (see Apocrypha□) and sometimes to reduce it, denying Shakespeare some plays such as *Pericles, Henry VIII* and parts of *Henry VI*; but Heminge□ and Condell,□ the editors of the First Folio, seem to have done an accurate editorial job conscientiously in deciding which plays Shakespeare actually wrote.

Censorship. Early in Elizabeth's reign, in 1559, a proclamation required local officials (mayors and justices) to examine interludes□ and plays to prevent discussion in them of 'matters of religion or of the governance of the estate of the common weale'. In 1581 a court official, the Master of the Revels,□ was given the power 'to order and reform, authorise and put down as shall be thought meet or unmeet to himself' all plays everywhere in Britain. (This was in fact meant also to authorise plays and to overrule the Mayor and Corporation of London which had tried to suppress the theatre throughout London and its suburbs. The Court preserved and encouraged the theatre, which the City tried to abolish.) From 1581 plays had to be submitted to the Master of the Revels for approval. In 1606 an act 'to restrain the abuses of the players' in the matter of the use of oaths and of the name of God was passed, and in the following year texts of plays intended to be printed had also to be sent to the Master for censoring. Shakespeare seems to have suffered little from censorship. He was clearly not in any way subversive, or anything but a loyal subject and supporter of the Tudor regime and dynasty. But the deposition scene in *Richard II* was not printed in the first three quarto□ editions of the play, not until the fourth quarto in 1608, dangerous parallels with the Essex rebellion of 1601 being seen in it. See also Licensing.□

Chamberlain's Men, the Lord. This company was formed in 1594, chiefly from the former Lord Strange's Men. Their patron the Lord Chamberlain was one of the chief officials of the Royal Household, responsible for the sovereign's accommodation and travel, for the Chapel Royal and its music and also for the royal entertainment. The Master of the Revels□ was his subordinate. Successive Chamberlains, who were noblemen, were keenly interested in the emerging professional theatre and especially in the company of which they were patrons. Shakespeare, Richard Burbage,□ Will Kempe the comic actor, and John Heminge,□ later one of the two editors of the First Folio,□ were members of the Lord Chamberlain's men from 1594, at The Theatre, perhaps briefly at the Swan□ in 1596, and the Curtain in 1598 (where they played Ben Jonson's□ *Every Man in His Humour*). By 1599 the Burbages had built the Globe□ where for the next ten years they reigned unchallenged as the leading company, and had Shakespeare's greatest works written for them. In 1603 when King James I came to the throne they became known as the King's Men. From 1608 they also had the Blackfriars,□ which, though smaller, made more profit because of higher admission charges. They played here, as it was an indoor theatre, in the colder and winter months. Shakespeare was a sharer□ or shareholder in the company.

Chaucer, Geoffrey (?1340–1400). The greatest English writer of the Middle Ages who virtually established the modern English language and the forms and development of English literature. Shakespeare knew his work but is surprisingly little indebted to him, even in *Troilus and Cressida* in which he treats cynically the love-affair so compassionately examined in Chaucer's *Troilus and Criseyde*. Even his Pandarus is deprived of the affectionate sympathy Chaucer showed. But Shakespeare followed the order of the action of Chaucer's poem. He possibly got some suggestions – the relaxed and humorous Theseus and the rival lovers – for *A Midsummer Night's Dream* from 'The Knight's Tale' in *The Canterbury Tales*. This was also the source for the play *The Two Noble Kinsmen* by John Fletcher in which some think Shakespeare had a hand.

Children's companies. See Actors□ and Actors' companies□.

Chorus. A few of Shakespeare's plays have a Chorus, a person who introduces the play, giving helpful information to the audience and/or telling it details of the plot which have not been actually shown. But the Chorus rarely comments on the action, or is seen with or talking to other characters. In Greek tragedy the Chorus is a group of persons usually representing ordinary people (such as the citizens of Athens). *Romeo and Juliet* has a Chorus for the first two acts. Rumour as a sort of Chorus introduces *Henry IV, Part 2*; a Chorus opens *Henry VIII* and one introduces each act of *Henry V*. In *Pericles* the character Gower (who is based on the English writer John Gower,□ contemporary with Chaucer, from whom Shakespeare got much of the plot) introduces each act and sometimes comments on the action. 'Time, the Chorus' tells the audience in a speech of sixteen couplets of the passing of sixteen years between Acts III and IV of *The Winter's Tale*.

The Chronicles of England, Scotland and Ireland (1577). A part of an intended history of the world with descriptions of geography and societies. The chief part, the historical, on England, was by Raphael Holinshed,□ as was the history of Scotland (though this was largely a translation of a history of Scotland by Hector Boece). A second edition was published in 1587. The work was Shakespeare's chief source for most of the historical plays, and for *Macbeth*; and elsewhere (*King Lear*, *Cymbeline)* he made some use of Holinshed. (But see Hall, Edward□).

Chronicle plays. It used to be thought that there was a strong *corpus* of chronicle plays, dealing with events in English history, which Shakespeare developed into his masterly history plays. In fact none exist or even survive indisputably as recorded titles, and even Marlowe's□ *Edward II* is now believed to have been influenced by Shakespeare (the first tetralogy□) rather than the other way round. Shakespeare may well have originated the genre.

Chronology. There has been endless discussion of the order and timing of the plays but certainties about the time of writing are few. Dates of entries in the Stationers' Register,□ the list of plays given by Francis Meres in his *Palladis Tamia*□ (1598), dates of first printing, evidence of performance sometimes given on title-pages, occasional contemporary references and allusions, which are in fact very few, all contribute something to the picture. Internal evidence of style has been used for dating, and computers have been used in this task. Shakespeare began writing in about 1588 or 1589; by March 1592 there is a record of 'Harey the Sixth' by Strange's Men, almost certainly a part of Shakespeare's *Henry VI*. By September 1592 the writer and dramatist Robert Greene□ had published an indirect attack on Shakespeare as thinking himself 'the only Shake-scene in a country' in *A Groatsworth of Wit*, which implied that the young man from the country was already well known in the theatre in London. Shakespeare seems to have written at least one play every year, in many years two, from about 1588 or 1589 until 1612. Some of the early plays may have been written in some form earlier still and revised, adapted or rewritten. It seems clear that the *Henry VI* plays and *Titus Andronicus* are the earliest and were written in their present form some time between 1588 and 1591. The order of composition of the plays is probably something like this:

1588–94	*Love's Labour's Lost*
Titus Andronicus	*Richard III*
Henry VI, Part 1	*The Taming of the Shrew*
The Comedy of Errors	**1594–6**
The Two Gentlemen of Verona	*Romeo and Juliet*
Henry VI, Part 2	*Richard II*
Henry VI, Part 3	*A Midsummer Night's Dream*
King John	*Henry IV, Parts 1 and 2*

1596–8	*Othello*
The Merry Wives of Windsor	*King Lear*
The Merchant of Venice	*Macbeth*
Henry V	**1607–10**
Much Ado About Nothing	*Timon of Athens*
1599–1601	*Antony and Cleopatra*
As You Like It	*Coriolanus*
Twelfth Night	*Pericles*
Julius Caesar	*Cymbeline*
Hamlet	**1611–13**
1602–6	*The Winter's Tale*
All's Well That Ends Well	*The Tempest*
Troilus and Cressida	*Henry VIII*
Measure for Measure	

Cinthio. The name by which Giovanni Battista Giraldi (1504–73), an Italian who was a professor of rhetoric at Pavia and a copious writer, is usually known. He is celebrated for his *Hecatommithi* (1565) ('One Thousand Tales'), a collection of tales of romance and sexual intrigue not unlike those of Bandello□ and Boccaccio.□ Shakespeare got the story of *Othello* from Cinthio, and also, via George Whetstone's English version *Promos and Cassandra* (1578), the plot of *Measure for Measure*.

Civile Warres, The '. . . *between the Houses of Lancaster and York*' (first part 1595, second part 1609). An historical epic poem by Samuel Daniel□ (1562–1619). It dealt with English history from the reign of Richard II (1377–99) to 1485 when Henry VII came to the throne. His victory over Richard III at the battle of Bosworth Field in 1485 and his firm rule finally ended the long contention between the leading (related) families for the throne, the Wars of the Roses□ (white for York, red for Lancaster). The first part was a useful source for *Richard II* and seems to have been used also for *Henry IV* and *Henry V*. Daniel's revision for his expanded second edition seems to show the influence of Shakespeare, especially in the changes made in the portrayal of Richard II.

Clown. Usually a foolish servant or rustic (compare the adjective 'clownish' which is related to 'clod', 'clot', 'lout' and 'lump'). Shakespeare's clowns, such as Costard, Launce, Launcelot Gobbo, Dogberry, are to be distinguished from his intelligent witty 'professional' fools□ or jesters such as Touchstone, Feste and Lear's Fool. In addition to the slow-witted, puzzled, ignorant dolts who provoke much laughter in the audience, there are often quick-witted servants such as the Dromio twins, Speed, Tranio and Grumio. These are like their counterparts and probable inspirers, the *zanni* (from which we get the word 'zany') of Italian *commedia dell'arte*□ and are often called 'clowns' or 'fools'. Clowns tend to be rural or urban; fools belong to the courts of nobles and kings.

Comedy of Errors, The. An early comedy, perhaps the earliest, probably dating from 1589. It is the shortest of Shakespeare's plays (less than 1,800 lines).

Act I: The beginning seems to promise tragedy, as old Aegeon is sentenced to death by the Duke of Ephesus. As a Syracusan his life is forfeit, because of the enmity between the two cities, unless he can pay the required ransom. Asked why he thus contravened the law, he tells of a storm many years before in which he had lost his wife and one of their infant identical twins; also lost was one of another pair of infant identical twins, who had been born at the same time and whom Aegeon had bought from their poor parents, to be brought up as servants. Aegeon had been rescued with one of his own twins and one of the 'servant' twins. Eighteen years had passed, and his Antipholus, now grown up, had left Syracuse with the servant twin Dromio to seek their twin brothers. They had disappeared, however, and in searching distractedly for them Aegeon had risked putting ashore in enemy Ephesus. Touched by the tale, the Duke allows him twenty-four hours to try to find the money to pay the fine. Scene 2 introduces this son, Antipholus of Syracuse, newly arrived in Ephesus with his servant Dromio of Syracuse, whom he despatches with money to the Centaur inn, where they will be staying. Very soon, his servant seems to return, but it is in fact the other Dromio, (of Ephesus) who calls on him to hasten home to dinner. Antipholus thinks this is one of his Dromio's jokes, and the twin Dromio is equally puzzled. His master demands to know what has happened to the thousand marks, while Dromio of Ephesus keeps referring to the anger of his mistress – and this Antipholus is not married! He is not to know that his long-lost brother is alive and in Ephesus, with the twin-Dromio as his servant. Antipholus remembers he has been told that Ephesus is a town of cozenage, sorcery and witchcraft.

Act II: This introduces Adriana, the wife of Antipholus of Ephesus, and her young unmarried sister Luciana. Adriana is something of a scold. To them comes their puzzled servant Dromio of Ephesus and tells of being beaten by his master, who had also declared that he had 'no house, no wife, no mistress'. Adriana begins to worry about her husband's fidelity. In Scene 2 the newly arrived Antipholus of Syracuse is now joined by his true servant Dromio of Syracuse, and a new misunderstanding develops as he berates him for speaking of his mistress's waiting dinner for him and denying that he had been sent with one thousand marks to the Centaur inn. This Dromio is now perplexed, and is beaten, and the mystery – to all – deepens when Adriana and Luciana enter. After many confused and confusing interchanges Adriana 'forgives' him and says they will dine intimately alone, and the perplexed Antipholus of Syracuse decides to take a chance and go with her and her sister.

Act III: Adriana's husband, Antipholus of Ephesus, arranges with Angelo, a goldsmith, about a necklace for his wife, hurrying because he is late for dinner. He is denied entrance by the other Dromio within, and then by Adriana (within), because of course an Antipholus (of Syracuse) is dining with her, and a Dromio (of Syracuse) keeping the door. Antipholus of Ephesus, thus thwarted, decides to go to the house of a courtesan to dine, and asks Angelo to bring the necklace in an hour's time to her house, for he will now give it to her, not to his wife. Luciana gently asks Antipholus (of Syracuse) to treat Adriana more kindly and considerately; he, of course still puzzled, has fallen in love with Luciana and declares it to her, to her embarrassment. As she leaves the stage Dromio of Syracuse enters, ludicrously terrified because he has been claimed – in mistake for Dromio of Ephesus – by the fat kitchen-wench. Antipholus of Syracuse, further convinced that Ephesus is a place of sorcery, decides to leave, despite his growing love for Luciana, and sends his Dromio to see if any ships are about to leave. The goldsmith Angelo appears with the necklace ordered by the other Antipholus, insists on his taking it and says he will call at supper-time for the money.

Act IV: This opens with a merchant demanding of Angelo repayment of a debt. Antipholus of Ephesus is just emerging from the courtesan's, with his Dromio, whom he sends to buy a rope's end (with which to beat his wife for locking him out), and then turns to rebuke Angelo for not bringing the necklace in time. Angelo asks for the money to pay off his creditor but Antipholus of Ephesus will not pay because he has not received the necklace, although Angelo protests he gave it him half an hour ago. Antipholus of Ephesus is arrested just as Dromio of Syracuse enters to report that he has found a ship they can leave by and has put their goods on board. This is nonsense to Antipholus of Ephesus, but he sends the servant to his house to tell his wife Adriana to send money for bail, and the Syracusan Dromio reluctantly sets off to the house where he will have to encounter the fat serving-wench again. Adriana sadly hears from her sister that her husband has apparently declared his love for her briefly, rails at him but concludes 'Ah, but I think him better than I say' and 'My heart prays for him, though my tongue do curse'. The Syracusan Dromio rushes in, reports the arrest of Antipholus (of Ephesus) and asks for and receives the money. When he goes to give this money (five hundred ducats) to his master Antipholus (of Syracuse), the latter is of course bewildered, and this is increased when the Courtesan enters and asks for the necklace she has been promised by Antipholus (of Ephesus) or else the ring she had given him then. Convinced that mad sorcery is rife in Ephesus, Antipholus of Syracuse goes off with his Dromio, while the Courtesan thinks Antipholus must be mad and decides to go to his house here in Ephesus to tell his wife that he is mad and has taken her ring worth forty ducats. Dromio of Ephesus comes to his master – in the custody of an officer – who thinks he has brought the five hundred ducats from Adriana, only to find that Dromio has only brought the rope's end, whereupon he beats him. Adriana, with Luciana and the Courtesan, brings Dr Pinch, a schoolmaster and exorciser, to try to expel her husband's evil spirits that have made him mad. Raging with puzzlement and frustration, Antipholus of Ephesus is eventually caught and bound and his Dromio with him and they are taken off. The scene and act end when Antipholus of Syracuse and his Dromio enter with drawn rapiers prepared to fight their way if necessary through this bewitched city to the harbour, frightening Adriana and Luciana who think the other – arrested – pair have escaped their captors.

Act V: This act consists of a single long scene in which the confusions are disentangled. The Syracusan master and servant run into a nearby priory; the prioress emerges (her first appearance in the play), listens to Adriana's story but refuses to hand Antipholus over and goes back inside. The Duke passes in procession with the prisoner Aegeon going to execution, and Adriana calls on him for 'justice ... against the abbess' for refusing to hand over her 'husband'; but suddenly word comes that Antipholus of Ephesus and his Dromio have broken free from *their* captivity, and in a few moments they come on to the scene. Antipholus of Ephesus complains to the Duke and seeks justice from him. The Duke questions him, which naturally elicits a recounting of many of the 'errors' or confusions. The Duke concludes that 'all have drunk of Circe's cup' (are bewitched and transformed). Old Aegeon speaks to Antipholus of Ephesus and his Dromio, thinking they are Antipholus of Syracuse and his Dromio. He is amazed that they cannot remember their old father from whom they have only been parted five or seven years. When the Abbess reappears she realises that Aegeon must be her long-lost husband. Happy reunions of parents and children and of brothers take place all round, now that the errors have been cleared up; Aegeon is freed, Antipholus of Syracuse resumes his wooing of Luciana, and Ephesian Dromio, meeting his hitherto-unmet brother for the first time, says 'I see by you I am a sweet-fac'd youth.'

SOURCE   The chief source was a play by Plautus,□ the Roman comic dramatist (*c*.254–184BC), called *Menaechmi*, about two twins each called Menaechmus who are constantly confused with each other; the quarrel with the wife, the dinner with the courtesan, the present of jewellery and the apparent madness in *A Comedy of Errors* all come from this play. Shakespeare chose to set it in Ephesus; that city had a reputation for sorcery, witchcraft, magic and deceit. His most original change was to create twin servants as well as twin masters, thus doubling the possibilities for comic confusion. He also set it in a serious frame, taking the story of Aegeon and his long-lost wife from the story of Apollonius of Tyre (which he later used again in *Pericles*), possibly from a version in the *Confessio Amantis* (Confession of a Lover) by John Gower,□ a contemporary of Chaucer.

TEXT   The play appears only in the First Folio□ (1623); it was probably printed from a manuscript of the author's.

Commedia dell'arte. The popular comic drama of sixteenth- and seventeenth-century Italy which used a varying collection of stock characters in slick conventional plots of love, duping and intrigue. There was no firm written dialogue but instead the actors improvised the speech. (No doubt a kind of standard text often established itself with repeated performances by the same players.) The stock characters included young lovers, an old dotard in love (who was sometimes the pedant or doctor), a tyrannical and/or duped father, a pedant (doctor, schoolmaster or priest), a braggart or in other ways offensive, but usually comic, soldier and *zanni* – clowns or witty servants often used to promote further intrigues. Many of Shakespeare's comic characters have more than a hint of these types, which he may have known from travelling companies of Italian actors, or from the plays of Lyly,□ but they themselves derive from the stock characters of Roman classical comedy (see Plautus,□ Terence□). These he might well have seen in private theatres played by children's companies, but Plautus and Terence he would have read, studied and even acted in at school (see Education,□ Shakespeare's). Shakespeare invests his personages with humour and idiosyncrasy, and gives a sense of their human (and usually English) reality and worth, absent from the Roman and Italian plays.

Condell, Henry (?–1627). An actor who was in the Lord Chamberlain's Men□ by 1598. He was one of the twenty-six actors who performed Shakespeare's plays listed in the First Folio.□ He became a housekeeper□ of the Globe□ in 1599 and later of the Blackfriars.□ But his chief fame is that he was co-editor, with John Heminge,□ of the First Folio.

Copy. The manuscript or text from which a printer (or his compositor or typesetter) works. In the case of Shakespeare's plays this might be:

(*a*) his 'foul papers'□ or draft of the text.

(*b*) his 'fair copy', revised, corrected and copied out again either by Shakespeare or by a professional copier or scribe.

(*c*) the prompt-book□ of the company, held by the book-keeper,□ or a transcript of it.

(*d*) a 'memorial reconstruction'□ pieced together by actors and written down from dictation.

(*e*) a text taken from a shorthand report made during a performance or rehearsals.

(*f*) an 'assembled' text got by assembling together the separate actors' parts (which the book-keeper of the company prepared) and the plot□ (or scene-by-scene outline, also prepared in the theatre and hung up for members of the company to refer to during a performance or rehearsal).

(*g*) an earlier printed version, perhaps corrected or adapted.

Of the above, (*a*), (*b*), (*c*) and perhaps (*f*) are more likely to have been authorised. (*d*) and (*e*) especially might be what are known as 'bad' (usually 'bad' quartos□), pirated or stolen. The editors of the First Folio,□ Heminge□ and Condell,□ were very good editors on the whole, and used a high proportion of copy either directly from Shakespeare or closely derived from his papers. As old colleagues and friends they were in a uniquely good position to do so.

Copyright. To 'enter' a book title in the Stationers' Register,□ kept by the Stationers' Company of London, for a fee, in theory ensured copyright (namely that no one else was entitled to print or publish it). In practice it was not until the first Copyright Act of 1710 that there was much legal force.

Coriolanus. A Roman tragedy of early 1608.

Act I: A crowd of citizens, mutinous because of grain shortages – and their suspicion that the patricians (upper and ruling classes) are exploiting the situation for their own benefit – especially inveigh against Caius Martius, 'chief enemy of the people'. They declare that the great deeds he has admittedly done were done not for the state, as one claimed, but 'to please his mother, and to be partly proud'. A friend of his, and one loved by the people, Menenius Agrippa, tells the crowd that the patricians have 'most charitable care' of them and it is the gods, not the patricians, that are responsible for the famine. He tells the famous story of the belly and the members, in which he amusingly likens the senators of Rome to the belly, and the mob to the other organs of the body which have complained of the belly's greed and inaction; they could not survive without the belly, 'the storehouse and the shop' which sends the food through the body to every organ and every part. Caius Martius enters, contemptuous and tactlessly abusive about the common man's cowardice, pride, unreliability and envy. He reports that another restive mob elsewhere in the city has gained a concession: five tribunes to represent the people to the Senate. Suddenly news is brought that the Volscians, led by Tullus Aufidius, are in arms. Titus Lartius and Cominius with Caius Martius are to lead the expedition against them. We meet Caius Martius's mother, Volumnia, a heroic

hero-making Roman matriarch, and his wife Virgilia, who shrinks
from the martial spirit and has resolved not to leave the house until
her husband returns from the war.

The action moves to Corioli, the Volscian capital. The Romans
attempt to capture it but are driven back to their trenches; Caius
Martius rallies them with curses. In the renewed assault he enters the
city and the gates close behind him. Later he re-emerges covered in
blood; Titus Lartius and other Romans join him, and they enter and
capture the city. Some looting Romans are cursed by Caius Martius.
The Roman leader, Cominius, fighting elsewhere, receives a report of
the earlier Roman repulse but Caius appears, tells him Titus Lartius
holds the city, and, being told where Tullus Aufidius is with his troops,
goes to fight him. The Volscian general is defeated, and Cominius
honours Caius Martius with the additional name of 'Coriolanus' to
mark his victory. Aufidius, now for the fifth time defeated by
Coriolanus, vows to overcome him.

Act II: The two tribunes of the people Sicinius and Brutus denigrate
Coriolanus for his pride to his friend Menenius Agrippa, who boisterously mocks them for their own pride. Coriolanus receives a hero's
welcome; his mother is proud of his wounds, his wife weeps with relief.
The two tribunes fear that Coriolanus will be made consul, as he now
has such a following of enthusiastic supporters. There are two other
contenders for the office. Menenius Agrippa proposes Coriolanus, and
the tribunes express the hope that he will give 'a kinder value of the
people than / He hath hereto priz'd them at'. Coriolanus is extremely
reluctant to stay and hear his deeds recited, but is prevailed upon to
stand for election; he is even less inclined to wear the customary gown
of humility, speak to the people and show his wounds. In spite of his
impatient, scornful manner to representative citizens, they support him;
but they soon reflect on his contempt, and, worked upon by the
tribunes – who say 'they have chose a consul that will from them take /
Their liberties, make them of no more voice / Than dogs' – they
'repent in their election'.

Act III: Coriolanus hears that Tullus Aufidius, disaffected with the
Volscians after the defeat at Corioli, has moved to Antium and is raising
a new force, and still vowing revenge on him. The tribunes, again treated
tactlessly and contemptuously by Coriolanus, report that the people
have turned against him and no longer support him for consul; they
remember his opposing the distribution of free corn during the famine.
Coriolanus angrily comments that they 'did not deserve corn gratis.
Being i' th' war, / Their mutinies and revolts, wherein they show'd /
Most valour, spoke not for them.' Menenius tries to calm things down,
especially during a confrontation between patricians and plebeians
(the people) when the two tribunes incite the mob further to seize

Coriolanus. Coriolanus draws his sword and disperses them. The tribunes are determined to bring Coriolanus down and have him exe- cuted. Menenius still attempts to pacify them in the interests of Rome and promises to bring Coriolanus to the Forum to answer the mob's charges. Volumnia, the hero's mother, thinks he is unwise to antago- nise them: 'I would have had you put your power well on / Before you had worn it out'; and Menenius comes to tell him that he must confront the mob and mollify them. He angrily refuses but eventually yields to the authority and wise advice of his mother, who urges him to combine 'honour and policy'. Contemptuously he says he'll 'mountebank their loves, / Cog their hearts from them, and come home belov'd / Of all the trades in Rome'. The tribunes Sicinius and Brutus have prepared for Coriolanus's appearance, having planned deliberately to anger him and decided how they will stir up the mob. Their plan quickly succeeds: they accuse him of being a traitor to the people because of his tyrannical nature, which provokes him to wild denunciation, whereupon they banish him. Rounding on the people, the 'common cry of curs', he declares 'I banish you' and sweeps out, prophesying that, banishing those who have defended them, they will be conquered easily by a foe, as they cannot and will not defend themselves.

Act IV: Coriolanus leaves his sorrowing wife, mother and friends. Volumnia briefly reviles the two tribunes. A Roman in the pay of the Volsces tells a Volscian of the 'insurrection' of the people against the patricians, and of Coriolanus's banishment, and is told of Volscian preparedness to seize the opportunity of 'division' in Rome to attack. Coriolanus comes disguised 'in mean attire' to Antium: 'My birthplace hate I, and my love's upon / This enemy town.' Going to Tullus Aufidius's house, he reveals who he is and offers either his throat to be cut or his 'revengeful services' (against his own 'canker'd country') to his old enemy. Aufidius gladly, almost lovingly, welcomes him. In Rome, the satisfaction of the tribunes at their success in getting rid of Coriolanus is changed to anxiety when news comes of his joining with Aufidius and his threat to Rome, and the plebeians begin to convince themselves that they had always felt is was a 'pity' to banish Coriolanus. Tullus Aufidius begins to resent Coriolanus's masterful pride and his popularity, but thinks that, although they will be successful and Coriolanus will be again acclaimed in Rome, some defect in his nature – arrogance, mistaken judgement, the need to dominate – will nullify the achievement, and then his own opportunity will come.

Act V: Cominius has been to the Volscian camp to intercede on Rome's behalf, and has been rebuffed. Old Menenius Agrippa at first will not go; he tells the tribunes, who had banished Coriolanus, to go and 'A mile before his tent fall down, and knee / The way into his mercy'. However, he yields to their request. In the Volscian camp, after being hindered by servants, he meets Coriolanus, who rejects his plea to him to pardon Rome, though he does give him a letter he had already written to him. Coriolanus and Aufidius, advancing towards Rome, are met by Volumnia, Virgilia and Coriolanus's young son. Although he embraces his wife and kneels to his mother, Coriolanus at first resists their appeals to spare Rome: 'Desire not / T'allay my rages and revenges with / Your colder reasons.' Volumnia speaks of her own tragic predicament, loving both Rome and her son, and begs him not to abandon the Volscians, but to reconcile them and the Romans; and eventually, as he says, she wins 'a happy victory to Rome', although he tells her she has 'most dangerously. . . with him prevail'd'. He turns to Aufidius, who seems to agree to a peace but who reveals in an aside that he sees an opportunity here for his own advantage. Coriolanus leaves Rome and Aufidius returns home. The Romans rejoice, and applaud Volumnia. Aufidius plots with three or four henchmen to revenge himself on Coriolanus for first usurping his position and then abandoning the Volscian cause when victory was certain. When Coriolanus returns, welcomed by the Volscian crowd, with the treaty of peace, Aufidius calls him a treacherous boy and the conspirators attack and kill Coriolanus.

SOURCE   The 'Life of Coriolanus' in Plutarch's□ *Lives* translated by Sir Thomas North□ (second edition 1595). As usual Shakespeare condenses and concentrates the action. He develops the character of Menenius Agrippa greatly, makes Tullus Aufidius (only named in Plutarch when Coriolanus goes to Antium) a more significant rival / equal, and humanises Volumnia and Virgilia.

TEXT   The play appears only in the First Folio□ (1623). Probably printed from Shakespeare's manuscript, perhaps with some corrections and marking by the book-keeper□ in the theatre.

Costume. The players mostly wore contemporary Elizabethan/Jacobean costume, except for Roman and Greek parts and conspicuous foreigners' parts (like Moors, Turks). The costumes were rich, grand and colourful, and very expensive. Costumes of foreigners or those representing persons of classical or ancient times hinted rather than achieved or aimed at accuracy. The richness of materials and the colour made up for the bare stages and lack of scenery.

Cymbeline. A late romance, of 1609 or 1610.

Act I: The situation at the beginning of the play, which is set in ancient Britain, is that the old king Cymbeline has imprisoned his daughter Imogen for marrying against his will, and has banished her husband Posthumus Leonatus. Under the wicked influence of his recently married wife, he had sought to marry Imogen to his stepson, the Queen's doltish son by a former marriage, Cloten, 'a thing / Too bad for bad report'. We also learn that twenty years earlier Cymbeline's two sons had been stolen away when very young. On parting, Imogen gives Posthumus a diamond ring and he gives her a bracelet. Posthumus goes into banishment to Rome, to the house of his friend Philario. Here he meets a gallant, Iachimo, and, during a discussion of women's virtue, is provoked into wagering Imogen's diamond ring against ten thousand ducats that Iachimo cannot win or seduce her: 'My mistress exceeds in goodness the hugeness of your unworthy thinking.'

In Britain, Imogen is still a prisoner, in the custody of the wicked Queen. The latter has commissioned a doctor, Cornelius, to make her a box of poisonous compounds, but, suspecting her intentions, he in fact gives her harmless substances which will only induce deep sleep. Unaware of this the Queen conveys the box to Posthumus's servant Pisanio, telling him it contains a life-restoring drug; she also tries to persuade him to desert his banished master and to prevail upon Imogen to love her son Cloten, promising him great rewards. Pisanio says little, but lets us know he will not betray Posthumus.

Iachimo comes to Britain and visits Imogen, bringing a letter of introduction from Posthumus. When he sees her, he recognises her virtue and knows that he will have to use deceitful tricks if he is to win the wager, so he tells her that Posthumus is unfaithful to her in Rome, wantoning with women. Iachimo then flatters her and proposes himself to her as her lover. Imogen immediately reviles him angrily, whereupon he persuades her that he was simply testing her devotion to Posthumus and begs her pardon, which she graciously gives. He then tells her that Posthumus, he and other Roman lords have joined together to buy valuable presents for the Emperor, which he wishes to leave in safe keeping for the night before returning home, and she agrees to the chest being deposited in her bedchamber.

Act II: In a short scene Cloten's boorish stupidity is again shown. Imogen goes to bed and sleeps; Iachimo emerges from the chest, wonders at her beauty, notes details of the room to report to Posthumus and notes particularly the mole on her breast, five-spotted 'like the crimson drops/ I'th' bottom of a cowslip', and takes from her arm the bracelet given her by Posthumus. Thus he reckons to be able to convince Posthumus that he has 'won' her. He then returns to his hiding-place in the trunk. Early the next morning Cloten comes with singers to serenade Imogen. When she appears, he woos her; her natural courtesy is soon turned to contemptuous dismissal when Cloten persists, and she tells him that Posthumus's meanest garment is dearer to her. She finds that she has mislaid her bracelet (taken by Iachimo while she slept). Posthumus's host in Rome, Philario, is discussing with him the Roman mission – demanding tribute – to Britain, which the Briton thinks will lead to

British defiance and so to war, when Iachimo returns. Describing Imogen's bedchamber and bodily beauty and showing the bracelet, he rather easily convinces Posthumus of her unfaithfulness. In anguish, grief and rage Posthumus curses her and all women and vows vengeance.

Act III: The Roman emissary Lucius comes to the British court demanding the unpaid tribute, but is defied by the King, the Queen and even by Cloten. Pisanio receives a terrible letter from Posthumus accusing Imogen of adultery and calling on him to murder her. He is appalled. There is also a deceitful letter from Posthumus to Imogen, telling her that he is in Britain, at Milford Haven in West Wales, and asking her to meet him there; there he intends Pisanio shall murder her. Imogen is overjoyed and bids Pisanio hasten to get ready and to provide her with a riding suit, for she intends immediately to go to Milford Haven with all speed.

In Wales we meet old Morgan and two young men, Polydore and Cadwal, who all live by hunting and whose dwelling is a cave. Morgan in a soliloquy reveals that he is in fact a courtier, Belarius, who twenty years before had been wrongly accused to Cymbeline and banished; in revenge, to deprive the King of heirs, he had stolen away the King's two young sons Guiderius and Arviragus (Polydore and Cadwal) whom he has brought up in the wild as his own sons. Pisanio and Imogen arrive in West Wales; he shows her Posthumus's letter demanding that he murder her. Incredulous and distressed she bitterly rounds on her absent husband, condemns all male falseness and calls on Pisanio to obey the command and kill her there and then. Of course he will not, and persuades her to put on male disguise (which he has brought with him) and to seek service with Lucius the Roman ambassador who, he has heard, will be arriving in Milford Haven on the following day. Thus she will be able to go with him and perhaps get sight of Posthumus. Pisanio will send some bloody cloth to Posthumus to convince him that he has obeyed and killed Imogen, and he gives her the box of medicine – which he believes to be restorative, though in fact it is the sleep drug – which he had received from the Queen.

Lucius leaves the court as the King prepares for war. Imogen's disappearance is discovered. Pisanio returns to the court from West Wales and is pounced on by Cloten who seeks to know where Imogen is. Pisanio gives him a letter containing Posthumus's decision to have her murdered, whereupon Cloten vows vengeance, presses Pisanio into his service, and tells him to bring him some of Posthumus's clothes, for he intends to go thus disguised to Milford Haven to kill Posthumus and secure Imogen. Imogen comes to Belarius's cave, and, weary, goes into it to sleep. Belarius, Guiderius and Arviragus return to find her there – of course in boy's attire, and calling herself Fidele (faithful) – and make her welcome. In Rome it is decided that orders shall be sent to Lucius to take command of Roman forces in Gaul in order to invade Britain.

Act IV: Cloten, dressed in clothes belonging to Posthumus, arrives in West Wales intending to kill Posthumus and ravish Imogen. Near by, Belarius and the two young men, going hunting, leave Imogen behind in the cave. She is, as she says to herself, 'sick still, heart-sick', and takes some of the drug given her by Pisanio. Meanwhile, Cloten has been seen by Belarius, who recognises him and fears he has come to find them as they are outlaws. Guiderius challenges him while Belarius and Arviragus depart. Cloten is killed by Guiderius and beheaded. Imogen is discovered in the cave and believed dead, to the grief of the three. Guiderius and Arviragus lay her body down and speak the song 'Fear no more the heat o' th' sun' as her dirge, and Belarius lays the corpse of Cloten (for 'He was a queen's son, boys') beside her, and flowers are strewn over them. They depart, and Imogen, recovering consciousness, is horrified to find what seems to be the dead and headless body of her husband beside her. While she is grieving over it, Lucius and his staff approach, and Imogen/Fidele is taken into his service. At court, Cymbeline, distracted by the disappearance of his daughter and the feverish illness of his wife, learns of the Roman landing. Pisanio wonders why he has heard nothing from his master Posthumus since he had written to tell the (untrue) news of Imogen's death, nor from her; nor does he know what has become of Cloten. In Wales Belarius thinks they must move higher into the mountains, away from the battles, for he cannot join the king's party, as a banished man. But the two young men are eager to change their lonely, isolated existence and prevail on him to go with them to join in the war.

Act V: Posthumus has arrived in Wales with the Roman forces. Grieving over the supposed death of his wife Imogen, and bitterly repenting his order to Pisanio to murder her, he resolves to join the British forces and to fight to the death against the invaders. Iachimo is now one of the Roman leaders; Posthumus dressed as a poor British soldier encounters and vanquishes him and departs. Iachimo expresses his guilt and grief at having 'belied a lady,/ The princess of this country' and sees his defeat and present weariness as punishment. In the general battle, Cymbeline is captured and the British retreat, until Belarius, Guiderius and Arviragus appear and rescue the King. Posthumus tells a British lord of the unbelievable exploits of the three in stopping the flight of the army down a narrow lane and how he had joined them in encouraging renewed assaults that brought victory. He is then, as a Roman soldier, captured.

While under arrest that night and chained, Posthumus deeply repents of his murderous intent towards his wife and then, sleeping, sees in a vision the ghosts of his aged father and mother and his two young brothers who briefly recite his life story, speak of his bravery in the battle and call on Jupiter to 'take off his miseries'. Jupiter descends, riding on his eagle, and comforts them: 'He shall be lord of lady Imogen,/ And happier much by his affliction made'; he gives them a book which is to be laid on Posthumus's breast. The latter awakes, reads in the book a prophecy of the end of his miseries and of the restoration of the British to 'flourish in peace and plenty', but he dismisses it as 'a dream' or 'senseless' (mad). Gaolers come to take him away to be hanged, to which he is indifferent, but suddenly the order is cancelled and he is to be freed.

Cymbeline, celebrating the three who ensured his victory, each of whom he creates a knight, laments that the poor soldier who joined them in their heroic exploit cannot be found. The physician Cornelius enters to report the death of the Queen, mad with remorse and confessing her abhorrence – concealed by pretence – of the King, her hatred of Imogen and her ambition for Cloten to come to the throne. Lucius, Iachimo and other Roman prisoners are brought in before execution; Lucius asks for his page Fidele (Imogen) to be spared, which Cymbeline grants. Belarius and his two 'sons' are puzzled at seeing Fidele whom they thought dead, and Pisanio realises that it is indeed his living mistress, Imogen; but the attention of all is drawn to Iachimo when Imogen, granted a boon by the king, asks the Italian where he obtained the diamond ring he wears. Iachimo then confesses his trickery, recounting the whole story of the wager with Posthumus in Rome and the bedchamber visitation. At this Posthumus advances, reviling himself bitterly for his own treachery and lack of faith, and calling out in grief Imogen's name. Imogen/Fidele cries out to him but Posthumus strikes her to the ground as an interfering page, whereupon Pisanio reveals that it is Imogen, to the amazement and joy of Cymbeline. Imogen, recovering, reviles Pisanio for giving her poison, but Pisanio quickly convinces her that he was ignorant of the drug's power, having been deceived by the Queen who had given it him. Imogen and Posthumus, restored to each other, embrace, and she kneels for her father the King's blessing. Now Pisanio reveals Cloten's villainy and Guiderius reports that he slew him, whereupon he is sorrowfully condemned to death by the King, in spite of his heroic part in the battle. At this Belarius reveals himself and identifies his two heroic 'sons' as the long-lost sons of Cymbeline, to the great joy of the King, and of Imogen, thus endowed with two brothers whom as strangers she already loved.

In the general happiness at all these reunions, Cymbeline frees

Lucius and his fellow-prisoners. At this point Posthumus reveals that he was the soldier 'in poor beseeming' who had fought with the heroic three, calling on Iachimo, whom he had worsted in the battle, to confirm it. The repentant Iachimo does so and asks for death at Posthumus's hands, but the latter spares him: 'The power that I have on you, is to spare you: / The malice towards you, to forgive you', and Cymbeline, crying 'Nobly doom'd' (judged), says 'Pardon's the word to all'. A soothsayer interprets the prophetic message Jupiter had left for Posthumus, most of which has now been fulfilled, and the rest – that 'Britain be fortunate, and flourish in peace and plenty' – is implied in 'the harmony of this peace', which is rounded off by Cymbeline's deciding that Britain will pay the 'wonted tribute' to Rome, and Britain and Rome live 'Friendly together'.

SOURCE   The 'historical' parts come from Holinshed's☐ *Chronicles of England, Scotland and Ireland*☐ (2nd edition, 1589), there sketchily put together. The heroism of Belarius, Guiderius and Arviragus comes from the Scottish section of the *Chronicles*, an account of a brave Scot and his two sons who defeated a Danish force. The wager part seems to be drawn from Boccaccio's☐ *Decameron*, the ninth novel of the second day, but even more from a version called *Frederyke of Jennen* (Genoa), which was an English translation (1518 and reprinted) of a Dutch version of a German version which probably derived from an Italian tale which Boccaccio knew. The Belarius and the long-lost princes plot was probably inspired by a romantic drama, *The Rare Triumphs of Love and Fortune*, performed before Queen Elizabeth at Windsor in December 1582; it was first printed in 1589. The wicked stepmother does not appear in any of the sources, though a boorish gentleman is to be found in *The Rare Triumphs* as the heroine's brother.

TEXT   The play appears only in the First Folio☐ (1623), entitled *The Tragedy of Cymbeline*, probably from a good copy of Shakespeare's, perhaps with the book-keeper's☐ additions of some stage-directions.

D

Daniel, Samuel (1562–1619). Writer of an academic tragedy *Cleopatra* (which was indebted to Shakespeare's play) and the epic historical poem *The Civile Warres*,☐ which Shakespeare made some use of for several of his historical plays.

Decameron, The. See Boccaccio.

Degree. The 'degree' or order of the world was a crucial concept in Elizabethan literature. God at the Creation had carefully worked out the proper degree from highest to lowest of every created thing, thus repeating on earth the order which existed in Heaven, where even the angels were graded in rank. Indeed the created world was a microcosm (little world) that repeated the order and degree of the macrocosm (great world) of Heaven. A complete system of correspondences existed within the created world and related to the heavenly creation. Because of this connection, any breaking of earthly order or degree (the abdication, deposition or murder of a king, for example) produced terrible repercussions in the heavens and in Nature. Examples in Shakespeare are the storm in *King Lear*, and terrible happenings such as the reports of horses eating each other after the murder of Duncan in *Macbeth*. Ulysses in *Troilus and Cressida* makes a famous speech about degree (I.3.83ff.); the history plays and the tragedies especially show the chaos of disorder and the misery which going against God's natural order will cause. The idea of degree is strongly shown in imagery, with correspondences such as God-king-sun-lion-eagle-oak-dolphin taken for granted: each item is chief or principal in its group or kind.

Dumbshow. The brief mimed interludes, 'dumb' because no words are spoken, which suggest, represent or symbolise the action that has happened or is about to happen in Tudor and Elizabethan drama. There are about 150 examples altogether in surviving plays, from the first example in *Gorboduc*□ (1562) to about 1630. In that play an elaborate dumbshow introduces each of the five acts. Sometimes, as before Act I, it is a symbolic presentation making a moral didactic point; sometimes it anticipates the action to come. In *Gorboduc*, a rather static 'classical' play (though on a supposedly historical English chronicle subject), a play of speeches rather than action, the dumbshows provide some interesting concentrated action in addition to pointing the moral significance, making the plot clear and informing the audience of things that could not easily be expressed in dialogue. Shakespeare possibly intended a dumbshow in *A Midsummer Night's Dream*, to show in advance the action of the play by the mechanicals (craftsmen, Quince and his fellows), *Pyramus and Thisbe*, before the court, although the use of the word 'show' here may refer simply to the humble actors introducing themselves in turn to the noble audience, and no stage-direction details any action. In the most famous dumbshow of all, in *Hamlet*, the whole action of the 'Mousetrap' play is mimed before the 'play' begins. This is exceptionally rare, if not unique, and is almost certainly in order that the audience may know what is to happen in the 'play' and can accordingly concentrate on the reactions of the king and of the intently watching Hamlet. In *Macbeth* there is not exactly a dumbshow but a 'show' of kings, an armed head, a bloody child, presented by spirits summoned by the witches; there are brief 'visions', like small dumbshows, in *Pericles*, *Cymbeline* and *Henry VIII*; and in *The Tempest* there are 'shows' by spirits presenting a feast.

E

Education, Shakespeare's. Although there is no actual proof that Shakespeare was educated at the Grammar School at Stratford-on-Avon it would be surprising if not incredible if he had not been. His father was a prominent citizen, an alderman who served his turn as mayor. Shakespeare was clearly well educated and well read. The main function of a Tudor/Elizabethan grammar school was to teach Latin. After learning the grammar a boy would learn by heart *Sententiae Puerilae*, a collection of memorable moral sayings, then Cato's (234–149BC) proverbs. A Latin Aesop's (6th century BC) *Fables*, Latin pastorals of Baptista Spagnuoli (1448–1516) known as the Mantuan, Cicero's (106–43BC) *Letters* and Virgil's (70–19BC) pastoral eclogues .followed, leading on to the *Metamorphoses*□ of Ovid (43BC–AD18). Ovid's *Heroides*, moving letters from 'heroines', and Virgil's epic poem the *Aeneid* were then studied. In the higher forms the Latin comedies of Plautus□ and Terence□ were read, and probably acted, and probably the tragedies of Seneca. A lot of classical rhetoric and Roman history was also studied. In several plays Shakespeare writes about schooling or schoolmasters: the boy William in *The Merry Wives of Windsor* is tested in Latin grammar by the parson Sir Hugh Evans; Holofernes is a pedantic bore of a schoolmaster in *Love's Labour's Lost*.The curriculum of a grammar school provided an ideal education for a would-be writer and dramatist of the time. Shakespeare's work everywhere shows how much he learned, how much of it he remembered and how much it influenced him.

Elizabeth, Queen (1533–1603). Elizabeth was the only surviving child of Henry VIII and Anne Boleyn (or Bullen). She became queen in 1558 on the death of her older sister, the Catholic Queen Mary Tudor (who had herself succeeded her younger brother Edward VI – a Protestant king). She was twenty-five when she came to the throne, to a realm threatened by religious and other divisions within, and by the Catholic powers of Europe without, led by her brother-in-law, King Philip II of Spain, widower of Mary Tudor. Invasion was imminent then, and the threat was not removed until the defeat of the Armada thirty years later in 1588. By a combination of intelligent ruthlessness and clear-sighted purpose, helped by able ministers such as Lord Burghley, she preserved Protestantism and English independence of Rome and of Catholic Europe, and encouraged a slow-rising but extraordinarily powerful upsurge of patriotic feeling and of national achievement in all aspects of the country's life. As in other periods in British history, a long-reigning queen was to become a focus for national unity and purpose, and Elizabeth I became also, as Virgin Queen, a symbol of virtue, beauty and power for the nation, and especially for its writers (Edmund Spenser□ above all) who themselves fostered and extended the worship.

Elizabeth was a generous patron of the theatre and some think that without her support and her encouragement of the drama, both personally and through giving greater powers to the Lord Chamberlain (see Chamberlain's Men, the Lord□) and the Master of the Revels,□ the hostility of the City of London and of Puritan strength in the Church might have killed the drama. She increasingly entertained at court with theatrical presentations, and Shakespeare's company performed at court twice as often as any other company, and its members were Grooms of the Chamber.□ Shakespeare rarely refers to her directly, but the greatest speech in *Henry VIII* at the baptism of the baby Elizabeth is a noble implied tribute to 'A pattern to all princes living with her/ And all that shall succeed' (though some think the speech may not have been written by Shakespeare). There is a famous story that after *Henry IV* she commanded him to write another play to show Falstaff in love: this was *The Merry Wives of Windsor*. Much of Shakespeare's English history writing was inspired by and supported the Tudor settlement (when, after years of faction and civil wars, the Wars of the Roses□ were concluded towards the end of the fifteenth century by the victory of Henry Richmond, crowned king as Henry VII and grandfather of Queen Elizabeth, over Richard III). Elizabeth died in 1603 after reigning for forty-five years and ensuring the greatness of Britain as a world power, its unity and its continued Protestantism.

F

Florio, Giovanni (?1553–1625). Born in England of resident Italian parents, Florio was the author of a well-known Italian grammar and dictionary. If Shakespeare knew Italian, which is very likely, he probably used Florio's books. He certainly knew Florio's famous translation (published 1603) of the *Essays* of Montaigne□ (1533–92), and was consciously (many words and phrases especially in *King Lear* and *The Tempest*) or unconsciously (the questioning introspection of Hamlet) influenced by and indebted to it. Florio's translation appeared in 1603 but it seems likely that the two knew each other, as both were known to and favoured by the Earl of Southampton, and the dramatist may well have seen the translation before it was published.

Folio, the First. The first edition of all of Shakespeare's plays (except *Pericles*) in one volume, published in 1623, 'containing all his

Comedies, Histories and Tragedies: Truely set forth, according to their first originall' as the title-page in many copies records. The title-page also carries the names of the principal actors, beginning with Shakespeare and Richard Burbage□ and including, among the twenty-six names recorded, John Heminge□ or Heminges and Henry Condell,□ the two editors of the volume. In many copies, the title-page carries an engraving of the portrait of the dramatist by Martin Droeshout (see Plate 1 on page 6). The printers were William Jaggard and his son Isaac. Eighteen of the thirty-six plays had never been printed before. The plays are presented in three sections, with separate numbering of the pages: Comedies, Histories, Tragedies. One or two are oddly placed, *Cymbeline* for example being with the Tragedies and called *The Tragedie of Cymbeline*; *Troilus and Cressida* appears between the Histories and the Tragedies; and almost the last of all the plays, *The Tempest*, comes first of all. There are 907 pages. It is called the Folio because of the page-size. To printers a folio book was made up of sheets folded once to form two leaves (that is, four pages or 'sides') of a size varying from 11 to 16 inches deep by 8 to 11 inches wide (about 27 to 40cm by 20 to 28cm). There was probably a printing of about 1,000 copies, and of these about 240 survive, many of them damaged and incomplete. Any of the plays which had been published previously had been single editions in quarto,□ a much smaller size. Later folios of the complete plays were F2 (1632), a reprint of F1; F3 (1663), a second impression of which in 1664 added *Pericles* and six plays wrongly attributed at that time to Shakespeare (see Apocrypha□); and F4 (1685). Each of these was based on the one before, always with some corrections and some new errors.

Fools. Fools in Shakespeare are to be distinguished from clowns□ and witty servants. They are based on the professional fools who served in royal courts and noble households. There was a convention of their being 'all-licensed' to say whatever they liked, as Goneril complains of the Fool in *King Lear*. (The matter is complicated a little by the fact that 'fools' in great houses were sometimes, as the name suggests, harmless lunatics or weak-wits kept because their antics gave amusements.) Lear's Fool is the chief Shakespearian fool, with an intelligent and (vainly) warning function in recognising and commenting on his master's folly. His relationship with the King and his power to move an audience are unique. The amiably cynical Touchstone of *As You Like It* and the musical Feste of *Twelfth Night* (who as well as jesting and entertaining takes a prominent part in the sub-plot) are the other leading fools. But Shakespeare sometimes has characters call fools 'clowns' as well. Some think these witty intelligent questioning parts, especially Feste and Lear's Fool, were written for the actor Robert

Armin who joined the company in 1599, and the earlier jesters and the clowns for William Kempe.

Forest of Arden. See Arden, Forest of.

'foul papers'. Either the author's original manuscript or rough copy or last completed draft, which was then made into a fair copy. Shakespeare seems not to have made fair copies himself. A number of quarto□ editions of separate plays and three plays in the First Folio□ are thought to have been printed from his foul papers, which cannot have been very foul (and the editors in the preface to the First Folio recorded that they 'scarce received from him a blot in his papers').

Foxe, John (1516–87). Foxe, a dedicated Protestant, took himself off to Germany during the reign of the Catholic Queen Mary Tudor (1553–8). Here he completed in Latin his *Book of Martyrs,*□ a collection of accounts of Christian martyrs, and added accounts of the Protestant martyrs of his own century. It was published in 1559, in which year he returned to England, Protestantism having been re-established with the accession of Queen Elizabeth the year before. He prepared an English edition – *Actes and Monuments of these Latter and Perilous Days* – which was published in 1563, by which time he had entered the Church and become prebendary of Salisbury. Enormously popular, copies of it were placed in most churches. Shakespeare found it useful for *King John* and *Henry VI, Part 2*, and for Cranmer material in *Henry VIII*.

G

Ghosts. Elizabethans on the whole believed in ghosts, and the Elizabethan drama inherited a tradition of tragic ghostly intervention in human affairs from the tragedies of Seneca□ which showed most clearly in revenge tragedy. Shakespeare presents ghosts in five plays. In *Richard III* the ghosts of the king's murdered victims come threateningly in his dreams, and also appear to his virtuous rival Richmond, encouragingly, on the night before the battle. In *Julius Caesar* the ghost of murdered Caesar appears to Brutus, the chief of those who had murdered him. The ghost of murdered Banquo in *Macbeth* comes to the banquet (but is seen only by the guilty king, not by Lady Macbeth or the other guests). In *Hamlet* his father's ghost comes to tell Hamlet of his murder by his brother Claudius, and is seen and spoken to by the prince and his companions; but later, appearing in the Queen's bed-chamber, it is seen by Hamlet but not by her. In *Cymbeline* the benign ghosts of Posthumus's father, mother and brothers appear in a vision appealing to the god Jupiter to help him. Shakespeare's use of what in his contemporaries was usually merely theatrical and sensational

shows his characteristic development in subtlety and meaning. The
ghosts have great theatrical impact, especially in the two great tragedies, but are also excellent devices used by the dramatist to show the
troubled mind or sick conscience, and to convince the audience of the
terrible demands, whether internal (when the ghost is not seen by
others) or external, laid upon the tragic hero and constituting the crux
of his moral dilemma. The suggestion – or proof – of the existence
of a supernatural world beyond the world of men is a significant
element in all great tragedy, whether Christian or pre-Christian. The
helplessness of man caught and isolated in a pattern of events finally
beyond his control is a recurrent idea of great power, uniting an
audience in a bond of sympathy with the noble victim, however erring
he may be. (The idea is strongly realised in all the great Shakespearian
tragedies whether or not ghosts actually appear.)

Globe Theatre. The Globe was the home of the Lord Chamberlain's
Men,□ later the King's Men, of which Shakespeare was a member. He
was also a housekeeper□ of the Globe. It was built in 1598-9. The
Burbages (see, Burbage, Richard□), owners of the playhouse called
The Theatre but not owners of the land on which it stood, were refused
a renewal of the lease of the site, the owner intending to pull it down.
But the Burbages had the building dismantled and the materials (wood
chiefly) removed to a site on the other side of the River Thames at
Southwark, where they built the Globe. (We know of this from records
of a lawsuit brought by the owner of the land on which The Theatre
had stood, in 1602.) We do not know exactly what the Globe was like,
but we do know some of the dimensions of the Fortune, built the following year, 1600, by the same carpenter-builder, Peter Streete, because
the contract for that survives. Unfortunately, the Fortune was rectangular whereas the Globe was almost certainly polygonal. Furthermore, the contract records that the Fortune stage is to be in all 'propor-
tions contrived and fashioned like unto the stage of the . . . Globe' but
does not give those dimensions. The Fortune had three galleries; the
Globe almost certainly had the same and certainly had thatched roofs
over the galleries and stage, for during a performance in June 1613,
believed to be of *Henry VIII*, the thatch was ignited when a salute was
fired for an entry to a banquet, and the Globe was burned to the ground.
It was rebuilt and re-opened the following year. John Orrell, in *The
Quest for Shakespeare's Globe*, Cambridge University Press, 1983,
calculates that Shakespeare's Globe – whether the first Globe or its
successor, which he claims was the same size, being built on the earlier
foundations – was roughly 100 ft. (about 30½m.) across in total,
with a stage width of about 50 ft. (about 15¼m.), and that it could
accommodate an audience of well over 3,000 people.

We can obtain some idea of what the Globe looked like by studying

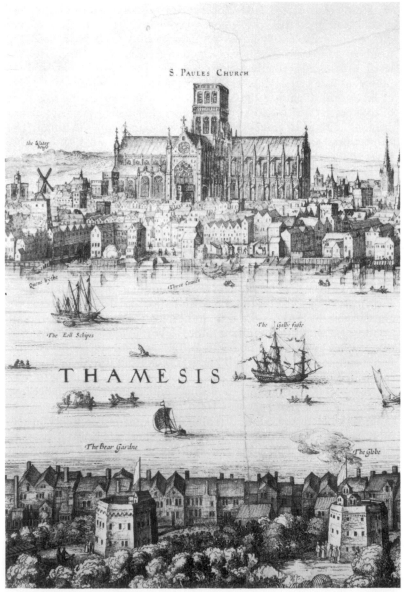

PLATE 2: Detail from an engraving by C. J. Visscher, *c*.1600, in which the first Globe is clearly polygonal. But Visscher may have transposed the names of the Globe and the Bear Garden, as Hollar, who based his engraving (1649) partly on Visscher, certainly did.

contemporary illustrations. The engraving by the Dutch artist C. J. Visscher (1586–1652), from a drawing of about 1600, shows a clearly polygonal first Globe (see Plate 2).The equally famous drawing of the interior of the Swan□ theatre by J. de Witt of about1596, which looks like a rough sketch meant only to give a general impression, probably gives a pretty good idea of the interior of an open (outdoor, unroofed) Elizabethan theatre like the Globe (see page 142). Such visual and written documentation was used to form the basis of C. W. Hodges' 'conjectural reconstruction of the Globe' (see page 123). See also Playhouses.□

Golding, Arthur (?1536–?1605). Elizabethan translator, especially of Ovid's *Metamorphoses*□ which he published in 1567. Translated into 'fourteeners' (fourteen syllables to the line), the Roman poet's collection of the principal legends and myths of Greece and Rome, written about the first decade of the Christian era in exile at Tomi on the Black Sea, contained a number of myths concerning the metamorphoses or bodily transformations of gods and nymphs, often in the interests of sexual pursuit or evasion. The original was well known to Shakespeare and greatly loved. Although he would have read Ovid at school there are enough echoes of Golding's translation for us to be sure he knew the translation well.

Gorboduc. An early tragedy (1562) by Thomas Norton and Thomas Sackville written for the Christmas revels of the gentlemen of the Inner Temple (one of the great London 'colleges' for lawyers) and presented before the Queen at Whitehall two weeks later. The first play in blank verse,□ it is a Senecan□ tragedy with a Chorus,□ five acts and dumb-shows,□ a tragedy of blood dealing with the murder and civil strife that follow the division of his kingdom by the old king Gorboduc. It was a very influential though not a very good play, and indirectly had some influence on Shakespeare's *King Lear*.

Gower, John (?1330–1408). Poet and moral writer contemporary with Chaucer,□ who called him 'moral Gower'. In the English *Confessio Amantis* (?1380–90) ('Confession of a Lover'), published by William Caxton in 1482, a lover is questioned by and confesses to a confessor his sins against love, which are discussed between them under the headings of the Seven Deadly Sins – Pride, Lust, Greed, Anger, Envy, Avarice and Sloth – and illustrated by many tales. Gower's long tale of 'Apollonius of Tyre' was a chief source for *Pericles, Prince of Tyre*, and Shakespeare makes this even clearer by having the figure of Gower in his play as a kind of Chorus□ who presents the story, filling in gaps of time where necessary and introducing each act as well as summarising the plot in the Epilogue. His part is written mostly in the octosyllabic (eight-syllabled, four-stress) couplet form used by John Gower in *Confessio Amantis*.

Greene, Robert (1558–92). Elizabethan writer, pamphleteer and dramatist. His prose romance *Pandosto, the Triumph of Time* (1588) gave the
main plot and idea of *The Winter's Tale*. His own plays *Friar Bacon
and Friar Bungay* and *James IV*, both of 1590 or 1591, although not at
all 'Shakespearian', have a number of elements and modes which may
have pointed the way for the early Shakespeare (though we cannot be
sure the influence was not the other way round) – romantic comedy
with charming heroines of spirit and intelligence (Margaret, Ida and
Dorothea), humour, delightful Englishness of setting and of characters as well as interest in history, and a relaxed mixture of humour,
fantasy, magic and drama. It was Greene who first recorded, in his
Groatsworth of Wit, published in 1592 just after his death, the rise of
Shakespeare, attacking him as an 'upstart crow' of a player and
writer invading the London theatrical scene and thinking himself
'the only Shake-scene in a country'.

Grooms of the Chamber. The actors of the Lord Chamberlain's Men,□
Shakespeare's company, later called the King's Men after the
accession of James I in 1603, together with other players under royal
patronage (the Queen's Men in Elizabeth's reign and in James's the
Prince's Men), were also Grooms of the Chamber under the Lord
Chamberlain. They were not paid, except for some special occasions,
but received livery (uniform and ceremonial clothes). Shakespeare
headed the list of nine members of his company who received 4½
yards of scarlet cloth for the coronation procession in March 1604,
for example. Below the rank of Gentlemen of the Chamber and
above that of Yeomen, they formed part of the Lord Chamberlain's
staff. It is further indication of the standing of actors and of
Shakespeare, as well as of royal interest in drama: actors were, or
could be, men of some rank and position as well as of substance.

Groundlings. These were the poorer members of the audience in the
London playhouses□ who stood on the ground in the yard, not
sitting – at a higher charge – in the galleries.

H

Hall (Halle), Edward (?1498–1547). A historian and lawyer who was the
author of the chronicle *The Union of the Two Noble and Illustre Famelies
of Lancastre and York* (1548) which influenced all Tudor and Elizabethan historians. It records the history of England from the reign of
Henry IV up to and including the reign of Henry VIII (under whom
Hall held high legal appointments). It takes a moralistic view of
history as providing a warning to princes and rulers. It celebrates the
end of the Wars of the Roses□ with the overthrow of the usurper

Richard III by Henry Richmond (Henry VII), founder of the Tudor
line, father of Henry VIII and so grandfather of Queen Elizabeth.
Shakespeare is greatly indebted to Hall, as was his other principal
source for English history, Holinshed.□

Hamlet. A tragedy of 1600–1.

Act I: The ghost□ of Hamlet the recently dead King of Denmark has
twice been seen on the battlements. His son's friend Horatio joins the
two officers of the guard, sceptically, to watch, and the ghost appears
for a third time; Horatio fears it 'bodes some strange eruption to our
state'. The state of Denmark is already under threat from Fortinbras,
the young King of Norway, whose father had been defeated and killed
by old Hamlet, and many warlike preparations are being made.
Horatio decides to tell Hamlet about the ghost. Claudius, the new
King, has married old Hamlet's widow, Gertrude, very soon after his
death. In court, he sends emissaries to Norway, and permits Laertes,
son of Polonius (his chief state official and adviser), to return to
France; but he requests his new stepson, young Hamlet, not to return,
as Hamlet wishes, to his German university at Wittenberg. Hamlet is
sullen and still grieving over his father's recent death, but accedes to
his mother's further urging. Left alone on stage, in his first soliloquy
he passionately expresses his grief and depression and his shocked
anger at how quickly his mother has remarried – and that to
Claudius, a 'satyr' (half-beast, half-man) in comparison with old
Hamlet ('Hyperion', the sun-god). To him comes Horatio and tells
him of the ghost, and Hamlet resolves to go on the watch himself.

Laertes takes leave of his sister, Ophelia, warning her to be careful
of Hamlet and his professed love; and their father, Polonius, after
giving the famous parting advice to Laertes – 'And these few
precepts in thy memory / Look thou character' – similarly fears for
her, assuming, cynically, that the Prince's 'love' may be more selfish
and worldly than her innocence can understand; he forbids her to
meet or correspond with Hamlet. Hamlet goes on watch on the
battlements that night; the ghost appears, beckons to Hamlet to leave
his companions and follow him, and tells him that his death was
murder by poison at the hands of Claudius, who had already 'won
to his shameful lust/The will of my most seeming-virtuous queen'.
He calls on Hamlet to remember, and to revenge. Hamlet, while not
revealing what passed with the ghost, swears Horatio and his
companion to secrecy, and also makes them swear not to betray him
if he 'shall think meet/To put an antic disposition on'.

Act II: We see another side of Polonius as he commissions Reynaldo
to go to Paris to spy on his son Laertes's behaviour. A frightened
Ophelia reports to her father a visit from Hamlet, distraught, his
clothes disordered and neglected; it sounds like a sad, mad, regretful

farewell, but Polonius assumes that 'this is the very ecstasy of love'. It is also the first sign of Hamlet's 'transformation', perhaps the first 'antic disposition'. Polonius hastens to tell Claudius and Gertrude. They are welcoming two former friends of Hamlet, Rosencrantz and Guildenstern, and asking them to pick up the old friendship in order to find out the cause of Hamlet's 'transformation'. The emissaries return, successful, from Norway, reporting that young Fortinbras has been restrained and now seeks permission to pass through Denmark to attack Poland, which is agreed. Now Polonius with comic circumlocution tells the King and Queen that on his instructions his daughter Ophelia has refused Hamlet's love, and it is this that has brought on 'the madness wherein now he raves'. Polonius encounters Hamlet and is treated by the Prince with mad, insulting but pointed rudeness. (This is the first we have *seen* of Hamlet's 'antic disposition'.) Rosencrantz and Guildenstern enter. Hamlet suspects they are acting for the King, and they are forced to admit it.

A troupe of players known to Hamlet has come to the court. He welcomes them, asks them for a speech, which he begins himself (about the murder of King Priam by Pyrrhus). He asks them to put on a play the following night, *The Murder of Gonzago*. Left on stage alone, he speaks the second soliloquy: 'O what a rogue and peasant slave am I!' in which he reflects how the chief actor in giving the speech had 'in a fiction, in a dream of passion' brought tears to 'his eyes, distraction in's aspect', while he, Hamlet, with so great a 'motive and . . . cue for passion' has done nothing. But now he will do something: 'I'll have these players / Play something like the murder of my father / Before mine uncle.' By the King's reaction Hamlet will know whether the Ghost is to be believed about Claudius's guilt.

Act III: The King and Polonius hide as, by arrangement, Ophelia is to encounter Hamlet, so that they can determine whether or not his 'confusion' is caused by love of her. Hamlet enters, gives the third soliloquy, 'To be, or not to be, that is the question', is approached by Ophelia and cruelly, tormentingly, rejects and insults her. The King now knows that love is not the cause, but does not believe that what they have seen was actual madness. 'There's something in his soul / O'er which his melancholy sits on brood', he says, and, fearing what this may be, resolves to despatch him to England. Polonius suggests that Gertrude should see him after the play and try to find the truth, and this is agreed. Hamlet briefs the players, and talks to his admired friend Horatio ('just' and one who 'is not passion's slave'), telling him to watch intently the King's reactions to the play. The royal party enters and the dumbshow (in which the action of the play about to be seen is presented briefly) is played. The action shows a loving king and queen, the poisoning of the king, the grief of the queen, her wooing

by the murderer and then her acceptance of him. Then the play begins.
After Hamlet has identified the murderer as 'nephew to the king' and
he has poured poison in the 'king's' ears, the King rises, Polonius stops
the play and the royal party leaves hastily. Hamlet excitedly cries out
that the Ghost's story of his own murder must be true, and Horatio
agrees. Rosencrantz and Guildenstern come to summon Hamlet to
the Queen. The King is now convinced that he is in danger from
Hamlet and charges Rosencrantz and Guildenstern to be his escort to
England. Polonius reports Hamlet's approach to his mother's
chamber and says that he will hide behind the arras there to observe.

The King in a soliloquy acknowledges his guilt, of 'the primal eldest
curse' – a brother's murder – and kneels and tries to pray, but cannot.
Hamlet comes upon him, unsheathes his sword to kill him but draws
back, with the cold explanation that to kill Claudius at his prayers
would send him straight to heaven. Equally cruelly he berates his
mother, frightening her into crying out; Polonius, behind the arras,
calls out, and Hamlet, believing it to be Claudius, stabs through the
curtain and kills him. He returns to chiding his mother for her betrayal
of his father and sexual indulgence with his murderer, at which point
the Ghost appears briefly to him (but not to Gertrude) to remind
Hamlet of his task. Hamlet again urges repentance and chastity upon
her, and commands her not to reveal to Claudius that his 'madness' is
assumed. He knows of the plan to send him to England.

Act IV: Claudius comes to Gertrude and is told of Hamlet's madness
and of his killing of Polonius. Hamlet is placed under arrest, but continues with sardonic wit mordantly to suggest elated madness, and is
lyingly told by Claudius that he is being sent to England for his own
safety, which he accepts although he guesses the truth – which is
that he is to be killed on arrival. On the journey to the port Hamlet
encounters Fortinbras's army, and in the fourth soliloquy, 'How all
occasions do inform against me' he contrasts his failure so far to carry
out his dead father's commands with the energy and spirit of young
Fortinbras. In Elsinore, Ophelia has lapsed into madness. Laertes
returns from France in anger, having heard of Polonius's death, and
is supported by a mob demanding that he be made king; while
Claudius is placating him and trying to explain, his grief is heightened
by the entry of his mad sister. Letters come from Hamlet for Horatio
and for the King and Queen, announcing his return. Claudius plots
the murder of Hamlet, to be made to seem an accident: Laertes, a
good fencer, is to take part in a contest, with a naked sword (not a
practice-sword) which he himself will also dip in poison. At this point
the Queen brings news that Ophelia has drowned herself.

Act V: Hamlet, accompanied by Horatio, stops to talk to two grave-
diggers in a churchyard. Jokingly they discuss death and the identity

of some of the skulls turned up. He is unaware that the grave they have been digging is for Ophelia, but soon the funeral procession enters and he discovers this; passionate with grief he proclaims his love for the dead girl, which involves him in a scuffle with her brother. In the castle Hamlet tells Horatio of his discovery of the plot to kill him, and of how he had instead ensured the deaths of Rosencrantz and Guildenstern; a foppish courtier, Osric, informs Hamlet of the proposed contest with Laertes, which the Prince accepts, though, as he suddenly says to his friend, 'thou wouldst not think how ill all's here about my heart'. The royal party enters. When the fencing match begins, the King drops a poisoned pearl into a cup which is offered to Hamlet during a pause in the match. Hamlet declines; the Queen in ignorance takes it up to drink his health, the King being unable to forestall her. Hamlet is wounded; in scuffling they exchange rapiers and Laertes is wounded. As the Queen calls out that the cup is poisoned, swoons and dies, the dying Laertes reveals the treachery of the poisoned foil, incriminating the King. Hamlet rushes at Claudius and kills him; Laertes dies, asking forgiveness which Hamlet freely gives. As he is dying, Hamlet stops the faithful Horatio from killing himself, asking him to live and tell the whole story. He learns of the arrival of young Fortinbras of Norway and expresses the wish that he shall succeed to the crown, and dies. Fortinbras enters, claims the throne and orders 'soldier's music and the rites of war' for Hamlet.

SOURCE   An earlier Elizabethan play, not surviving and not known to have been printed, most probably by Thomas Kyd (1558–94), author of the famous revenge play *The Spanish Tragedy* (c.1589). The so-called *Ur-Hamlet* derived from the twelfth-century *Historiae Danicae* of Saxo Grammaticus, a mixture of folk-legend and Danish history, via François de Belleforest's□ *Histoires Tragiques* (1559–82).

TEXT   There are two quarto□ texts, Quarto 1 (1602), Quarto 2 (1604), and the First Folio (1623).□ Q1 is a 'bad' quarto, a pirated reconstruction, probably chiefly by the small-part actor or actors who played Marcellus, Lucianus and Voltemand (whose speeches correspond closely with those in Q2 and the Folio). Q2 is nearly twice as long (over 3,750 lines, the longest of all Shakespeare's plays), and was probably printed from Shakespeare's 'foul papers'□ to which had been added some playhouse notes, stage-directions, etc. The Folio text is about 230 lines shorter (it omits, for example, most of IV.4 including the fourth soliloquy, and a lot of Osric in V.2). Most editors now base their editions on Q2, but with additions, etc. from the Folio text.

Heavens. Two great pillars set on the stage seem to have supported a roof or cover known as the 'heavens'. Painted cloth or cloths could be suspended from the roof, which provided concealment from which properties or machinery could be lowered on to the stage and from which gods, etc. could appear. The painted ceiling and pillars also provided some colour and splendour for the bare stage area.

Hecatommithi. See Cinthio.

Heminge, or Heminges, John (?–1630). An actor with the Lord Chamberlain's Men□ from 1594. He was a good man of business and seems to have become a sort of business manager for the company, of which he was a large 'sharer';□ at his death he had a quarter share in the Globe□ as a housekeeper,□ and also in the Blackfriars.□ He produced with his fellow-actor Henry Condell□ the First Folio□ of Shakespeare's plays, 'without ambition either of self-profit, or fame: only to keep the memory of so worthy a Friend, and Fellow alive, as was our Shakespeare'.

Henry IV, Part 1. A history play, dating probably from late 1596.

Act I: It is a year since the murder of Richard II. The King, Henry IV, hopes that England has seen an end to civil disturbance – 'No more the thirsty entrance of this soil/ Shall daub her lips with her own children's blood' – and intends to hasten on the pilgrimage to the Holy Land he wants to make. But news comes of a Welsh rising under Glendower and of his capture of Mortimer, followed immediately by word of another outbreak on the Scottish border, in which, however, Douglas has been defeated by Henry Percy (Hotspur). Hotspur, despite the fact that he has arrogantly refused to hand over his prisoners, is admired by the King, who sees in him the virtues of honour and sense of duty sadly lacking in his own son. Straight away we meet that son, Prince Hal, in the unseemly company of Sir John Falstaff, sublimely witty and amusing but a drunken old roysterer and reprobate. A highway robbery is being planned by Gadshill, and the Prince is persuaded to take part in it. Ned Poins proposes secretly that Hal and he shall wait and then rob the robbers, Falstaff, Gadshill, Bardolph and Peto; he thinks Falstaff will be exposed as a coward and then as a lying braggart. Left alone, the Prince reveals in a soliloquy that although he 'will awhile uphold/ The unyok'd humour' of his low associates, it will only be like the sun's beauty 'smothered' from the world by 'base contagious clouds', and when the time comes, he will shine forth to the people more gloriously. The King rebukes Hotspur; his uncle Worcester reminds the King that he owes his position to the Percies, and is angrily dismissed. Hotspur explains why he refused to hand over the prisoners, and declares he will only do so if the King ransoms his brother-in-law, Mortimer, whom the King thinks of as in traitorous association with Glendower. When the King departs, the Percy family–Northumberland, Worcester and Hotspur – plot rebellion, and hope to involve Mortimer, Glendower, Douglas and the Archbishop of York.

Act II: The 'hold-up' takes place as planned, Hal and Poins in disguise threatening the others who have robbed the travellers and succeeding in getting the booty when Falstaff and the others run away. Hotspur and his wife (sister of Mortimer) are shown in affectionate banter; he is getting ready for the rebellion, she chides him for his recent neglect of her and fears her brother Mortimer is about to press his (good) claim to the Throne, and is involving Hotspur. At the Boar's Head Tavern the 'robbers' forgather, Falstaff tells a tale of valour, of how he fought with a number of travellers – an ever-increasing number as he tells it – and reviles the Prince for not having been there. When Hal reveals the true story, Falstaff instantly produces his excuse: that he knew it was Hal he was fighting, and 'was it for me to kill the heir-apparent?' A messenger comes to order the Prince to attend at court the following day, for the rebellion – Percy, Glendower, Mortimer, Northumberland – has begun. The spirit of festivity, however, is not quelled, and Falstaff, suggesting that the King will be angry with his son, proposes that Hal shall 'practise an answer'. Falstaff first plays the King, rebuking Hal for taking part in a robbery and keeping bad company but lavishly praising 'a virtuous man', 'a goodly portly man . . . of a cheerful look, a pleasing eye, and a most noble carriage', among Hal's companions. Hal ripostes when, playing the part of his father, he refers to the 'old fat man . . . that villainous abominable misleader of youth, Falstaff, that old white-bearded Satan'. At this point, the sheriff comes to the tavern, seeking the thieves; Falstaff and the others hide and Hal covers up for them.

Act III: In Wales, Glendower, Mortimer and Hotspur are about to divide England and Wales between them on a map. Hotspur is dissatisfied, and also impatiently argumentative with the Welsh leader, but all is resolved by Glendower's complaisance. Mortimer and his wife, Glendower's daughter, who cannot speak each other's language, say farewell through him as interpreter, and Hotspur and his amusing forthright wife also say farewell. In London, the King rebukes Hal for his unworthy and irresponsible way of life; he sees him as a second Richard II, and wonders whether this is God's punishment for some fault of his own. Hal is so 'lavish' of his presence, 'So stale and cheap to vulgar company', just like that 'skipping King'; he would that Hal were as seldom seen as he himself had been – 'Not an eye / But is a-weary of thy common sight'. A contrite Hal, after the King has referred to Hotspur as being like he himself had been, a resolute warrior, vows that he will out-do Hotspur in worth and honour. Before this reformation, however, we see him again with Falstaff; he has paid back the stolen money, has procured a military position for Falstaff and tells him to prepare for the rebellion – 'The land is burning, Percy stands on high/And either we or they must lower lie.'

Act IV: All is not going well for the rebels. At their camp near Shrewsbury, Hotspur learns that his father Northumberland is ill, and unable, with his supporters, to join them; then that Glendower's forces cannot be with them for fourteen days. Worcester is anxious, but Hotspur remains buoyant although they will now be outnumbered. Falstaff on the road towards Shrewsbury with a feeble body of conscripted men meets Hal and Westmoreland, who urge haste on him. At Shrewsbury, Hotspur is eager for action, but caution is urged upon him by others, as their forces have not yet all arrived. Suddenly a messenger from the King arrives with a conciliatory message, requesting to know 'the nature of your griefs' and offering pardon; but Hotspur angrily reminds the others of earlier promises and of the apparent tractability of Bolingbroke just before he seized the throne. Yet Hotspur decides to pause for a night.

Act V: Worcester and Vernon go early in the morning to the King's camp. In reply to the King's claim on his subjects' obedience, Worcester recites the grievances of his family, the Percy family, 'the first and dearest' of the King's friends, now treated with enmity, and charges the King with breaking his word and with rejecting them, when as Bolingbroke he returned from exile. Hal offers to meet Hotspur in single combat. The King, though, again offers peace. Falstaff, who was present at the foregoing meeting, muses cynically about honour in a famous speech. Worcester and Vernon, returned to their own camp, resolve not to report the King's pacific offer – 'it cannot be, / The King should keep his word in loving us; / He will suspect us still'. So battle is joined. Hal fights heroically, saves his father from the Scot, Douglas, and defeats and kills Hotspur. Falstaff, encountering Douglas, falls down feigning dead, and is found, apparently dead, by Hal – 'Poor Jack, farewell! / I could have better spar'd a better man.' Hal departing, Falstaff arises, finds the corpse of Hotspur near him and takes it up on his back, claiming to have killed him in fight. He maintains this even to Hal, who does not press for the truth – 'if a lie may do thee grace, / I'll gild it with the happiest terms I have'. The King is victorious. Worcester and Vernon are sentenced to death, and the valiant Scot, Douglas, spared. The plays ends with the King making plans to complete the suppression of the rebellion by sending forces rapidly to York to attack Northumberland and to Wales to deal with Glendower and Mortimer.

SOURCES   Chiefly (*a*) Holinshed,□ *Chronicles of England, Scotland and Ireland*□ (2nd edition, 1587), Shakespeare omitting and adding where he chose. The development of Hotspur and Hal, and of the Boar's Head world, and the creation of Falstaff, are Shakespeare's own; (*b*) from Samuel Daniel's□ *The Civile Warres*□ (1595) he probably got the idea of changing Hotspur's age so that he becomes a contemporary of and significant contrast to Hal.

TEXT   The First Quarto□ (1598), which seems to have been set up from revised 'foul papers'.□ Other quartos followed, five in all, before the First Folio□ (1623), which was set up from Q5 (1613).

Henry IV, Part 2. Late 1596 or early 1597.

Act I: The play begins with the figure of Rumour as 'presenter' or prologue and immediately we hear rumour and counter-rumour about the result of the Battle of Shrewsbury. The Earl of Northumberland, at first misinformed, learns of the defeat of the rebels and the death of his son Hotspur, and that Prince Hal's younger brother, John of Lancaster, is marching to attack with Westmoreland. Northumberland, crying 'Let order die', resolves on resistance and revenge. Falstaff, in London, about to be sent with messages to John of Lancaster, reluctantly encounters the Lord Chief Justice, but his 'night's exploit on Gad's Hill' (the highway robbery in Part I) is thought of as mitigated by his 'day's service at Shrewsbury' (his supposed bravery in the battle). At York, the Archbishop confers with Mowbray the Earl Marshal, Hastings and Lord Bardolph; they have twenty-five thousand men, and are not quite confident whether without Northumberland (who, they remember, let Hotspur down at Shrewsbury) they dare risk the fight. They decide they may, as the royal forces are divided into three – one force against the Welsh under Glendower, one against the French and one against them – and as the common people have turned against the King.

Act II: Mistress Quickly of the Boar's Head Tavern in Eastcheap attempts to have Falstaff arrested for his debts to her. Their altercation is interrupted by the arrival of the Lord Chief Justice, who reproaches Falstaff and tells him to pay her and repent. Falstaff manages to cajole her into lending more and inviting him to supper. News comes of troop movements. Prince Hal and Poins, hearing of the planned supper, decide to disguise themselves as drawers (inn servants) and see how he disports himself with Mistress Quickly and Doll Tearsheet, a young harlot. Meanwhile, in the North, Northumberland's wife and Lady Percy, his son Hotspur's widow, persuade him not to join the other rebels. In a long scene at the tavern, the drunken Pistol is thrust out and Hal and Poins, disguised as drawers, see Falstaff affectionately fondling Doll, and hear him disparage them amusingly before they reveal themselves. The scene ends abruptly when Hal and Falstaff are both summoned to arms; Prince Hal feels himself 'much to blame, / So idly to profane the previous time, / When tempest of commotion, . . . doth begin to melt / And drop upon our bare unarmed heads'.

Act III: The King, ill and tired, soliloquises on his anxieties and sleep-

lessness – 'Uneasy lies the head that wears a crown' – and then discusses with Warwick and Surrey 'the body of our kingdom/ How foul it is, what rank diseases grow'. Talking of the rebellion, he speaks of how loyalties and allegiances change (Northumberland is chiefly in his mind), fears the size of Northumberland's and the Archbishop of York's joint forces, and is reassured on this point by Warwick who also tells him of the death of Glendower, the Welsh rebel. In Gloucestershire, Falstaff calls on an ancient acquaintance, Justice Shallow, and chooses unlikely recruits in Feeble, Shadow and Wart.
Act IV: In Yorkshire, the Archbishop reports Northumberland's defection to Mowbray and Hastings. Westmoreland comes to them from John of Lancaster, Hal's brother and the young commander of the royal forces. The Archbishop speaks of their grievances, finding 'our griefs heavier than our offences'; he deplores the sad state of the realm, and declares that they are in arms 'Not to break peace, or any branch of it,/ But to establish here a peace indeed'. Westmoreland indicates some willingness to investigate the 'griefs', and says that John of Lancaster will listen to their demands, a list of which the Archbishop then hands over. While Mowbray is unhappy about this procedure not believing peace can be made, or can be lasting if made, York and Hastings feel that the King wants a settlement. At the meeting with Lancaster, Lancaster promises speedy redress of their grievances, and suggests that both armies should disperse and the leaders celebrate 'restored love and amity'. But Mowbray's reluctance is justified when, the rebel army having dispersed as arranged, Lancaster, his forces intact, orders the arrest of the three rebellious leaders for high treason. Falstaff in the field takes a prisoner, Sir John Coleville, and tries to get credit for bravery from John of Lancaster. Lancaster and his entourage leave for London, leaving Falstaff on the stage to speak of Lancaster's inhuman coldness, which he attributes to abstaining from wine. In London the King welcomes the victory and news of the defeat of Northumberland and the Scots, and looks forward to national peace. Worries about Hal's way of life still perturb him despite Warwick's assurance that 'The Prince will, in the perfectness of time,/ Cast off his followers', and suddenly he is taken ill. Lying alone at his own request, he is visited while sleeping by Hal, who thinks he is dead and grievingly takes the crown, places it on his head and leaves. When the King wakes, finds the crown gone and hears that Hal has visited him, he is bitterly distressed at what he thinks is Hal's apparent eagerness to succeed him. Warwick, however, reports finding Hal in the next room 'Washing with kindly tears his gentle cheeks,/With such a deep demeanour in great sorrow', and by his sincere grief and repentance Hal soon convinces his father of his reformation and serious commitment to his future

duty as king. The King, still troubled as always in his conscience about the 'by-paths and indirect crook'd ways' by which he had gained the crown, is comforted by his son's new sense of duty and is pleased to learn that the chamber was called the Jerusalem Chamber; he had for long hoped to make a pilgrimage to Jerusalem.

Act V: Falstaff revisits Shallow in Gloucestershire. His old enemy the Lord Chief Justice in London fears for his position now that Hal is king (as Henry V) but is reassured by Hal's praising him for having done his duty, even when it had once meant imprisoning the young prince. When Pistol brings news of the King's death to Falstaff feasting in Gloucestershire, the knight rises immediately to set out for London, showering promises of bounty on his companion, for now that Hal is king 'the laws of England are at my commandment . . . and woe to my Lord Chief Justice'.

But when the scene shifts to London we find Mrs Quickly and Doll Tearsheet being arrested, and when Falstaff, in the crowd for the royal procession after the coronation, calls out and greets his old friend Hal, the King austerely rebukes him with 'I know thee not, old man. Fall to thy prayers./How ill white hairs become a fool and jester.' But though Falstaff is to be temporarily held in custody and is to be 'banished' to a distance of at least ten miles from the new king, he and his followers are to be 'very well provided for . . . till their conversations/Appear more wise and modest to the world'. In the last speech John of Lancaster prophesies that there will be war in France before the year is past, so anticipating *Henry V*.

SOURCES   As for *Henry IV Part 1*.

TEXT   The First Quarto□ (1600), reprinted in the same year with the present Act III Scene 1 added; it was set up from the author's original manuscript. The First Folio□ (1623) text was set up from this or from a transcript of the prompt-book□ but with some additions, chiefly the replacing of passages deleted from the quarto for political reasons; it had also had all uses of 'God', 'Christ', 'the Trinity' and so on excised, in obedience to an act of Parliament of 1606.

Henry V. A history play, concluding the second tetralogy□ from *Richard II* through *Henry IV* Parts 1 and 2. It was probably written in mid-1599. (Each act – uniquely – begins with a Prologue spoken by a Chorus.)

Act I: We learn from a conversation between the Archbishop of Canterbury and the Bishop of Ely, who are anxious about threatened confiscation of Church property, that the new king, after his wild youth, is 'full of grace and fair regard. . . And a true lover of the holy Church'; they think he will be sympathetic to the Church's fears. At the court, the King calls on the Archbishop to interpret the Salic Law by which, the French claim, Henry's right to the French throne through his great-great-grandmother is not valid. The Archbishop refutes this, and urges the king to heroic action – to invade France, for which he promises generous financial support from the church. The French ambassadors are then called in; they make an insulting gift of tennis balls, implying that Henry's reputation for frivolity and irresponsibility means that his claims to territory in France cannot be taken seriously – 'You cannot revel into dukedoms there.' Henry tells them to tell the Dauphin (heir to the French throne) that he will 'show (his) sail of greatness', 'will dazzle all the eyes of France, / Yea, strike the Dauphin blind to look on us' and that many thousands of French widows will curse the Dauphin's jest.

Act II: Some of Falstaff's old associates meet in a London preparing for the war. Pistol has married Mrs Quickly, to whom Nym had been betrothed, and the two rivals squabble but are reconciled by Bardolph. Quickly is called out to Falstaff, suddenly taken ill; as she goes off, 'The king has killed his heart' she says. The Prologue to Act II had told of a conspiracy between the Earl of Cambridge, Lord Scroop and Sir Thomas Gray, to assassinate the King before he took ship at Southampton. We now see them with Henry at Southampton. They are exposed and sentenced to death. Pistol, Bardolph and Nym, about to leave London for Southampton, hear from Mrs Pistol (ex-Quickly) of Falstaff's affecting death, with its famous description 'his nose was a sharp as a pen, and a' babbled of green fields'. In France the French king (Charles VI) speaks of the threat posed by Henry; his son the Dauphin scornfully denigrates the 'vain, giddy, shallow, humorous youth', but the Constable of France speaks of Henry as now 'terrible in constant resolution' and with all 'his vanities forespent'. To them comes Exeter as emissary, demanding on the King's behalf that the King of France shall give up the throne and save his country and people the devastation of war.

Act III: In France now, Henry exhorts his men in the siege of Harfleur near Le Havre ('Once more unto the breach, dear friends, once more, / Or close the wall up with our English dead.') Nym, Bardolph, Pistol and Falstaff's 'Boy' are also there at the siege, not liking it very much, and indeed dodging as much as they can, as the Boy makes clear to us; he resolves 'to leave them and seek some better service'. We meet Gower the English captain, and the Welsh, Scottish and Irish officers, Fluellen, Jamey and Macmorris. Henry calls on the citizens of Harfleur to surrender, painting a grim picture of the violence, loot and rapine that they will suffer unless they do – 'the gates of mercy shall be all shut up'. The Governor appears, and, having heard that the help he expected from the Dauphin is not coming, surrenders. Henry orders 'Use mercy to them all', and decides, as winter is coming on, to move most of the army into winter quarters in Calais. The Princess Katharine of France has an English lesson; also in the Palace at Rouen, King Charles calls on his nobles to rally and assail the weakened English force as it marches towards Calais. It is thought they will give in and Henry offer ransom. We learn of the seizing of an important bridge by an advance force led by Exeter. Fluellen tells of Pistol's bravery there, but the English captain Gower knows him to be a lying braggart. Pistol vainly asks Fluellen to intercede on behalf of his mate Bardolph, who is to be hanged for looting from a church. The King confirms his order about such offences and gives orders requiring strict discipline and sensitivity by his troops towards the local inhabitants, 'for when lenity and cruelty play for a kingdom, the gentler gamester is the soonest winner'. Montjoy, Herald of France, enters with King Charles's message; the French have been patient so far, but will be so no longer, and Henry should now give in and pay ransom, as his defeat is certain. Henry frankly admits the poor condition of his troops, that they are outnumbered and that he would not *seek* battle at the present time, but proudly sends his defiance. The French are supremely confident as they prepare for battle near Agincourt. Their leaders jauntily look forward to battle, the Dauphin being especially boastful and buoyant, though when he goes off to arm at midnight, the Constable questions the genuineness of his bravery.

Act IV: The Chorus contrasts 'the confident and over-lusty French' with the 'poor condemned English', ill-fed, ill-clad and seriously outnumbered, but tells of Henry's 'cheerful semblance and sweet majesty' . . . 'that every wretch. . . plucks comfort from his looks'. We then see Henry, wearing a borrowed cloak, going about the English camp at night, meeting first Pistol and then three soldiers, Bates, Court and Michael Williams. With the last particularly he talks seriously and frankly, discussing fear, responsibility, the King's responsibility for his men as for the whole action. The sceptical soldier cannot help thinking that when all their throats are cut, the King 'may be ransomed, and we ne'er the wiser' which angers Henry, and he exchanges a glove with Williams so that if they meet after the battle, they can finish the argument. The King, alone, muses on the cares and responsibilities of kingship and invokes God's help, asking Him not to think of his father's (Bolingbroke's) 'fault . . . in compassing the crown'.

At dawn, the French nobles confidently and contemptuously prepare for their easy task of overwhelming the sorry English. The latter, outnumbered five to one, are addressed by the King who urges them to glory on this St Crispin's Day (25 October) and says he is glad they are few – the lesser loss if they lose, and 'the greater share of honour' if they win. Yet again a messenger comes from the French, Montjoy proposing that Henry should come to terms and be ransomed, but the suggestion is firmly but courteously rejected. The battle of Agincourt ensues. A brief comic interlude shows Pistol with a French soldier at his mercy whom he spares for two hundred crowns. French nobles are seen in panic disorder; Henry hears of noble English deeds but also of French reinforcements, and orders the killing of prisoners. In another comic interlude, Fluellen for Gower's benefit laboriously compares Henry to Alexander the Great. Montjoy comes to ask for permission to look for and bury their dead, by which Henry first realises that the battle is won; the soldier Williams comes wearing the King's glove in his cap, and is sent on his way, the King then for a joke asking Fluellen to wear the other glove (Williams's) in his hat, saying that it is a French duke's glove and knowing it 'may haply purchase him a box o' th' ear'. This happens in the next scene, when the King identifies himself and orders the glove to be filled with crowns for Williams. The French losses are ten thousand and the English only about thirty, and the King says 'O God, Thy arm was here:/ And not to us, but to Thy arm alone,/ Ascribe we all.'

Act V: The Chorus tells of Henry's triumphant reception in London and of his return to France to conclude a treaty of peace. At the English camp in France, Fluellen repays previous insults by forcing Pistol to eat a leek (which the Welsh wear on St David's Day (1 March), in commemoration, it is said, of some early victory in a field of leeks). In the French King's palace at Troyes, the English and French kings meet in amity. Burgundy delivers a plea for peace, using the imagery of ordered and fertile gardens which should now replace the wilderness brought about by war and hatred. While the details of the peace treaty are being discussed off-stage, in a charming scene Henry, presenting himself as a rough soldier, humorously woos the Princess Katharine of France, who with demure coquetry and broken English yields to his bold, direct and manly entreaty. The union, welcomed by the French King and Queen, symbolises and asserts concord between England and France.

SOURCES Hall's□ *Union of the Two Noble and Illustre Famelies of Lancastre and York* (1548) and the second edition (1587) of Holinshed's□ *Chronicles of England, Scotland and Ireland*□ (which was indebted to Hall).

TEXT The Quarto of 1600 was a 'bad' quarto,□ probably based on memorial reconstruction by actors. It was again printed in 1602, and in 1619 (though falsely dated 1608). It is over 1600 lines shorter than the First Folio□ (1623) text, which is probably from Shakespeare's manuscript.

Henry VI. An early historical sequence in three parts, part of the first tetralogy.□

PART ONE   This probably dates from 1588–9.

Act I: The play begins with the funeral of King Henry the Fifth, and shows immediately the rivalry between his brother, Humphrey, Duke of Gloucester, the Protector (a substitute ruler, for Henry the Sixth is a young boy) and Henry Beaufort, Bishop of Winchester, his and the late king's uncle. The chief subjects of the *Henry VI* sequence are announced within sixty lines of the opening, as Gloucester's brother, Duke of Bedford, the Regent, calls on the ghost of the dead king to 'Prosper this realm, keep it from civil broils', and news is immediately brought of the sudden loss of many cities and areas in France, of the crowning of the Dauphin as King of France, and of the wounding and capture of the great English leader and hero Lord Talbot. In France at Orleans, after a French reverse, Joan la Pucelle ('maid'), a shepherd's daughter who claims that the Virgin Mary appeared to her in a vision telling her to take up arms to free France from England, is entrusted with military authority. She re-takes Orleans, after an amazed Talbot (freed when the English captured it) has fought briefly with her. He ashamedly acknowledges temporary English defeat. He thinks of Joan as a witch; the French rulers and leaders regard her as 'France's saint'.

Act II: Swiftly Talbot and the English recapture Orleans; the Duke of Burgundy has allied himself to them. In London we observe the quarrel between Richard Plantagenet and John Beaufort, Earl of Somerset, over the former's claim to the throne. In a celebrated scene in a garden, Plantagenet, later Duke of York, plucks a white rose and calls on those who support him to do the same, and Somerset picks a red one. This symbolic scene marks the beginning of the struggle between the Houses of York and Lancaster, a major theme of Parts 2 and 3 of this work and of *Richard III*. The question of the legitimacy of Plantagenet's claims is raised again in a scene in which he visits his dying uncle, Mortimer.

Act III: The other chief enmity comes to the fore again as Protector Gloucester and the Bishop of Winchester quarrel violently before the gentle young king Henry VI; the quarrel extends to their followers. The Earl of Warwick, who has joined the Yorkist side, acts as peacemaker, and the King restores to Plantagenet his property and his title of Duke of York, before setting out for France to be crowned there, as proposed by Humphrey, Duke of Gloucester. This first scene of Act III ends with the old Duke of Exeter foreseeing that the rivalry between York and Somerset 'Burns under feigned ashes of forg'd love, / And will at last break out into a flame'. In France, Joan captures Rouen by a ruse, but Talbot re-takes it the same day. Sir John Fastolfe makes a brief cowardly appearance and the old Duke of Bedford dies. Joan pleads with the Duke of Burgundy to 'see the pining malady of France' and to return 'with a flood of tears, / And wash away thy country's stained spots', and succeeds in arousing his old patriotism and detaching him from the English. Talbot is rewarded by the King by being created Earl of Shrewsbury.

Act IV: At Henry VI's coronation in Paris, Fastolfe brings a letter from Burgundy announcing his abandoning of the English cause; Talbot tears the Garter, sign of membership of the noblest English order of chivalry, from Fastolfe's leg because of his cowardice; and the enmity between York and Somerset comes to the fore again. It is controlled by the young king, who calls on both his cousins to 'be at peace', and emphasises the benefit to the French 'if they perceive dissension in our looks'. He puts on a red rose (the Lancastrian colour) saying that this means nothing and that he loves them both, makes York his Regent in France and asks Somerset to join his cavalry with York's infantry. The old Duke of Exeter ends the scene (IV.i) as he did III.i. with words fearful of the future because of the envy and division in the court. Talbot, outside Bordeaux, calls for the city's surrender but is trapped by superior French forces; York, in response to an urgent message from Talbot, declares that he cannot help because Somerset has failed to send his cavalry to join York's force. Somerset eventually agrees to do this, but it is too late and the heroic Talbot is thus destroyed by the hostility between York and Somerset. He had urged his son to escape the battle but John Talbot refused, and Talbot himself died of his wounds holding his dead son in his arms.

Act V: In London, Gloucester reports to the King that the Pope and others are urging a peaceful settlement. Henry VI concurs in this and agrees to marry the daughter of Armagnac, close kin to Charles, king of France. The Bishop of Winchester, now Cardinal (Exeter expresses foreboding about this elevation) is sent to France to begin peace talks. Before he gets there, Joan, deserted by the evil spirits she has called to her aid, is defeated and captured by York. The Earl of Suffolk captures Margaret, daughter of the Duke of Anjou, is captivated by her, desires her and proposes to marry her to King Henry, to which both she and her father agree. Joan, condemned to death by burning, contemptuously rebuffs her old shepherd father, claiming to be of royal descent; in vain she begs York for mercy, declaring that she is pregnant. When Beaufort, now Cardinal, comes to discuss peace, York is outraged, as is King Charles of France when he hears the terms; but the latter eventually accepts even though he must swear allegiance to Henry VI and serve him only as his Viceroy in France. The play ends with Henry resolving to follow Suffolk's plan and marry Margaret, despite Gloucester's reminding him that he is already betrothed.

PART TWO   This probably dates from 1590.
Act I: Although the King is deeply happy at the marriage, others, especially the Protector Gloucester, Salisbury, his son Warwick and

York are angry to discover that the marriage contract drawn up by
Suffolk ceded Anjou and Maine to the new Queen Margaret's needy
father, the Duke of Anjou. Gloucester, 'good Duke Humphrey', has
a strong claim to the throne, and is indeed heir-presumptive (he would
succeed if the king did not have children); his enemy Cardinal Beaufort
plans with Suffolk, Somerset and Buckingham to oust him from power.
Salisbury, Warwick and York support Gloucester, though York only
intends to support him as long as it suits him. The York-Lancaster
rivalry deepens: York despises the young king, a Lancastrian, and is
ambitious to possess the crown himself. Another with ambitions for
the crown is Eleanor, wife of Gloucester, whom she urges to 'Put forth
thy hand, reach at the glorious gold', but the duke is virtuous and loyal
and calls on her to 'Banish the canker of ambitious thoughts'. Soon
the duchess is caught by York and Buckingham in the act of conjuring
a spirit which foretells the future, and she is arrested. We have already
seen the growing dominance of the Queen and the developing relationship between her and the ambitious Suffolk.

Act II: This begins at St Albans with further animosity between
Gloucester and Cardinal Beaufort to the grief of the King, and with
the exposure of a rogue who claims to have had his sight restored; and
Buckingham brings news of the arrest of Eleanor. The claims of York
to the throne are acknowledged by Salisbury and Warwick, and the
three agree to pursue this end in 'silent secrecy'. Eleanor is banished,
her husband Gloucester deprived of the Protectorship; he is gentle and
loving and, when she warns him that his mildness increases the danger
he is in from his enemies, he replies that no harm can come to him as
he has committed no crimes or wrongs.

Act III: Gloucester, summoned to a special Parliament at Bury St
Edmunds, is arrested by Suffolk for treason, his character having been
blackened by the Queen, Suffolk, Cardinal Beaufort and York, who
all want to get rid of him; the weak King protests Gloucester's virtue
but is overruled. News is brought of serious losses of territory in
France, and then of rebellion in Ireland, and York is appointed to go to
Ireland. He suspects that he is being sent to get him out of the way, but
welcomes the task as it will put a large force of men at his disposal; he
plans to foment a rising in his absence led by Jack Cade, as a further
part of his ambitious aims. Gloucester is murdered swiftly, at Suffolk's
instigation, to the King's distress and grief. He begins to turn from his
powerful and wicked queen and her associates. Warwick reports
suspicion of the responsibility of Suffolk and the Cardinal for the
murder, and representatives of the people demand the death or
banishment of Suffolk. Henry banishes him, despite Queen Margaret's
pleading for him, and there is a passionate parting. Cardinal Beaufort
is taken ill, and in his delirium reveals his part in Gloucester's death.

Act IV: Suffolk, sailing to France, is murdered and decapitated. The rest of the act is taken up with the events of Jack Cade's rebellion. He claims to be John Mortimer and rightful heir to the throne, but leads a people's revolt especially hostile to the upper and educated classes. It is temporarily successful, but Cade loses support and is eventually killed by a Kentish gentleman called Iden.

Act V: York returns from Ireland with an Irish army intending secretly 'to pluck the crown from feeble Henry's head', but asserting to Buckingham, sent by the King to question him, that his intention is to dispose of the seditious Somerset. He then 'submits' willingly to the king, having been assured that Somerset is a prisoner in the Tower of London, but, finding this is not so, he comes out into the open and claims the crown, deriding the King as 'not fit to govern and rule' and more fit 'to grasp a palmer's staff' and lead a life of piety. Confronted by the Queen, Somerset and Clifford, he calls for Salisbury and his son Warwick, who support him in the ensuing battle of St Albans, in which he is triumphant. He kills Clifford, whose son vows revenge on the family of York; his own son Richard (later to be King Richard III) kills Somerset, and the King and Queen flee to London. The Wars of the Roses have begun.

PART THREE   This probably dates from 1590-1.

Act I: The victorious York comes to London with his two sons, the Earl of Warwick and his supporters wearing the white rose of York. He seats himself on the throne where he is found by Henry, Northumberland and others, wearing the red rose of Lancaster. Henry admits the weakness of his title to the crown (because of the usurpation of Richard II's throne by Henry of Lancaster (Bolingbroke, later Henry IV)) and weakly agrees to nominate York as his heir on condition that while he lives York will 'honour me as thy king and sovereign' – to the disgust and anger of his followers, and especially of the Queen, who resolves to take the field against York. The Queen with twenty thousand men of the northern lords defeats York with his five thousand outside Wakefield. York is brought as a prisoner before the Queen, who taunts him with a napkin stained with the blood of his youngest son, Rutland, killed by Clifford, and by thrusting a paper crown on his head, before he is slaughtered by Clifford and the Queen.

Act II: York's two sons, Edward and Richard, having escaped with their army, hear of his death and are joined by Warwick and his force. From him, they learn of a further defeat at the hands of the Queen at St Albans, but the three of them now resolve with their total of twenty-five thousand men to attack the Queen's thirty thousand. Queen Margaret exults and the King grieves at the sight of York's head set up on a gateway at York. The Yorkists enter, young Edward claiming the crown in a scene of anger and abuse between them and the royal

(Lancastrian) party. The battle of Towton takes place soon, near by. The gentle King Henry, having tried in vain to speak of the horror of civil war, has been sent away from the battlefield by the queen and Clifford, and, sitting on a mole-hill, muses on the felicities of the simple pastoral life compared with the cares of court. His grief over the 'Roses' struggle is emphasised by the entry of a soldier bearing the body of his victim, his own father, and of a father with his dead son whom he had similarly killed unknowingly. The Yorkists triumph; Warwick urges young Edward of York to go straight to London to be crowned, and proposes a marriage with the French Lady Bona, sister-in-law of the French king.

Act III: The royal party escapes to Scotland, but the deposed king, slipping over the border to see England again, is captured by two game-keepers. In London the new king, now Edward IV, has become enamoured of Lady Grey, whose husband had been slain at St Albans and his estate confiscated. She resists his amorous pressure, even at the expense of not having the estate restored, whereupon he resolves on honourable marriage to her – to the scorn and distaste of his brother Richard, now Duke of Gloucester, who wants no elder brother's heirs to keep him from the throne he is determined on achieving. The scene moves to Paris, where Queen Margaret, pleading for help from the French king, is interrupted by the arrival of Warwick with his offer of a marriage between Edward IV and the Lady Bona. King Lewis decides to support the cause of the new English king and to further the marriage. When news is brought of Edward's marriage to Lady Grey, however, Lewis changes his resolve, supporting Queen Margaret; an angered and outraged Warwick abandons Edward's cause and joins the other side in preparing, with French help, to unseat him.

Act IV: Edward's marriage has confounded his brothers. Clarence leaves him to join Queen Margaret and Warwick, but Richard of Gloucester out of policy protests his loyalty. Warwick lands in England with French troops and takes Edward prisoner in a surprise raid and uncrowns him. Edward is helped to escape to France by his younger brother Gloucester and Lord Hastings. Meanwhile Henry, restored to the throne, thanks his supporters, especially Warwick, to whom he resigns the government of the realm, and Clarence, who is also named Protector with him. But Edward returns with French help, captures York, proclaims himself king again, and, marching to London, captures Henry again and imprisons him in the Tower.

Act V: Warwick, surprised by Edward's sudden arrival at Coventry, refuses to submit, remaining loyal to King Henry. Edward's troops are quickly reinforced by Oxford, Montague, Somerset and then by Clarence, returning to his allegiance to his brother Edward and aban-doning the royal cause. Warwick is slain in a battle at Barnet. Queen

Margaret returns from France with an army and is defeated at the battle of Tewkesbury, and her son Prince Edward is stabbed to death by Edward IV, Clarence and Richard of Gloucester before her eyes. Richard then hastens to the Tower and murders King Henry VI, and reveals in a soliloquy his resolve to get to the throne, although the King, Clarence and others stand in his way. The play ends with Edward IV apparently secure on the throne, and with a son and heir.

SOURCES   Hall's□ *Union of the Two Noble and Illustre Famelies of Lancastre and York* (1548) and the second edition (1587) of Holinshed's□ *Chronicles of England, Scotland and Ireland*□ are prime sources; Shakespeare took many liberties with the chronology and with historical facts, but his account of the weak reign of Henry VI and the rivalry between the houses of York and Lancaster (deriving from Bolingbroke's usurpation of the throne of Richard II – explored in the *Richard II, Henry IV* and *Henry V* sequence) is generally faithful.

TEXT   The First Folio□ (1623) is the authoritative text, but two of the plays first appeared in earlier separate quartos,□ Part 2 in 1594, Part 3 in 1595. These used to be thought of as earlier versions, but are now generally accepted as memorial reconstructions,□ put together by printers from actors' memories (probably actors of minor roles) of plays in which they had taken part.

Henry VIII. A history play, Shakespeare's last play, of 1613.

Act I: After a short prologue, in clumsy rhyming couplets, that does not sound or seem Shakespearian, we learn from a conversation between the Duke of Norfolk, the Duke of Buckingham and Lord Abergavenny about the meeting with magnificent pageantry at the 'Field of the Cloth of Gold' between Henry VIII and Francis I, King of France, engineered by Cardinal Wolsey, Archbishop of York. The three criticise Wolsey's ambitious greed for power; they agree that the 'peace' marked by the meeting was not worth the 'cost that did conclude it', for the French have already broken it, seizing English merchants' goods at Bordeaux and placing the ambassador under house arrest. But Buckingham claims that Wolsey had engineered the break with France and been rewarded by the King of Spain for so doing. Norfolk advises Buckingham, whose hatred of Wolsey is public knowledge, to be careful and secret, knowing 'the Cardinal's malice and his potency', and at that moment Wolsey passes across the stage, glowering disdainfully at Buckingham and speaking briefly but threateningly about the Duke to his secretary. Norfolk again tries to restrain Buckingham, who is determined to see the King and 'cry down/ This Ipswich fellow's insolence', complaining of his pride, corruption and treason. Almost at once Buckingham is arrested, with his son-in-law Abergavenny, and charged with treason.

The King, with Wolsey at his right hand, is preparing to hear the charges against Buckingham when he is interrupted by his Queen Katherine, who brings a plea on behalf of the clothiers of the kingdom to have unfair, excessive taxes on them, levied by Wolsey, reduced. Wolsey seeks to defend and justify himself, but the King orders the tax and action to punish those who had risen in protest to be revoked. Wolsey secretly orders his secretary to make sure that he and not the King receives credit for this clemency. Then Buckingham's surveyor, recently dismissed, is questioned and swears that the Duke was ambitious for the crown and had even been contemplating killing the King. A fairly short scene follows in which the Lord Chamberlain and Lord Sandys, on their way to a banquet given by Wolsey, mockingly deride foreign fashions and their popularity in London. To this banquet, the King and others come, uninvited, masked and in shepherd dress; the King here meets and dances with the Lady Ann Bullen and is immediately attracted to her.

Act II: 'Bounteous Buckingham, / The mirror of all courtesy', we learn from the conversation of two gentlemen, is found guilty of treason. He enters under guard, on the way to execution, declares his innocence of the charges, and in noble charitable speeches commends others as well as himself to God's mercy. The two gentlemen then discuss the latest rumour, of the King's separation from Queen Katherine, which they ascribe to Cardinal Wolsey's machinations. We learn more of Wolsey's schemes from the Dukes of Norfolk and Suffolk in conversation with the Lord Chamberlain. The Cardinal has now broken the alliance with Charles V (King of Spain and Holy Roman Emperor) who is Queen Katherine's nephew, and seeks to break her marriage to King Henry and to ally him with the sister of the French King; the pretext is that Henry's twenty-year-old marriage was invalid. Norfolk and Suffolk are angrily rebuffed by Henry but he gladly welcomes the proud Cardinal and Cardinal Campeius whom he has invited from Rome to advise on the validity of the marriage. Anne Bullen, in conversation with a shrewd and worldly old lady of the court, laments the rejection of the good Queen after twenty years of loving loyalty to the King, and says 'I swear, 'tis better to be lowly born . . . Than to be peak'd up in a glist'ring grief / And wear a golden sorrow'; almost at once the Lord Chamberlain comes to tell her the King has made her Marchioness of Pembroke and granted her a thousand pounds a year.

In a grand assembly at which the legality of the King's marriage is to be resolved, Katherine speaks of her long love and obedience, of the care taken over legality by her father, King of Spain, and by King Henry VII at the time of her marriage. Accusing Wolsey of enmity for her and of cunning, arrogance, pride and ambition, and calling for her case to be considered by the Pope himself, she leaves the court.

Henry pays tribute to her virtues, asserting that the only reason for this 'trial' is his anxious conscience, and his fear that in the marriage he 'stood not in the smile of heaven'. The fact that although many children have been born to Katherine, no male child has survived, seems to be a judgement on him. All he hopes for, he says, is that the marriage be proved lawful, and he calls for judgement now, but Cardinal Campeius demands an adjournment because of the absence of the Queen.

Act III: The Queen (with her ladies, one of whom sings the song 'Orpheus with his lute'), is visited by Wolsey and Campeius, ostensibly to help and advise her; but she is openly critical and suspicious of them and wants 'time and counsel' to consult 'friends . . . in mine own country', as she now feels 'friendless, hopeless' in England. They urge her to submit to the King, and although she cries 'Alas, 'has banish'd me his bed already,/ His love, too long ago', in the end she agrees to listen to their counsels and reaffirms her obedience to her husband.

Now comes the fall of Cardinal Wolsey. Secret letters he despatched to the Pope urging him to delay his decision about the marriage to Katherine, in order to frustrate the King's proposed new marriage to Anne Bullen, a Protestant, have come to the King. By chance the King has also seen an inventory of Wolsey's possessions, indicating his immense wealth. The Cardinal knows that he has 'touch'd the highest point of all [his] greatness'. Norfolk and Suffolk come to demand the great seal from him – which he refuses – and abuse him, Surrey accuses him over the execution of his father-in-law Buckingham, and they all three recite examples of his pride and ambition. He is ordered into house arrest. Left alone briefly he bids 'a long farewell to all my greatness', and, when his servant Thomas Cromwell comes, in speeches of noble resignation and contrition he acknowledges his pride and urges Cromwell to 'fling away ambition'. He concludes, 'Had I but serv'd my God with half the zeal/ I serv'd my king, he would not in mine age/ Have left me naked to mine enemies.'

Act IV: The two gentlemen (of II.1), awaiting the coronation procession of Queen Anne, discuss the promotions of Suffolk and Norfolk and the divorce and illness of Queen Katherine, now known as Princess Dowager. After the procession has passed, a third gentleman describes the service in Westminster Abbey and the wonderful impression made by the new queen, and reports the quick rise of Wolsey's servant Thomas Cromwell. The dying Katherine learns from her gentleman-usher Griffith of the death of Wolsey, speaks condemningly of him but permits Griffith to 'speak his good now' and then speaks forgivingly. To 'sad and solemn music' she falls asleep, and a small wordless masque (her vision) takes place – not seen by Griffith or her lady Patience – in which six white-robed figures dance and honour her. In her sleep she 'makes signs of rejoicing, and holdeth up her hands to heaven'. Capucius, an emissary from Charles V (the Emperor, her nephew) visits her, bringing also a message, intended to be of comfort, from the King; but, as she says, 'That comfort comes too late . . . That gentle physic given in time, had cur'd me'. She gives him a letter she has had written to the King, commending their young daughter (the future Queen Mary) to his care and concern, and asking for him to help and support her faithful household; 'Tell him in death I bless'd him'.

Act V: Gardiner, the Bishop of Winchester, originally a favourite of Wolsey's and advanced by him to be the King's Secretary (II.2), discusses in a chance meeting at night with Sir Thomas Lovell the new Queen's plight in labour, and deplores her Protestantism; and they agree in denouncing Cranmer, Archbishop of Canterbury, and Cromwell, now promoted still further. Gardiner has prevailed on the lords of the council to summon Cranmer before them on a complaint of heresy the following day. The King too waits up for news of the birth, and also for Cranmer whom he has sent for to discuss this summons; convinced by the archbishop's candour and quiet confidence, he warns him of danger and gives him a ring as a sign of his support. The old lady (of II.3) brings word to the King of the birth of a daughter. The archbishop, Cranmer, is forced to wait outside the council chamber like an underling, an insult which is brought to the King's notice. When admitted to the chamber he is accused of Protestant heresy by Gardiner, who orders him to be committed to the Tower. He shows the King's ring, and the King, entering and rebuffing Gardiner's hypocritical obsequiousness, makes clear his support for Cranmer and takes him off to christen the baby and to be its godfather. A brief comic scene shows the rowdy interest in the christening shown by ordinary citizens – offstage – trying to get into the court past a harassed porter. Then the royal procession comes on to the stage and the child is christened Elizabeth by Cranmer, who pronounces a moving speech about the peace and glory this child will bring to England and foretells her long reign as the virgin queen.

SOURCES   Holinshed's□ *Chronicles of England, Scotland and Ireland,*□ (2nd edition, 1587), with some material from Hall's□ *Union of the Two Noble and Illustre Famelies of Lancaster and York* (1548) and some details from Foxe's□ *Actes and Monuments* (1563), popularly known as the *Book of Martyrs.*□

TEXT   The First Folio□ (1623), apparently from a careful transcript of Shakespeare's manuscript, with full and unusually detailed stage-directions especially of pageantry and processions. Some lame passages and the episodic nature of the play have led many to believe it was a collaborative effort, John Fletcher (1579–1625), who succeeded Shakespeare as the principal playwright of the King's company on the latter's retirement, being thought of as the most likely joint-author. Some parts of one or two scenes, or at least a few speeches, may be another's work, and probably Fletcher's, but the play as a whole, which has unity of purpose despite its episodic form, and many signs of the thematic preoccupations of late Shakespeare – a concern for integrity, honour, repentance of sin, and a movement (here rather forced against the grain of the action) towards reconciliation and harmony – is Shakespeare's in design and execution. It would be tempting to think that originally it was an earlier chronicle play by Shakespeare which celebrated at the end the birth and future glory of Elizabeth actually during her reign, but if so, it was certainly rewritten. In any case, in February 1613 King James I's daughter Elizabeth was married in London to the Elector Palatine, a leading German Protestant prince; the praise of the earlier Elizabeth and the sympathetic presentation of Cranmer, soon a leading architect of Protestantism, and the treatment of the overthrow of proud Catholics like Wolsey, would not have been inappropriate or have passed notice, and the play was first produced at this time.

Henryson, Robert (*c*.1430–1500). A Scottish poet and author of a lively poetic version of the 'Moral Fables of Aesop' and of a powerful tragic poem *The Testament of Cresseid* (published in 1593) from which Shakespeare may have got the idea of a much harsher condemnation of Cressida's unfaithfulness than Chaucer gave. *The Testament* was normally printed with Chaucer's *Troilus and Criseyde* in the sixteenth century as if it were a sequel. Shakespeare certainly knew it, for he refers to Cressida as a beggar in *Twelfth Night* and as a whore in *Henry V*.

Henslowe, Philip (?–1616). The great theatre-owner and manager. He began with bear-baiting management (the Bear Garden or Paris Garden house was near where the Globe was built in Southwark, south of the Thames) and in 1587 he built the Rose Theatre, of which he took half the proceeds of the galleries in return for being responsible for the licensing fee and for keeping the building in good repair. He 'shared' with the actor Edward Alleyn□ in the Fortune, built in 1600, and later in the Hope. He also owned a lot of other property in London. His *Diary* and other papers were inherited by Alleyn, who bequeathed them to the school which he founded, Dulwich College, where they still are. The *Diary* covers the years 1592–1603; it is an account, record and memorandum book rather than a diary. It records the companies performing at his theatres during the period, names the plays performed, records his 'take' as housekeeper,□ and later records the money he advanced for buying plays and costumes and for licensing, and the money he lent to players, revealing the great control he exercised and the hold he had over the players. His papers, not really known about until found in the library by Edward Malone in 1790, have contributed more to our knowledge of Elizabethan/Jacobean theatrical operation than anything else. We can only regret that he was not the owner/manager/ keeper of Shakespeare's theatre or company, so that we could have had much more detail of the great dramatist's professional life. On the other hand, probably Shakespeare could not have endured the dominance and power of Henslowe's operations: he himself belonged to a much more democratic organisation.

Holinshed, Raphael (?1530–?80). Holinshed contributed the *History of England* and the *History of Scotland* (the latter largely a translation of a history by Hector Boece) to a projected but unfinished history of the world, which appeared as *The Chronicles of England, Scotland and Ireland*□ in 1577. There was a second edition in 1587, enlarged but without the illustrations, and this is the edition Shakespeare used. It provided material for most of the history plays and, to a lesser degree, for *Macbeth* and *Cymbeline*. Holinshed, who was himself also greatly indebted to Hall,□ was the greatest source for Shakespeare's maturer history plays – *Richard II* to *Henry V*, and *Henry VIII* – and, together with Hall, for the early *Henry VI* to *Richard III* sequence.

Homilies. Printed sermons or moral and religious addresses required to be read aloud in churches after England's separation from Roman Catholicism 'by all Parsons, Vicars and Curates every Sunday and Holyday . . . for the better understanding of the simple people' and 'to avoid the manifold enormities which heretofore by false doctrine have crept into the Church . . .'. The intention was to teach and promote the new English Protestant religion and to ensure its uniformity. In 1547 Archbishop Cranmer had edited *Certaine Sermons or Homilies*, and, after the break following Edward VI's death after a short reign, when the Catholic Queen Mary Tudor reigned for six years, *The Second Tome of Homilies* (Tome = volume) appeared in 1563. Because church attendance was compulsory, everyone in theory heard these homilies, and heard them repeatedly, so their influence on Elizabethan ideas and beliefs was great. It was very strong of course on Shakespeare, and many of the topics, on the divine right of kings, on obedience, on love and charity, on rebellion, on strife and contention, on order and degree□ and the divine ordering of the universe, and also some of the phrasing of the homilies, are to be traced readily in his works. They were models of simplicity and directness.

Housekeeper. An owner of a substantial interest in a playhouse□ as distinct from a sharer□ who was a part-owner of an acting company. The Globe□ housekeepers were originally (1599) the brothers Cuthbert and Richard Burbage□ who owned 25 per cent each, and Shakespeare, Heminge□ and three other actors the other half, that is 10 per cent each. When the company took over the Blackfriars□ as well in 1608, the two Burbages, Shakespeare, Heminge, Condell□ (the co-editor with Heminge of the First Folio□ of 1623) and two others held equal shares. They were all also sharers in the company, but this seems to have been unusual, for the great rival theatre was solely owned by Philip Henslowe□ who was also a large sharer.

I

Inns of Court. The 'colleges' which provided legal training in London. There were four in Elizabethan times: Gray's Inn, the Inner Temple, the Middle Temple and Lincoln's Inn. As early as about 1470 it had been written, by Sir John Fortescue, that the students learned not only law and divinity but also music and dancing 'so that these hostels, being nurseries or seminaries of the Court, are therefore called Inns of Court'. Masques□ and plays were put on by students, as in some colleges at Oxford and Cambridge, and sometimes professional companies were engaged. Their interest much encouraged the growth of the drama in London especially in the private theatres.

Inn-yards. Before the building of the first theatre in London (James Burbage's The Theatre in 1576) plays were put on in inn-yards. They could be quite large, accommodating many standing spectators, and also had galleries for more at first-floor level running along some or all of the four sides. (The best surviving example is a provincial one, the New Inn at Gloucester.) Innkeepers welcomed the extra trade, but eventually the City authorities in 1574 forbade the performing of plays in them, because of the drunkenness, noisy assembly and petty crime that they provoked. This led to the building of professional theatres, the design of which was certainly influenced by the form and amenities of the inn-yards.

Interlude. A vague term used for a wide variety of more or less dramatic pieces in the early and middle sixteenth century. As the name implies they were originally short and formed only part of an evening's or occasion's entertainment. The oldest known surviving interlude, *Fulgens and Lucrece* by Henry Medwall, of about 1497, was first performed in a banqueting hall during the actual banquet itself, the characters several times referring to the guests/spectators. Religious matters – there were in different reigns both Protestant and Catholic interludes – and moral instruction, the virtues and vices being common characters in them, were the chief topics, but comedy and indeed farce were not far away. Beginning with a didactic (or teaching) purpose, they became more positively entertaining, more comic and dramatic. In this respect and in the development of the serio-comic Vice☐ character they lead towards the Elizabethan drama, which eclipsed them, and to the glories of Shakespeare. A late example such as *Cambyses* by Thomas Preston, of about 1569, is characteristic of the interlude's transforming itself: 'An interlude a lamentable Tragedy full of pleasant myrth', as it is described in the Stationers' Register,☐ it is based on a classical story of a king of Persia but has comic scenes and characters, including a notable crafty comic rogue of a Vice, called Ambidexter. Most interludes were comparatively short, about 1000 lines, and most were for indoor performance but John Skelton's *Magnificence* (?1530) has over 2,500 lines and the Scottish *A Satire of the Three Estates* by David Lindsay, first performed out of doors, had over 4,600 (but see Morality plays.☐) As some later interludes, including the comic ones attributed to John Heywood (1497–?1580), such as *The Pardoner and the Friar* and *Johan Johan*, carry no explicit moral and have real characters rather than the personifications and abstractions of the early successors to the morality plays, it is obvious that the term 'interlude' is a loose one and covers a wide variety of dramatic moralisings, debates, anecdotes and entertainments.

J

Jews. Edward I had expelled Jews from England in 1291 and few Elizabethans would ever have met one, though there were some in London and elsewhere. (They could enter a house of instruction, *domus conversorum* (house of converts), and after baptism as Christians enter ordinary society.) In spite of the fact that there were very few of them (and those in fact Christian), feeling against Jews existed because of the betrayal and crucifixion of Jesus Christ, and the Jew remained in the popular imagination as a kind of anti-Christ, begotten of the devil. The medieval church, and the mystery cycles☐ in which Jews were uncompromisingly shown and condemned, kept vivid the Jewish 'crime'. The best-known Jew of Elizabethan times was Roderigo Lopez, a Portuguese physician who became the Queen's personal doctor in 1586. He was accused of being involved in a plot to poison the Queen and Don Antonio, the pretender to the throne of Portugal, and was hanged in 1594. Many think that to some extent Shylock, the Jewish merchant and usurer in *The Merchant of Venice*, was suggested by the alleged villainy of Lopez – and of course the Merchant of Venice himself is called Antonio. Yet Shakespeare's presentation of Shylock is far from the demon-travesty of Marlowe's□ Barabas in *The Jew of Malta* (?1590). Animosity against the Jews was religious, not really racial, in Elizabethan England, although some modern productions have sought to make race-hatred and contempt a strong force in the Shakespeare play. The Church of England has always prayed – for example in the collect for Good Friday, the day on which the death and sacrifice of Christ are commemorated – for 'all Jews' (and indeed for Turks, infidels and heretics).

Jonson, Ben (1572–1637). Jonson stands second only to Shakespeare among dramatists of the time, but is completely different, his plays being classically regular and often heartless and satirical. *Every Man in His Humour* (1598) was originally acted by the Lord Chamberlain's Men□ with Shakespeare playing a part, possibly Elder Knowell. Jonson's encomium, a great tribute to Shakespeare's memory, appears in the First Folio.□ In *Timber, or Discoveries*, not published until 1640, he wrote: 'I lov'd the man, and doe honour his memory (on this side idolatry) as much as any.' But he did not wholeheartedly admire Shakespeare's free fancy and imagination, especially in the Romances, and is recorded as saying that 'Shakespeare wanted [lacked] art.' Shakespeare might have riposted that Jonson lacked 'nature'.

Julius Caesar. The earliest of the mature tragedies, dating from 1599.

Act I: Julius Caesar, successful in a civil war, has returned in triumph to Rome. In the first scene the two tribunes of the people reprove some workmen for not being at work and for celebrating Caesar's triumph, which they themselves deplore, as his victory was against fellow-Romans, the two sons of the great Pompey. They fear the rise of Caesar to this great position and popularity. Two others who are similarly apprehensive are Brutus and Cassius, and when they hear offstage great shouts from the crowd they instantly assume great honours are being heaped on Caesar. They learn from Casca that Mark Antony has three times offered Caesar the crown, which the victor has three times, but with increasing reluctance, refused. Cassius secretly plans to arrange for a number of letters, apparently from different people, to be thrown through Brutus's windows that night, to convince him that many are fearful of Caesar's ambition and think of Brutus as a potential natural leader of the opposition. That night there is a fierce thunderstorm and strange and unnatural happenings are reported (for example, a slave's hand flamed and burned 'like twenty torches' without getting scorched, and Casca encountered a lion near the Capitol which 'glaz'd upon me, And went surly by,/ Without annoying me'). Such frightening omens are seen by Cassius as 'instruments of fear and warning' from heaven, aghast at the ambitions of Caesar. Quickly Cassius begins to form a conspiracy.

Act II: Meanwhile Brutus, sleepless and anguished, debates with himself, torn between his honourable nature, his liking for Caesar and his fear of Caesar's possible tyranny. He has come to the conclusion that for Rome's sake Caesar must die, when the conspirators arrive. Although Cassius has formed the conspiracy, all look to Brutus as the natural leader. Brutus disagrees with Cassius, and has his way, in two matters. He does not think it necessary for them to swear an oath to bind themselves to perform the deed ('what need we any spur but our own cause'), and he refuses to countenance the murder of Mark Antony as well. He urges that they should 'be sacrificers, but not butchers', that they should kill 'boldly, but not wrathfully', and that Antony, who 'is given/ To sports, to wildness, and much company' can 'do no more than Caesar's arm/ When Caesar's head is off.' When the conspirators have gone, Brutus's wife Portia comes to him, sadly aware that something is troubling him and wanting to share it with him.

Then we see Caesar, also sleepless in this troubled night of storm. His wife Calpurnia has dreamed of Caesar being murdered and begs him not to go to the Capitol. His servant reports that the priests he has been sent to consult urge Caesar not to stir forth that day. Caesar scorns these fears but gives way to her entreaty. At this point Decius Brutus comes to escort him to the Capitol, and persuades him to go, because he will be thought to be afraid if he does not and because he is to be offered the crown that day. The other conspirators all come to accompany Caesar to the Capitol. We briefly observe Artemidorus, reading aloud a letter he has written to Caesar warning him of the conspiracy and naming the conspirators, which he intends to give to Caesar as he passes. Portia agitatedly sends the servant Lucius to the Capitol, and a soothsayer who earlier warned Caesar to 'Beware the Ides of March' (15 March), which it now is, passes on his way to warn Caesar again.

Act III: Caesar comes to the Capitol, brushing aside the soothsayer and Artemidorus with their warnings. In the Senate house, one of the conspirators – Trebonius – lures Antony away, and Caesar rejects an appeal by Metellus Cimber on behalf of his banished brother. The conspirators gather round as if to plead the banished man's cause and stab Caesar to death one by one, Brutus giving the final blow. Brutus reassures the senators and others present: no one else is in danger now that 'ambition's debt is paid' with the death of

Caesar. Cassius calls for 'Liberty, freedom and enfranchisement' to be cried out in the streets. Trebonius returns, reporting that Antony has fled to his house appalled; soon Antony's servant comes to say that his master will 'not love Caesar dead/ So well as Brutus living' if he can be 'resolv'd/ How Caesar hath deserv'd to lie in death', and is sent to fetch him. When Antony comes, he grieves over 'mighty Caesar' laid so low, 'finds no hour so fit/ As Caesar's death's hour' for his own death, and calls on the conspirators, if they intend to execute him, to kill him straight away. Reassured of their amity he shakes each bloody hand, at the same time asking dead Caesar's forgiveness. He asks permission to take Caesar's dead body to the market-place to speak at his funeral. The generous-spirited Brutus immediately agrees, though Cassius sees danger in this. When the conspirators withdraw, Antony in a soliloquy asks pardon of dead Caesar 'that I am meek and gentle with these butchers' and grimly prophesies bloodshed and civil strife.

In the forum (market-place) Brutus tells the crowd that despite his love for Caesar he loved Rome more, and that is why, 'as he was ambitious, I slew him'. Then Mark Antony enters with Caesar's body, and in a famous speech contrives to move from temperate praise of Brutus gradually to questioning his motives and action, and then, despite continual references to his 'honourable' nature, to incriminate him and the conspirators. He stirs the crowd to lament Caesar's death, pointing out that he had three times declined the offer of the crown, and holding up the torn and blood-stained mantle. Finally, he tells them that in his will Caesar had left his gardens to Rome and a sum of money to every citizen, thus inflaming them to mutiny and to seek revenge. After the people have carried off Caesar's body, news is brought to Antony that young Octavius Caesar has arrived in Rome, and that Brutus and Cassius have abruptly left the city. The first victim of the inflamed mob is Cinna the Poet, mistaken for Cinna the Conspirator.

Act IV: Antony, Octavius and Lepidus form the 'triumvirate' (rule of three men). They decide on who is to be executed, and when Lepidus is sent to fetch Caesar's will – Antony intending to meddle with its provisions and lessen the outgoing payments - Antony shows his real ruthlessness further in scornful denigration of Lepidus. In camp near Sardis we witness an angry quarrel between Brutus and Cassius, in which finally Brutus is placatory and Cassius quickly then responds. Brutus now reveals that he is 'sick of many griefs', the chief of them being the news he has received of his wife Portia's dreadful suicide. News is brought that Mark Antony and Octavius are advancing with their army to Philippi. Brutus proposes an immediate march and attack, but Cassius prefers to let the enemy seek them. Brutus dominates in this, claiming that their own forces are now 'at the height, ready to decline', and they should seize the initiative: 'There is a tide in the affairs of men, / Which, taken at the flood, leads on to fortune', and it is so agreed. That night, his boy Lucius having fallen asleep while playing and singing to him in his tent, Brutus is briefly visited by the ghost□ of Caesar, come as 'thy evil spirit, Brutus' to warn him that they will meet again at Philippi.

Act V: On the plains of Philippi Octavius observes with satisfaction that the enemy forces have come down off the hills. Brutus and Cassius confront Antony and Octavius in an angry exchange. Cassius, whose birthday it is, confides in Messala that it was against his will and advice that the decision has been taken to fight here, and refers to ill omens – ravens, crows and kites flying in the sky above their army. He and Brutus then part, before taking up their separate positions in the battle array: 'If we do meet again, why, we shall smile; / If not, why then this parting was well made'. In the battle Cassius's men flee, and, believing that Brutus's force has been surrounded and that the day is lost, Cassius calls on his servant to kill him, and dies. But in fact Brutus has overthrown Octavius. The victorious Brutus, learning of Cassius's voluntary death, feels that the spirit of Caesar (which had again appeared to him at night) 'walks abroad, and turns our swords / In our own proper entrails'. He sadly salutes his dead companion, and continues the fight, but there has been a reverse and Brutus, saddened by loss, death and ill omens, feels his hour has come and asks his friend Volumnius to kill him, which he refuses to do. But another, Strato, agrees to hold the sword while Brutus runs on to it. The victors Antony and Octavius enter, and Antony pays tribute to Brutus, 'the noblest Roman of them all. / All the conspirators save only he / Did that they did in envy of great Caesar; / He only, in general honest thought, / And common good to all . . '

SOURCES   Plutarch's□ *Lives* of Marcus Brutus, Julius Caesar and of Marcus Antonius, in North's□ translation. As usual Shakespeare telescoped and compressed much of the action, and, while greatly indebted to Plutarch for the characterisation, he increased the human interest, emphasising Brutus's gentleness and considerateness and Cassius's impetuosity, making him more likeable, and balancing Caesar's ambition more strongly with his human frailties. There are known references to earlier plays on the subject but they probably did not influence Shakespeare.

TEXT   The play appears only in the First Folio□ (1623) and was probably set up from the playhouse manuscript or the prompt-book.□

K

King John. An early history play. Those who believe the play derived from *The Troublesome Raigne of John, King of England* (see below, 'Source') date it between 1593 and 1596. E. A. Honigmann, the proposer of the opposite view, convincingly dates it 1590–1.

Act I: An ambassador from the King of France demands that King John shall give up his throne and lands in France to his nephew, Arthur, Duke of Brittany, son of John's older brother. This is angrily rejected by the King, who swears he will go to war. Then come to the court two young men, Robert Faulconbridge and Philip his bastard elder brother, who are in dispute over their inheritance. Philip is recognised as the bastard son of Richard Coeur de Lion (Richard I), King John's elder brother and his predecessor as king. The King knights him, dubbing him Sir Richard Plantagenet and he resigns his family claim to his younger brother Robert. Briefly his mother appears, and confirms his parentage.

Act II: In France, outside the city of Angiers, King Philip, Louis the Dauphin, Constance and her son Arthur, together with the allied Duke of Austria and their forces, are resolved to win for Arthur not only the French lands controlled by England but England itself. The ambassador returns with King John's defiance, closely followed by John, his mother Queen Eleanor, his niece Blanche and Faulconbridge. After angry interchanges, especially between the Queen and Constance, and between Faulconbridge and the Duke of Austria, Hubert de Burgh appears on the walls, and is called on to surrender by each side in turn. Hubert requires to be assured whether John or his nephew Arthur is the rightful king, whereupon, prompted by Faulconbridge, all agree to join in capturing the defiant city; but Hubert finds a solution, proposing a marriage between John's niece Blanche and Philip of France's son, Lewis. The Bastard Faulconbridge, alone on the stage, expresses his contempt for this folly, recognising it as a probably fated compromise. Constance, when she is told, is angered and grieved by what she sees as the loss of her son Arthur's rights of succession.

Act III: Constance condemns the marriage, which has made peace between the Kings of England and France, saying to Philip 'You came in arms to spill mine enemies' blood/ But now in arms you strengthen it with yours.' But the peace is short-lived. The Pope's representative Pandulph comes, demanding that John shall cease to reject the Pope's nominee as Archbishop of Canterbury. John dismisses this demand and is excommunicated, and Pandulph successfully calls on Philip to support the Papacy and withdraw from the agreement with England. In the battle of Angiers which follows, the English are victorious. The young prince Arthur has been captured and is put by John into the keeping of Hubert, but the King suborns Hubert to kill him. The Bastard is despatched in haste to England to seize the riches of the monasteries. Constance grieves for her captured son. Pandulph predicts to Lewis the Dauphin that John will have Arthur killed – 'that John may stand, then, Arthur needs must fall' – and declares that the Dauphin's claim to England will thereby be strengthened.

Act IV: In England, Hubert, as instructed by the King, prepares to blind Arthur, but the boy's grace and composure win him round and he decides to spare him but let the King think he is dead. At court, the King is pressed by the Earl of Pembroke to release Arthur. Learning of the boy's death Pembroke and Salisbury suspect foul play and leave the King, to whom immediately news comes of a French invasion, of the death of his mother, Queen Eleanor, and of Lady Constance, and, from Faulconbridge, of prophecies of his imminent abdication. He learns of growing anger at his suspected responsibility for Arthur's death, and reviles Hubert for effecting it, whereupon Hubert reveals that Arthur is still alive. However, almost at once Arthur in fact dies, in a fall while trying to escape from his prison. His body is found by Pembroke, Salisbury and Faulconbridge; the two former, 'stifled with this smell of sin', decide to throw in their lot with the invaders, but Faulconbridge, convinced by Hubert that he and the King were not responsible for the boy's death, remains steadfast.

Act V: The King gives up his defiance of the Pope in order to ensure that the French attack will be called off. Faulconbridge reports that the people of Kent and in London have already welcomed the Dauphin and his forces and many nobles have gone 'to offer service to the enemy'. When told by the King of the peace moves he is outraged and calls for resistance, and the King yields – 'Have thou the ordering of this present time'. (Although Salisbury with others has signed a compact with Lewis the Dauphin, he is deeply grieved at the thought of marching on 'the gentle bosom' of his own land, filling up 'her enemies' ranks'.) Pandulph comes to report John's submission to Rome, but Lewis is bent on war to win his claim to England, and Faulconbridge soon enters and proclaims England's defiance. In the ensuing battle, the French forces are faltering; a wounded French lord, Melun, reveals to Salisbury and Pembroke Lewis's secret intention, if victorious, to have them both assassinated, whereupon they rejoin the English forces. John falls ill of a fever, and dies poisoned by a monk in the abbey where he had taken refuge, but not before pardoning Salisbury and Pembroke at the request of his own son, Prince Henry. The French make peace,

Prince Henry will succeed to the throne, and the play ends with Faulconbridge's famous speech with its conclusion 'Nought shall make us rue / If England to itself do rest but true!'

SOURCE The primary source is Holinshed's□ *Chronicles of England, Scotland and Ireland*□ (2nd edition, 1587). (Some historical details come from *Actes and Monuments* (1563), popularly known as *The Book of Martyrs,*□ by John Foxe□ (1516–87), a collection of accounts of the deaths of Protestant martyrs.) It was for long assumed that the chief source was an anonymous play *The Troublesome Raigne of John, King of England*, published in 1591, but it seems more probable that that was dependent on Shakespeare's play, with a much stronger anti-Catholic preoccupation.

TEXT The play appears only in the First Folio□ (1623) and was probably set up from Shakespeare's 'foul papers'.□

King Lear. A tragedy, of late 1605 or early 1606.

Act I: We are immediately introduced to the upright Earl of Kent, the Earl of Gloucester and his bastard son Edmund, before the old King Lear enters with his three daughters and two sons-in-law. He has re-solved to divide his kingdom among them, giving the largest share to the daughter who convinces him that she loves him most. Goneril, wife of the Duke of Albany, and Regan, wife of the Duke of Cornwall, are lavish in their protestations of love, but the youngest, Cordelia – whose suitors the King of France and the Duke of Burgundy attend without – is able only to 'Love, and be silent'; 'I cannot heave / My heart into my mouth', and all she can say is 'Nothing, my lord.' The old king is so angered by this honest loving daughter's refusal to match her sisters' (insincere) declarations of love that he disclaims her, and gives her share of the kingdom to Goneril and Regan. He intends thereafter with a hundred knights to live in turn, month by month, with each of them. The Earl of Kent intervenes on Cordelia's behalf, bravely telling the raging king that he does evil, and for this he is instantly banished. The two French suitors for Cordelia's hand are admitted; Burgundy withdraws his suit when he hears that she is disgraced and dowerless, but the King of France remains constant. As she leaves with him she urges her sisters – though not very confident of their goodwill to him – to care for their father lovingly. Left alone, they coldly discuss 'the infirmity of his age: yet he hath ever but slenderly known himself' and prepare to act together if in future the old king is troublesome to them.

The illegitimate son of Gloucester, Edmund, resentful of his disadvantages as a bastard, contrives by trickery to incriminate his brother, the legitimate son Edgar, of a supposed plot to kill his father, Gloucester. The old king, staying in Goneril's house, is treated with neglect and disrespect by her servants, one of whom, Oswald her steward, she encourages particularly in insolence to her father. The faithful Kent, disguised, has followed his older master in spite of being banished, and is taken into service. The Fool pointedly makes jokes about the old king's folly in handing over power to his two older daughters and banishing the youngest. When Goneril enters we see with what contemptuous harshness she treats her father, complaining about his followers' behaviour and determining to reduce his train. Lear curses Goneril and leaves for his second daughter's house. Goneril's husband Albany knows nothing of the causes she alleges to explain her cruel behaviour. Lear for the first time expresses his fear: 'O! let me not be mad, not mad, sweet heaven'.

Act II: Edmund fully incriminates his brother Edgar of intending to kill Gloucester. To Gloucester's castle come Cornwall and his wife Regan; they have heard from Goneril and have left their castle to avoid receiving Lear and his train. Kent and Oswald both arrive with messages from the King and Goneril respectively and quarrel, for which Kent is put in the stocks by Cornwall. Meanwhile Edgar, having escaped, takes on disguise as a Tom o'Bedlam, a mad itinerant beggar. Lear arrives at Gloucester's castle, and finding his man, the disguised Kent, in the stocks, angrily goes off to find and to demand an explanation of Regan, who he knows has come to Gloucester's castle. He returns with Gloucester, incredulous that they 'Deny to speak with me' and orders him to fetch Regan or Cornwall. When they come Kent is released from the stocks and Lear tries to control his rage, but Regan soon shows as cold a response as Goneril had, and defends her actions. Goneril arrives and the two daughters icily defy and humiliate him, refusing to house him unless his train of a hundred knights is disbanded. He turns from one to another, as it were playing for the higher bid, but they unite in denying him; why does he need even one follower, Regan finally asks. This final rejection and humiliation leads him to a pitiful rage, 'a poor old man, / As full of grief as age'. Vowing revenge on these 'unnatural hags', he rushes out, muttering 'O Fool! I shall go mad' as the first thunder of an approaching storm is heard.

Act III: This great storm rages throughout the Act. Kent, trying to find the king, meets a gentleman who reports Lear to be alone with the Fool on a heath in the storm. Kent tells him of dissension between Cornwall and Albany, and of a force from France that has landed at Dover. Lear defies the elements; they are not more cruel than his daughters. Kent finds him and the Fool and brings them to a hovel where they may shelter. Gloucester, ignorant of Edmund's villainy, tells him of the arrival of a relieving force from France.

Edmund resolves to betray this information to Cornwall, which 'must draw me / That which my father loses; no less than all'.

Lear, who is obsessed by the idea of filial ingratitude, though he tries not to think of it ('O! That way madness lies') is brought to the hovel, from which suddenly runs the madman (Edgar in disguise). Lear quickly settles down to wild conversation with him, saying it must have been cruel daughters that had brought him to madness, and madly tries to tear off his clothes to be more like the 'poor, bare, forked animal'. Gloucester, loyally searching for the king, finds him in this strange company and, unaware that both his old friend Kent and his son Edgar are there in the King's company in disguise as well as the faithful Fool, leads them all to 'where both fire and food is ready'. Meanwhile his bastard son Edmund, whom he still believes true, has betrayed him to Cornwall and has been rewarded already with the title Earl of Gloucester. In warmth and shelter at last Lear with his companions conducts an imaginary trial of his cruel daughters. Gloucester enters and hastens them away to safety, telling them to go towards Dover. Gloucester is arrested and brought before Cornwall and Regan, who question him about Lear's whereabouts. They damn him as a traitor and blind him, telling him that it was Edmund who betrayed him. A servant intervenes, wounding Cornwall who we hear later dies of the wound, before being himself killed by Regan.

Act IV: Edgar (Poor Tom) sees his blinded father, led by an old servant. Appalled, but retaining his disguise and 'madman' voice, he takes over, and is asked by Gloucester to lead him to Dover clifs. At Albany's house we learn that Goneril is in love with Edmund and despises and reviles her husband. For Albany has recoiled in horror at the savagery of his wife and her sister, and is now confirmed in his sense of their wickedness and inhumanity when news is brought of the blinding of Gloucester, which he vows to avenge. We learn of Cordelia's arrival with French forces at Dover, and of her grief at Lear's madness and the cruelty of her sisters, from a conversation between Kent and a gentleman. We then briefly see her, ordering a search to be made for the lost and wandering king. At Gloucester's castle, Regan discloses her desire for Edmund to Goneril's steward, wishing him to tell his mistress, of whom Regan is now jealous, about it; she licenses Oswald to kill Gloucester if he comes across him.

Gloucester asks 'Poor Tom' to take him to the cliffs. He is intent on suicide, but Edgar deliberately deceives him into jumping from a negligible height and then persuades him that he has indeed leaped from the cliff-top, and that 'the clearest Gods, who make them honours / Of men's impossibilities, have preserved thee'. Edgar now

presents himself as a sturdy peasant, no longer a Tom o'Bedlam.
Lear suddenly appears, 'fantastically dressed with wild flowers'.
Blind Gloucester recognises his voice, and the two stricken old men
converse. Lear is still obsessed with his daughters' behaviour, with
justice and injustice, social hypocrisy and with sexuality, and madly
jokes about Gloucester's lost eyes. When Cordelia's gentleman
comes with others, Lear escapes from them. Oswald enters and
attempts to kill Gloucester but is himself killed by Edgar. The
distant drum-beats of battle are heard. Lear has been found and
brought to Cordelia's camp. Cordelia expresses her gratitude to
Kent for his loving guard of her father. The old king wakens from
deep sleep. He thinks he is in hell, and is perplexed to find an angel,
as he thinks, beside his bed – 'a soul in bliss; but I am bound/
Upon a wheel of fire, that mine own tears/ Do scald like molten
lead'. But soon he is convinced that it is Cordelia.
Act V: At the British camp, Regan chides her lover Edmund with
loving her sister Goneril. The 'domestic broils' between Goneril and
Albany and Regan and her husband Cornwall (now dead) are
temporarily at rest. Albany demands that they distinguish between
the invading French forces – which they must oppose – and the
old king and his daughter. Edgar, still as a peasant, gives Albany the
letter (from Regan to Edmund) that he had found on Oswald's
body. Edmund in soliloquy cynically wonders whether to take
Regan or Goneril – 'Both? one? or neither?' – and resolves to
frustrate Albany's intended mercy towards Lear and Cordelia.
Cordelia and her French forces are defeated and she and Lear
captured. Now that his truly loving daughter has been restored to
him, Lear envisages a happy life together, even in prison: 'We two
alone will sing like birds i' th' cage'. But Edmund secretly orders
their execution. The victorious party is soon at strife: Regan and
Goneril openly quarrel over Edmund; Albany arrests Edmund and
challenges him to single combat unless at the sounding of a trumpet
someone else appears to fight with him. An unknown knight
delivers a challenge, fights and mortally wounds Edmund; it is
Edgar, who now tells Albany that old Gloucester has died: his heart
''Twixt two extremes of passion, joy and grief,/ Burst smilingly' on
learning that it was his true son Edgar who had guided him. We
learn now that Goneril, having poisoned Regan, has stabbed herself
to death. Kent arrives, and Edmund suddenly confesses that he has
ordered the deaths of Lear and Cordelia and urges haste to prevent
it. He is carried off, dying. The message has come too late and Lear
now enters carrying Cordelia dead in his arms, beside himself with
grief. Albany, the victor and leader, immediately resigns 'During the
life of this old Majesty,/ To him our absolute power'. But Lear dies.

Albany calls on Edgar and Kent to rule jointly, but Kent, faithful to the end to Lear, says that he has a 'journey shortly to go;/ My master calls me, I must not say no.'

SOURCES *The True Chronicle History of King Leir* is a crude early piece (published in 1605). It has the division of the kingdom, the two faithless daughters and the one true daughter (and those four names), but ends happily with the king's restoration to his throne. The story – legend, tradition – first appears in the *Historia Regum Britanniae* of about 1140 by Geoffrey of Monmouth (*d.*1154) and gradually became regarded as historical. Holinshed□ told it briefly in his *Chronicles of England, Scotland and Ireland*;□ it still recorded Lear's restoration and peaceful reign, and the succession to the throne of Cordelia, but ends with her eventual taking of her own life in prison after a civil war waged by two nephews. In none of these versions is Lear mad; this is Shakespeare's invention. In none is there a Gloucester character or sub-plot; this further brilliant addition to the story was inspired by scenes of a blind king, of Paphlagonia, in Sir Philip Sidney's (1554–86) pastoral romance *Arcadia*□ (1590).

TEXT The First Quarto□ (1608), where it is described on the title-page as a 'True Chronicle Historie', seems to have been partly a memorial reconstruction,□ partly from a prompt-book□ hurriedly copied; it is not a good text. The Second Quarto (1619) was printed from a copy of Q1. The First Folio□ (1623) text was printed from an imperfect copy of Q1, perhaps a corrected one but with many alterations, including the loss of about 300 lines and the addition of over 100. The Folio is generally accepted as the better text, but editors usually make judicious use of both Q1 and Folio.

King's Men, the. See Chamberlain's Men, the Lord.

L

Licensing. Three kinds of licensing (authorising, permitting) affected the theatre: (1) Plays had to be licensed for performance by the Master of the Revels□ originally for court performances only; but from 1574 the Earl of Leicester's Men were allowed to perform anywhere provided the Master of the Revels approved. From 1581 the Master's authority was extended to all plays. Fees were charged. (2) From 1586 all books had to be licensed for printing by the Archbishop of Canterbury or the Bishop of London or their deputy. Then (3) they had to be registered – with a fee – with the Stationers' Company□ when copyright was established. Plays were in fact often printed without the official authority of the Church but only that of the Stationers' Company, until the Archbishop and Bishop took action in 1599 to assert their authority.

Lodge, Thomas (?1588–1625). Elizabethan writer now remembered chiefly for his prose romance *Rosalynde* (1590) which provided Shakespeare with the main plot of *As You Like It*. Shakespeare created the easy-going ironic fool Touchstone and the affectedly melancholic Jacques, both of whom comment on the situations and amusingly discuss and dismiss the artificiality of pastoralism.☐ He also created in Rosalind the most delightful of all his heroines, witty, amusing, spontaneous, impulsive and tender-hearted.

Lord Chamberlain's Men. See Chamberlain's Men, the Lord.

Love's Labour's Lost. A fairly early comedy, probably dating from 1593, but there is some possibility that it was originally written for a children's company in 1588 and revised and enlarged later.

Act I: The King of Navarre and his friends Berowne, Dumain and Longaville have resolved to devote three years to study and ascetic life. Berowne is sceptical and protests: 'O these are barren tasks, too hard to keep, / Not to see ladies, study, fast, not sleep', but he agrees and declares he will keep to the agreement longer than the others. The King thinks they will find recreation in observing the 'child of fancy' the Spaniard Don Adriano de Armado, 'a man of fire-new words, fashion's own knight', and the clown Costard. Armado has sent an extravagant and ornate letter, complaining that Costard has been consorting with a wench Jacquenetta, thus breaking the royal command forbidding women to come within a mile of the court. Costard is sentenced to 'fast a week with bran and water' in the custody of Armado. Armado reveals to his page Moth that he is in love with Jacquenetta himself.

Act II: The Princess of France comes with her three ladies, Rosaline, Maria and Katharine to negotiate with the King of Navarre over her aged father's debt to him. Each of the ladies in turn meets one of the lords, the most notable encounter being that of Berowne and Rosaline who indulge in witty provocative banter.

Act III: Armado, after an elaborate discussion of love with young Moth, gives Costard a love-letter to give to Jacquenetta. Berowne also employs Costard as a messenger, telling us how he, who has been a scoffer at love, has fallen in love with Rosaline.

Act IV: Costard, however, coming upon the Princess and her ladies preparing to shoot at driven deer, gives Armado's letter to Jacquenetta to the Princess, who has the ridiculous inflated letter read aloud. Berowne's letter to Rosaline goes to Jacquenetta, who asks the parson Sir Nathaniel to read it aloud to her, as she cannot read. The parson admires Berowne's verse-letter more than his friend the schoolmaster Holofernes (both of whom we now meet for the first time, together with Dull the Constable). Scene 3 is devoted to the exposure, one by one, of the King and his three companions. Unwittingly, unaware that they are observed, they reveal their secret loving by reading aloud in turn love-poems they have written to the ladies, the King to the Princess, Longaville to Maria and Dumain to Katharine. Berowne, the first to fall, berates the others for breaking their promise to forswear women for three years, until the entry of Jacquenetta and Costard reveals his own letter to Rosaline. In a long, famous speech in praise of women and of love – '. . . love, first learned in a lady's eyes, . . ./ Courses as swift as thought in every power,/ And gives to every power a double power,/ Above their functions and their offices', - Berowne justifies them all, and they all agree to 'woo these girls of France' and 'win them too', and to entertain them with 'revels, dances, masks'.

Act V: This begins with another scene of pedantic discussion between Nathaniel and Holofernes, to whom comes Armado (with Moth, who again shows his superior wit) to say that the King has asked him to put on 'some delightful ostentation or show, or pageant, or antic' before the Princess. They all enthusiastically agree to help with it. The four ladies of France are wittily and mischievously discussing the letters and presents they have received from the four gentlemen of Navarre when Boyet enters with news that the four are about to present themselves disguised as Muscovites. When they come, the ladies have disguised their identity with masks and each of the four men mistakes the lady he singles out; they are treated with witty mockery and withdraw. When they return undisguised, the Princess laughingly tells them of the ridiculous Muscovites who had visited them. Ruefully, the gentlemen 'confess and turn it to a jest', led by Berowne who swears to give up affected language in furthering his courtship of Rosaline: his 'wooing mind' will be 'express'd/ In russet yeas and honest kersey noes'. Then the 'ostentation' of the Nine Worthies is presented before the court by the comic characters: Costard as Pompey, Nathaniel as Alexander, Moth as Hercules, Holofernes as Judas Maccabaeus and Armado as Hector. But the presentation is interrupted by a French lord, Marcade, bringing news of the sudden death of the Princess's father, and the witty rather cruel jesting is brought to an end. The Princess must return immediately to France with her ladies. Before they leave, in response to urgent appeals from their lovers, it is agreed that the Prince shall spend the next twelve months as a hermit, Berowne shall spend the year visiting and cheering the sick in hospital, and that the ladies will marry their suitors only at the end of that time. The play, so suddenly transformed into seriousness, ends with a sung dialogue between Spring and Winter, 'the one maintained by the owl, the other by the cuckoo'.

SOURCES   There is no written source, but the play parallels a real historical situation concerning the King of Navarre and a Princess of France, and a debt owed, in the period 1578–86. Some of the names (Berowne, Longaville, Dumain) reflect those of actual historical figures. Another indirect influence is the Italian *commedia dell'arte*□ for the figures of (as Berowne lists them) 'pedant, braggart, hedge-priest, the fool and the boy'; but Holofernes, Armado, Sir Nathaniel, Costard and Moth are given so much detail and humorous diversification that they far outgo the convention.

TEXT   The Quarto□ of 1598, probably set up from Shakespeare's own manuscript, but there is some evidence of later revision. The editors of the First Folio□ (1623) used the Quarto, correcting it in places and making new mistakes of their own.

Lyly, John (?1554–1606). His prose romance *Euphues* (1578) and a successor made him the most fashionable writer for a time. He wrote eight courtly comedies of love in classical or mythological settings (for example, *Campaspe*, *Gallathea* and the best-known, *Endimion*) which were performed before the court and in private theatres by children's companies in the decade before Shakespeare began to write. Stylish, witty, learned, and written in mannered rhetorical prose – only one, *The Woman in the Moon*, was in verse – they were admirable for their audience but did not survive the rise of the professional adult companies and of the popular theatre. But Lyly naturalised some valuable dramatic conventions from which Shakespeare and others profited, notably the use of stock characters – much fantasticated and embellished by him – from Latin comedy and *commedia dell'arte*,□ such as lovesick young men, the *senex amans* or aged lover, the braggart soldier and the comic wily servants who constantly exchange witty or abusive badinage. Above all, he established the tradition of the comedy of courtship, with clever wit-combats, raillery and the use of disguise – especially of girl as boy. His forging of the language into a subtle, complex, sophisticated medium, using rhetorical devices, much metaphor and simile, personification and allusion, although easily ridiculed or parodied (as Shakespeare did, especially in *Love's Labour's Lost* and *The Taming of the Shrew*), was of considerable importance at that stage in the development of the language for literary and theatrical purposes.

M

Macbeth. A tragedy dating from 1606 and probably performed at Court in that year before King James I (a Scot) and the King of Denmark. It is the shortest play (2100 lines) and would have benefited from indoor performance.

Act I: Three witches open the play; they are agreeing to meet again upon a heath, there to encounter Macbeth, a Scottish general. We learn of an insurrection against the king of Scotland, Duncan, in which Macbeth, Thane of Glamis, has performed heroically, ensuring victory. The Norwegian king, involved with the uprising, has made peace, and Duncan decrees the death of the rebel Thane of Cawdor, his title being granted to Macbeth. Macbeth and his fellow-general Banquo are hailed by the witches, who prophesy that Macbeth shall be Thane of Cawdor and king 'hereafter', and Banquo shall 'get Kings, though (he) be none'. Almost as soon as the witches have vanished, news is brought to Macbeth of his promotion to be Thane of Cawdor. At the court at Forres, Duncan warmly receives and gratefully congratulates Macbeth and Banquo. He announces his intention of honouring Macbeth and his wife by a visit. But he also names his son Malcolm as his successor, at which Macbeth mutters, aside, 'That is a step / On which I must fall down, or else o'erleap, / For in my way it lies.'

The action now moves to Macbeth's castle at Inverness, where Lady Macbeth reads a letter in which her husband reports his meeting with the witches, his promotion and the prophecy about the kingship. Then a messenger brings word of the King's impending visit, and instantly she begins to prepare herself for terrible deeds, calling on evil spirits ('unsex me here, / And fill me, from the crown to the toe, top-full / Of direst cruelty'). Macbeth arrives and she immediately conveys to him her resolve to achieve the last prophecy of the witches; they must kill the king that night. Macbeth temporises. Duncan arrives and is fulsomely welcomed by Lady Macbeth. That evening in a soliloquy Macbeth thinks over his wife's plan, recoils as he thinks of Duncan's virtues, and of his special position as king, kinsman and guest, and tells his wife 'We will proceed no further in this business.' Lady Macbeth, enraged and contemptuous, reviles him so powerfully that he weakens and agrees to her murder plan.

Act II: With anguished doubt and horror, increased by imagining he sees a dagger before him 'The handle toward my hand', Macbeth waits for the signal – a bell – and then goes towards the King's chamber saying 'Hear it not, Duncan; for it is a knell / That summons thee to Heaven or to Hell.' Lady Macbeth excitedly awaits his return from the murder. She has made the two chamber-grooms drunk so that they sleep, and the plan is to incriminate them. She is horrified to find that Macbeth has bemusedly brought the grooms' two daggers back with him. Macbeth is too appalled by what he has done to be able to return to the murder chamber, so Lady Macbeth seizes them and takes them back. A knocking at the castle gate is heard three times, and Macbeth mutters to himself 'Wake Duncan with thy knocking: I would thou couldst!' The knocking continues in the next short scene when the drunken Porter with comic irony thinks of himself as the porter of Hell-gate. The knocking is by the nobleman Macduff, come by previous order to wait on the King early. His companion Lennox talks with Macbeth and tells of the fearful night that had passed ('Lamentings heard i' th'air; strange screams of death' and rumour of earthquake) before Macduff enters having discovered the murdered King. Macbeth goes with Lennox to the royal chamber, and returns, reporting that he has killed the two grooms in fury; in the ensuing clamour, Lady Macbeth faints and the King's sons, Malcolm and Donalbain, decide to flee, fearful for their lives. We learn of other dreadful disturbances of nature that night, and also of the unnatural darkness of this early morning. The flight of the King's sons 'puts upon them / Suspicion of the deed'. Macbeth is swiftly named King.

Act III: Macbeth, now King, knows that according to the prophecy Banquo and his descendants will succeed to the throne. Macbeth's is 'a fruitless crown', his sceptre 'barren' while Banquo lives. While seeming exceptionally gracious to him, inviting him as chief guest to a feast, he plots his death. Two murderers are commissioned and told to waylay Banquo and his son Fleance that evening as they return from riding. Lady Macbeth, who has already discovered that 'Nought's had, all's spent, / Where our desire is got without content', is worried at Macbeth's melancholy mood and his secretiveness; though she seems to sense it, she is not told of the next murder which is about to take place. Banquo is murdered but in the struggle Fleance escapes. At the great feast which ensues almost immediately, the ghost□ of Banquo appears and takes his seat, visible only to Macbeth, who reacts distractedly, and the feast is broken off by Lady Macbeth. Macbeth, recovering, resolves to consult the witches again, and wonders about the absence of Macduff; he says 'For mine own good, / All causes shall give way: I am in blood / Stepp'd in so far . . .' Lennox and another lord (after a brief, probably non-Shakespearian, scene of the witches being reproved by their 'goddess' Hecate) discuss the murderous and fearful times. We hear of Malcolm at the pious King of England's court and that Macduff has gone thither to raise a force to rid

Scotland of its tyrant, and has refused an order from Macbeth to return.

Act IV: Macbeth visits the witches in their cave. They warn him to beware the Thane of Fife (Macduff), but assure him that 'none of woman born/ Shall harm Macbeth' and that he will not be vanquished unless Birnam Wood moves to Dunsinane. He inquires of them whether Banquo's children will ever reign, and is shown 'a show of eight kings' and Banquo's ghost. Then the witches vanish, and almost at once Lennox comes with news that Macduff has fled to England. Macbeth resolves to seize Macduff's castle and kill his wife and children, and in the next scene Lady Macduff and her young son are killed by assassins. In England Macduff (who does not know of this) visits Malcolm at the English court to enlist his support, but Malcolm ·is wary lest he be secretly an agent of Macbeth. Macduff's honest, appalled and grieved response convinces Malcolm of his integrity. Ross now comes and with difficulty reports to Macduff the murder of his wife and children. Malcolm and Macduff resolve to march north with their forces.

Act V: At Dunsinane, her physician and waiting-gentlewoman watch the sleep-walking of Lady Macbeth. Tormented and distraught by guilt and horror, she seemingly relives some of the terrible acts of murder, and in her deranged sleep still tries to wash blood from her hands. Some Scottish leaders, Lennox among them, resolve for the good of Scotland to join Malcolm's approaching forces near Birnam Wood. Macbeth is defiant, having fortified Dunsinane Castle and believing that 'Till Birnam wood remove to Dunsinane, I cannot faint with fear.' But he is also 'sick at heart'; his wife's mental illness disturbs him and he knows that he cannot hope to have 'that which should accompany old age/As honour, love, obedience, troops of friends'. Malcolm orders his soldiers to hew boughs from Birnam Wood and carry them before them so that the numbers of his army will be concealed. Macbeth hears of his wife's death and then of the apparent movement of Birnam Wood. He is dismayed but his courage and defiance are not weakened. He clings, too, to the prophecy that he cannot be harmed by any man born of woman. Macduff finds and challenges him; during the fight Macbeth tells him of this, whereupon Macduff reveals that he was 'from his mother's womb/Untimely ripp'd', and they fight their way offstage, fighting to the death. Soon Macduff returns with Macbeth's head, and Malcolm is acclaimed as King of Scotland.

SOURCE   Holinshed□ *Chronicles of England, Scotland and Ireland*□ (2nd edition 1587), to some extent re-arranged; for example, the murder of Duncan is taken from the account of the murder of another Scottish King (Duff).

TEXT   There is only the First Folio□ (1623) text, probably from the prompt-book□ or a transcript of it.

Marlowe, Christopher (1564–93). Born the same year as Shakespeare, Marlowe was established as a playwright before him despite a hectic career at Cambridge and apparently as a government agent or spy. *Tamburlaine the Great* (?1587), a great sprawling heroic 'tragedy' in two parts, and possibly *The Tragical History of Dr Faustus* (?1589; a version was published in 1604) and *The Jew of Malta* (?1590; not published until 1633) may be earlier than any of the plays of Shakespeare, although in recent years there has been a tendency to date Shakespeare's earliest plays in the late 1580s rather than in the early 1590s. Probably only *Tamburlaine* in fact ante-dated Shakespeare, and it is difficult to find any direct influence from it on anything he wrote. Yet Marlowe in this play lifted the drama, and poetic drama especially, to new levels of grandeur, force and fluency. *The Jew of Malta* certainly preceded *The Merchant of Venice*, and a measure of Shakespeare's sensibility and superiority may be found in the difference between Marlowe's gloating, crude, half-comic demon Jew□ and the human dignity and pathos (as well as the cleverness) of Shylock. Shakespeare's earliest history plays, the three parts of *Henry VI*, ante-dated Marlowe's *Edward II*.

Marlowe wrote great leading parts, though they were usually deficient in a sense of humanity. He wrote them for the Admiral's Men, which meant that the great Edward Alleyn□ created them on the stage. Whether Marlowe, who died before he was thirty, stabbed in a tavern, would have developed and how, we cannot tell: *Edward II* shows advances in plotting, in dramatic speech and in tragic feeling. He remains powerful but unsubtle compared with Shakespeare, who by the same age had written not only *Titus Andronicus*, full of violence and cruelty yet softened by more than Marlovian pity and sense of pathos and of justice, but also the tremendous, if flawed, trilogy *Henry VI*, the powerful *Richard III* and several varied comedies: *The Comedy of Errors*, *The Two Gentlemen of Verona*, and probably *The Taming of the Shrew*.

Masque. Originally in Tudor and Elizabethan times at a feast or celebration in a great house the guests would enter wearing masks, acting in dumbshow and dancing. (See the masquing in *Romeo and Juliet*.) Before long, shape was given to the combination of music, dance and song by attaching it to a small dramatic action, debate or argument, and from this the Elizabethan court masque developed. It was used especially to pay compliments to the Queen or royal or distinguished visitors, and to show the triumphs of virtue. Once plot and argument had come, giving shape and strength, the masque could and did become more elaborate and serious in subject-matter;

but it remained poetic and symbolic, never becoming naturalistic or very dramatic. It was always above all musical, with singing and dance. Allegory, in which ideas and teaching are presented not directly but in a disguised but discoverable form, played a big part in the masque, which also came to have more and more rich and varied settings, costumes and stage-machinery. Jonson□ established the elaborate, extended masque form, and seems to have originated the anti-masque□ which became a regular element: it provided a contrast between the gods, goddesses and courtly personages on the one hand and rural or low characters, comic and/or grotesque, or grotesque creatures of the imagination, on the other.

Shakespeare used masque or masque elements and techniques in *Love's Labour's Lost*, *Romeo and Juliet* and *Much Ado About Nothing* for pleasing and appropriate courtly spectacle and entertainment. In *The Merry Wives of Windsor* Falstaff is finally fooled in a sort of masque of 'fairies and goblins' at midnight in Windsor Forest; in *Timon of Athens* a masque shows the chief character's wealth and extravagance. There is a brief masque, a sad but hopeful vision, in *Henry VIII*. *A Midsummer Night's Dream* and *The Tempest*, which both contain much masque material, seem in some ways almost to become extended dramatic masques themselves – except that that is a contradiction in terms, for masque is spectacle, music and movement and not drama.

Master of the Revels. The court official who under the Lord Chamberlain was responsible for arranging and supervising all entertainment at court. Eventually he became virtually responsible for all theatrical production in London. (See Censorship□.) It was first a permanent office under Henry VIII.

Measure for Measure. A so-called problem play,□ probably written in the summer of 1604.

Act I: The Duke of Vienna, about to leave the city, appoints Angelo as his deputy, with the old Lord Escalus to help him. It is thought that he goes on a peace mission. We quickly learn of Angelo's vigorous actions, for Mistress Overdone, a bawd, tells Lucio and other gentlemen that the brothels are all to be closed and that young Claudio has been arrested and is to be executed for getting Juliet his betrothed with child. At this point Claudio enters, a prisoner, accompanied by the Provost and Lucio, to the latter of whom he asserts his true love for Juliet, but that Angelo has invoked an old law long ignored. He asks Lucio to go immediately to the nunnery which his young sister Isabella is about to enter and implore her to intercede with the Deputy on his behalf, 'For in her youth/There is a prone and speechless dialect/Such as move men'.

In fact the Duke has not left Vienna but, we now see, has taken on disguise. He explains to the Friar from whom he borrows a friar's habit that he has for years allowed the 'strict statutes and most biting laws' to be 'let slip'; he does not feel that he can now harshly re-impose them, and he has appointed Angelo to bring order and justice back to Vienna. He says that Angelo is 'a man of stricture and firm abstinence' yet he closes the scene with the significant remark 'Hence shall we see/If power change purpose, what our seemers be'. Lucio comes to the nunnery with the unhappy news, declaring 'All hope is gone,/Unless you have the grace by your fair prayer/To soften Angelo', and Isabella decides to try to move Angelo to mercy.

Act II: Escalus pleads with Angelo to mitigate the sentence on Claudio, asking him to consider whether at any time in his life he might not himself have 'err'd in this point, which now you censure him', but the Deputy replies: ''Tis one thing to be tempted, Escalus,/Another thing to fall' and insists on maintaining the full rigour of the law, ordering the execution to take place by nine o'clock on the following day. Pompey Bum, Mistress Overdone's man, and a silly gentleman called Froth, are brought before them by Elbow, a simple word-muddling constable, with a charge so comically rambling and obscure involving Elbow's wife that Angelo impatiently leaves the case to Escalus who humorously lets them off with a caution.

Next follows the scene of Isabella's pleading with Angelo for her brother's life, encouraged by Lucio's whispered promptings. Eventually he agrees to see her again the following morning (which means the postponement of Claudio's execution). Left alone, in an anguished soliloquy Angelo reveals that her beauty and purity have aroused his passion, making him 'desire her foully for those things/That make her good'. The Duke in disguise calls at the prison, meets Juliet and learns of her and Claudio's 'sin'; he establishes that both her love for Claudio and her repentance are sincere and tells her he will now visit and instruct her doomed lover. Isabella comes to an Angelo who has just shown us again in a soliloquy his troubled passion for her and the conflict in him between virtue and temptation. He asks her as if it were an academic question, whether she would rather see her brother were executed, 'or, to redeem him,/Give up your body to such sweet uncleanness/As she that he hath stain'd'. When she realises that this is actually the choice he is offering her, she is appalled and angrily reviles him. She cries 'Seeming, seeming!/I will proclaim thee, Angelo', to which he rejoins that his 'unsoil'd name, th' austereness of [his] life' will vouch against her, and declares that unless she will yield up her body to his will, not only will Claudio die but he will have him tortured before execution. He leaves her, giving her another day to change her mind. She is determined to remain true to her principles, thinks that her brother would refuse to contemplate such a sacrifice on her part and would rather die than see her defiled, and decides to tell Claudio of Angelo's monstrous demand.

Act III: The disguised Duke visits Claudio in prison and comforts him, helping him to prepare to meet death. They are joined by Isabella. The Duke and Provost retire while Claudio anxiously asks her the outcome of her visit to Angelo. He is shocked, but cannot help clinging to the hope of life – 'Death is a fearful thing' and 'Ay, but to die, and go we know not where;/ To lie in cold obstruction and to rot'. He implores her to yield and save his life, for which she reviles him. Hearing this the Duke comes forward, asks Isabella to withdraw for a moment, and tells Claudio that Angelo is only testing her virtue and 'had never the purpose to corrupt her' so Claudio should prepare for death. He then speaks privately to Isabella, unfolding a plan to solve all. He tells her of Mariana, Angelo's rejected betrothed, who still loves him. Isabella is to agree to meet Angelo secretly at night and Mariana is to be substituted for her; the result will be 'your brother saved, your honour untainted, the poor Mariana advantaged, and the corrupt deputy scaled'. Isabella agrees to this plot. The disguised Duke in the street comes on Pompey, again under arrest by Elbow, for procuring. When Lucio appears he jests at Pompey's plight but will not bail him out, and stays talking to the 'Friar' in the course of which he gossips about Angelo's prim nature and denial of 'lenity to lechery', comparing him unfavourably with the absent Duke whom he accuses jokingly of licentiousness – 'he had some feeling of the sport'. Next, Mistress Overdone is hauled off to prison; Escalus informs the Provost that Claudio's execution is fixed for the morrow, and the Act ends with the Duke alone on stage in a strange sequence of couplets commenting on Angelo's 'seeming' and vileness and very briefly summarising the ensuing night's plot – 'Craft against vice I must apply.'

Act IV: Isabella comes to the moated grange, where sad Mariana, Angelo's rejected lady, dwells. Isabella tells the Duke of the arrangements to meet Angelo, and these are communicated to Mariana, who agrees to the plot by which she will take Isabella's place for the assignation, reassured by the Duke that there is no sin in it because of her and Angelo's earlier pre-contract of marriage. In the prison the Provost asks Pompey to assist the executioner Abhorson, who lacks a helper in the execution of Claudio and another prisoner, Barnardine, fixed for the morrow. Claudio is told of the new time for the execution. The Duke comes to the Provost, both awaiting the reprieve which should be on its way if the bed-substitution plot has succeeded and Angelo keeps his word. A messenger comes; there is no reprieve; Claudio is to die by four o'clock, Barnardine in the afternoon. Barnardine is a dissolute and drunken man, and the Duke prevails upon the Provost, who has told him that he is 'a man that apprehends death no more dreadfully but as a drunken sleep', to delay Claudio's execution but to execute Barnardine in his place. But the prisoner declares he has been drinking all night and is not ready for death and 'will not consent to die this day'. Fortunately, another prisoner, more resembling Claudio, has just died and it is decided to send his head to Angelo as proof of Claudio's execution. The Duke keeps Isabella still in ignorance, tells her that her brother is dead and that the Duke returns tomorrow, and tells her to accuse Angelo of the crime. A worried Angelo awaits the arrival of the Duke, who has required him by letter to proclaim that 'if any crave redress of injustice, they should exhibit their petitions in the street'. In a short scene the Duke, now again ducally attired, gives last-minute orders and messages to the Friar.

Act V: The Duke is met by Angelo, Escalus and others, and at once Isabella emerges from the crowd asking for justice, and accusing Angelo of being a hypocrite, adulterer and murderer. The Duke, pretending not to believe her, orders her arrest and imprisonment. Mariana then appears, veiled, supporting Isabella's charge of fornication against Angelo and exposing him, as she unveils, as her husband; she reveals that she had taken Isabella's place in his bed that night, but is not believed. Suspicions have been raised about the 'Friar' (the disguised Duke) and Lucio takes the opportunity of slandering him – and of making comic and sardonic comments throughout the scene, to the Duke's annoyance. Angelo admits that there had been 'some speech of marriage' with Mariana five years before. The Duke orders the 'Friar' to be sent for, and leaves the stage, but quickly returns again in Friar's habit, with the Provost and Isabella. Denounced by Escalus, Lucio and Angelo, he says he is not subject to the Duke, and is un-hooded by Lucio and revealed as the Duke indeed. Angelo at once confesses, realising that 'your Grace, like power divine,/Hath looked upon my passes' and begs for 'immediate sentence . . . and sequent death'. But the Duke orders him to be married to Mariana immediately and then brought back, when he is sentenced to death. Mariana begs for him to be spared, and persuades Isabella to support her in this appeal, which the Duke rejects. There is further disentanglement to be done. Barnardine and another prisoner, blindfolded, are brought in. The Duke acquits Barnardine, Claudio is unblindfolded, pardoned and restored to Juliet, Angelo is reprieved and bidden to love his wife, the Duke asks for Isabella's hand in marriage, and only Lucio the gossip and slanderer is punished – a comic piece of poetic justice – by being forced to marry the whore he had got with child.

SOURCES   There are three traditional plot elements: the stories of the corrupt magistrate (or the monstrous ransom), the ruler in disguise, and the bed-substitution trick. The first is also to be found in Cinthio's□ (1504–73) *Hecatommithi* (1565), the fifth *novella* of the eighth day, of which George Whetstone (?1544–?1587) made a two-part play, *Promos and Cassandra* (1578), but also told in prose in his *Heptameron of Civil Discourses* (1582). Shakespeare took the broad outlines but made some changes, and complicated the plot by adding the other plot elements of the ruler in disguise (from no one particular source), and the bed-substitution, a variant of which he had used in *All's Well That Ends Well* and which probably came from Boccaccio.□

TEXT   The play appears only in the First Folio□ (1623). It is a sometimes corrupt text and may have descended from Shakespeare's own 'foul papers'.□

Memorial reconstruction. It is believed that some of the 'bad' quartos□ were put together by an actor or actors reconstructing a text from what they could remember of a play in which they had acted, either for illegal publication or for illegal use.

Merchant of Venice, The. A middle comedy, probably of late 1596.

Act I: The Venetian merchant Antonio, somewhat sad though he says he knows not why, is asked by his close friend (and debtor) Bassanio for more money in order to go to Belmont to woo the beautiful heiress Portia. Although Antonio is very willing, all his capital is tied up in his business enterprises at sea, but he is prepared to borrow on behalf of his friend. In Belmont, Portia with her sprightly waiting-woman and friend Nerissa bewails the terms of her late father's will, by which she must marry whichever suitor chooses the correct one of three caskets, and discusses, dismissively, six suitors of different nationalities who have already come to attempt the choice. Back in Venice, Bassanio asks the Jew Shylock for a loan of three thousand ducats, Antonio standing surety. This is agreed, after some discussion which shows that there has long been hostility between the two. Shylock proposes to take no interest but imposes, as he says 'in a merry sport', a penalty clause that if the money is not repaid within the three months Antonio shall forfeit a pound of his flesh. Bassanio is unhappy at this clause, but Antonio is confident his ships will have returned and the money will be available in time.

Act II: The Prince of Morocco, one of several new suitors, meets

Portia and is told the penalty of a mistaken choice of casket – never to marry. Shylock's servant, Launcelot Gobbo, who is planning to leave his service, unexpectedly meets his old near-blind father, and at first jokingly pretends to be someone else. He wants to work for Bassanio, and is taken into his service. When Launcelot says farewell to Shylock's daughter Jessica, she asks him to give a letter to Lorenzo, her lover and a guest of Bassanio. The letter contains Jessica's plan for Lorenzo to help her escape from her father's house, taking gold and jewels and disguised as a page. We see this escape, while Shylock is reluctantly a guest at Bassanio's, and then the action shifts to Belmont for the Prince of Morocco's unsuccessful attempt; he chooses the golden casket. Before the next suitor, the Prince of Arragon, comes and chooses – wrongly – the silver casket, we return briefly to Venice and learn of Bassanio's embarkation for Belmont, of Shylock's discovery of his double loss – daughter and ducats – of rumour of a lost merchant vessel and of Antonio's sadness at Bassanio's departure.

Act III: In Venice there is news that the wrecked ship was indeed one of Antonio's, and later, after Shylock, distractedly hoping for news of his daughter and his ducats, has exulted at the thought of Antonio's misfortune, the Jew makes his famous and moving speech 'Hath not a Jew eyes? . . . If you prick us do we not bleed? If you tickle us do we not laugh?' His fellow-Jew, Tubal, enters, having failed to trace the missing Jessica but with the news that Antonio has suffered another loss at sea. In Belmont, Bassanio makes the correct guess, choosing the leaden casket; he is not to be like 'the world . . . deceiv'd with ornament', to the relief and joy of both himself and his beloved, Portia, who immediately in a movingly generous speech commits herself humbly to him ('You see me Lord Bassanio where I stand'). His friend Gratiano then steps forward with Nerissa: 'You saw the mistress, I beheld the maid:/You lov'd, I lov'd. . .' The other lovers, Lorenzo and Shylock's daughter Jessica enter with Salerio, who brings bad news from Venice: Antonio is ruined, all his argosies lost, and Shylock is greedy for his revenge. Portia at once offers money and tells Bassanio that they will marry immediately and then he must go straight to Venice with her gold and save his friend. In Venice, Antonio is arrested, Shylock implacable. In Belmont, Portia leaves Lorenzo and Jessica to look after her house and estate while she and Nerissa, she says, will go to a nearby monastery until their husbands return. In fact, as she tells Nerissa, they are going to go in male disguise to Venice and 'see our husbands/Before they think of us'. Portia also sends a servant with a mysterious message to a kinsman, the lawyer Dr Bellario, 'And look what notes and garments he doth give thee'.

Act IV: In Venice Antonio and Shylock appear in court before the Duke, the Jew claiming his pound of flesh and refusing the offer from Bassanio of twice the amount of his debt. Portia, in disguise as 'Balthazar', a doctor of laws, comes with a letter of recommendation from Dr Bellario; 'he' upholds Shylock's legal right but urges him to show mercy and take the money without endangering Antonio's life. Shylock wants revenge against the Christians and demands his right, a pound of Antonio's flesh, but Portia frustrates him by pointing out that it must be an exact pound and no blood must be lost, or Shylock's life and property will be forfeited. When Shylock realises he is beaten by this impossible demand, he offers to settle for three thousand ducats, but Portia points out that anyone directly or indirectly seeking the life of a Venetian must surrender half his property to the intended victim and half to the state. Antonio asks that his half-share shall be given to Lorenzo, and that Shylock be required to become a Christian, and the Duke remits the state's half-share. The trial over, Antonio and Bassanio thank 'Balthazar' for his skill and success, wishing to give him the three thousand ducats. But all 'Balthazar' will take is Bassanio's ring given him by Portia. Bassanio reluctantly parts with it, persuaded by Antonio; and we learn that the lawyer's clerk (Nerissa) is also going to get from Gratiano, if she can, the ring that she had given him.

Act V: In the moonlit garden of Belmont the lovers Lorenzo and Jessica think of the famous lovers of classical times ('In such a night as this'); are interrupted by news of Portia's return from Venice and then of Bassanio's imminent arrival; and resume their lyrical love-talk: 'How sweet the moonlight sleeps upon this bank!' When Portia comes, and is joined by Bassanio and Gratiano and welcomes Antonio, there is a sudden disturbance of the mood of serene happiness when Gratiano is charged by Nerissa with having given her ring to the lawyer's clerk in Venice, and then when Bassanio is similarly accused by Portia. After much expostulation and explanation by the men, each lady pretends to forgive and each gives a ring, asking pardon at the same time for having slept with the 'lawyer' and the 'lawyer's clerk'. Bassanio and Gratiano recognise the rings as being the very same ones and Portia then reveals the whole story of their disguising. Lorenzo and Jessica are told of their inheritance, and Antonio hears from Portia that three of his argosies 'Are richly come to harbour suddenly'.

SOURCES The story of a bond for human flesh is ancient. Shakespeare probably got it from a version in a fourteenth-century Italian collection by Ser Giovanni Fiorentino, *Il Pecorone*, the first tale of the fourth day, printed in 1558, which has a Venetian merchant, a bond with a Jew for a pound of flesh, a 'Lady of

Belmonte', the lady coming disguised and winning the court case, and the business of the rings. The wooing test is different, and Shakespeare probably took it from an English translation (1577 and 1595) by Richard Robinson of stories from *Gesta Romanorum*, a vast compilation of medieval Latin tales compiled in the fourteenth century and translated into several European languages (the tale was also translated by Boccaccio,□ in the *Decameron*, 1353, and by Gower,□ in *Confessio Amantis*, 1390). Marlowe's□ *Jew of Malta* was also a cruel and vindictive wealthy Jew with one daughter, but without any of Shylock's undeniable human appeal. The Queen's personal physician, the Portuguese Jew Roderigo Lopez, was suspected of a plot on her life and executed in 1594, which increased anti-Semitic prejudice against the small number of Jews□ living in London.

TEXT The First Quarto□ (1600), probably printed from Shakespeare's 'foul papers'.□ Second Quarto 1619. The First Folio□ (1623) text was set up from Q1.

Mermaid Tavern. This was situated in Bread Street, Cheapside, near St Paul's cathedral. At one time, on the first Friday of the month according to Thomas Coryat, author of *Crudities* (1611), gentlemen, members of the Inns of Court,□ actors and playwrights including Ben Jonson,□ Francis Beaumont (who wrote a verse letter about meetings there to Jonson) and Shakespeare forgathered at the Mermaid. The pleasing legend may well be true, for the landlord was William Johnson who later acted as one of Shakespeare's trustees, lending him money for the purchase of the Blackfriars Gatehouse in 1613, a property he left to his daughter on his death.

Merry Wives of Windsor, The. An English comedy of late 1596 or early 1597. It was probably written for the feast of the Order of the Garter in 1597 (St George's Day, 23 April), and possibly between *Henry IV, Part 1* and the completing of *Henry IV, Part 2*.

Act I: Falstaff is staying at Windsor at the Garter Inn. Shallow, the Gloucestershire justice of the peace (magistrate), comes, accusing him and his associates Bardolph, Pistol and Nym of wronging him. Hugh Evans, the Welsh parson, the Host of the Garter Inn, and George Page, a substantial citizen of Windsor, are to be referees in the dispute. Shallow, abetted by Sir Hugh Evans, persuades the former's foolish cousin Slender to woo Page's daughter Anne, who has other suitors in Dr Caius (pronounced 'Keys'), a ridiculous French doctor, and a young gentleman named Fenton. Falstaff, now short of money, disposes of Bardolph to be a tapster at the inn, and discharges Pistol and Nym when they refuse to carry love-letters from him to Mrs Page and her friend Mrs Ford, both of whom he hopes to seduce and to fleece; in revenge they decide to tell the two husbands of Falstaff's plans. Simple, Slender's servant sent by Sir Hugh to Mrs Quickly, Dr Caius's housekeeper and a friend of Anne Page, to ask her to forward Slender's suit to Anne, is found by Caius hiding in a cupboard, and is sent by the excitable doctor to carry a challenge to the parson.

Act II: Mrs Page and Mrs Ford both receive Falstaff's identical love-letters and decide to make a fool of him by each pretending to encourage him. Page and Ford are told by Pistol and Nym of Falstaff's intention, and the Host comes to call them to watch the duel between parson and doctor. Ford is less trusting of his wife than Page, and decides to test her by visiting Falstaff, assuming the name of Brooke, and offering him money if he will 'lay an amiable siege to the honesty of this Ford's wife', which Falstaff gleefully agrees to. So Ford is bitterly confirmed in his suspicions, and resolves to go at eleven, at which time Mrs Ford had mischievously arranged a meeting. Parson Evans does not appear for the duel and the Host says he will lead the doctor to find him.

Act III: When the Host brings doctor and parson together, he reveals that he has purposely misled them, and calls on them to 'lay their swords to pawn', and to drink together as 'lads of peace'. Mrs Ford and Mrs Page plan the discomfiture of Falstaff; he enters and has hardly begun his courtship when Ford is reported to be returning, whereupon Falstaff hastily secretes himself in a laundry-basket and is carried off – and is dumped in a ditch by the Thames. While Ford and his companions the parson and the doctor search the house, the two wives plan to send Mrs Quickly to Falstaff to apologise for the mistake and to invite him to try again. Fenton tells Anne that he is making no headway with her parents, who distrust him as a spendthrift and an old acquaintance of Prince Hal ('My riots past, my wild societies'). (The timorous awkward Slender is favoured as a suitor by Page, and Dr Caius by Mrs Page.) Ford, as Brooke, hears from Falstaff of his ducking, and that the knight is to go to Mrs Ford again that morning.

Act IV: Falstaff again comes to Mrs Ford, and is again interrupted by word of Ford's imminent return. This time, in order to escape, he dresses in the gown of the maid's aunt, the fat woman of Brainford, and is beaten as he goes, for Ford has forbidden her the house. Ford then asks forgiveness of his wife for his groundless suspicions. Another plot to fool Falstaff is devised. He is to go to an old oak in Windsor Forest at midnight, known as Herne's oak, where the wives will meet him. There he will be suddenly assailed by a show of fairies, led by Anne Page; they will 'encircle him about, / And fairy-like to pinch the unclean knight'. But other plans are afoot for this winter midnight: Page secretly decides to arrange for Slender to steal

Anne away and marry her, while Mrs Page plans similarly on behalf of Dr Caius. But Anne has told Fenton of both her father's and her mother's instructions, and they have resolved to defeat both plans and to elope; Fenton persuades the Host to help them by arranging for the vicar to wait for them after midnight at the church in order to marry them.

Act V: The preparations for the duping of Falstaff go forward. He presents himself disguised as Herne the Hunter and with a pair of horns tied to his head. Mrs Ford comes to him, but is again joined by Mrs Page; and then the others gather, Evans disguised as a satyr, Pistol as Hobgoblin (Puck), Mistress Quickly as the Fairy Queen and Anne Page and children as fairies. The fairy rout frighten and pinch Falstaff who has lain flat on the ground at their approach, and burn him lightly with their tapers. While this is going on, Slender leads off a fairy in white, and Dr Caius one in green, each having been told by one of Anne Page's parents that she will be so dressed. Fenton comes and leads Anne away. 'Brooke' reveals himself as Ford and the exposure is complete, Falstaff quickly acknowledging 'that I am made an ass'. Slender and Caius both return, each having discovered that his 'fairy' Anne was only 'a great lubberly boy', but in the end all are reconciled except Dr Caius.

SOURCE No specific source, but many of the situations and incidents have English or Continental analogues and there is some kinship with *commedia dell'arte*◻ conventions, and with obscure contemporary events (the horse-stealing and the German duke). Traditionally, the play was written at Queen Elizabeth's◻ request, wanting to see Falstaff in love after she had enjoyed *Henry IV*.

TEXT The First Folio◻ (1623); probably from a transcript of the prompt-book.◻

Metamorphoses. A work by Ovid (43BC–AD18), the Latin poet probably best known to Shakespeare and most loved. The *Metamorphoses* is in fifteen books and is a collection of the chief myths and legends of Greece and Rome. Its name emphasises a particular kind of tale which concerns the change or bodily trans-formation of gods, nymphs and humans, sometimes in pursuit of amatory adventure – as in the tales of Jupiter's transformations into swan, bull or cloud – or in escape from it – as in Daphne's metamorphosis into a tree to escape from Apollo; sometimes the change is because of despair or grief. Shakespeare's narrative poem *Venus and Adonis* derives from Ovid, and there are innumerable references, allusions and smaller borrowings in the plays. He would have read and studied Ovid at school (see Education,◻

Shakespeare's) but he also makes use of the translation by Arthur Golding.

Ovid also wrote *Heroides*, a series of poetic love-letters, *Tristia*, a series of poems, often of complaint, occasioned by his exile at Tomi on the Black Sea, *Ars Amatoria*, a playful treatise on the art of love, and many other poems.

Midsummer Night's Dream, A. A high comedy. The play, which clearly celebrates marriage, was possibly written in the winter of 1595–6 to mark a great marriage, perhaps that of a god-daughter of the Queen, Elizabeth Carey, who was the grand-daughter of the Lord Chamberlain, Lord Hunsdon, patron of Shakespeare's company. It is a short play (only three are shorter), and this supports the view that it was written for a private stately occasion.

Act I: In Athens the Duke, Theseus, and Hippolyta, Queen of the Amazons, whose 'nuptial hour / Draws on apace', impatiently await the new moon, due in four days' time, when their marriage will take place. To their court comes Egeus, 'full of vexation' 'with complaint against [his] child' Hermia who refuses to marry Demetrius because she is in love with Lysander. Theseus repeats the law that if she refuses to marry her father's choice she must either be put to death or 'abjure / For ever the society of men' by becoming a nun. Lysander pleads his case, declaring that he loves Hermia and is loved by her, and that Demetrius in fact had paid court to another girl, Helena, who still dotes on him. Lysander and Hermia, left alone on the stage, plan to meet in the wood outside Athens the following night and to elope. Demetrius's old love, Helena, still in love with him, enters, and they tell her of their plan, which she secretly resolves to reveal to Demetrius, to gain favour with him, and hoping that he will then pursue Hermia and come to the wood.

Meanwhile a group of Athenian craftsmen (with very English and comical names) meet under Quince the carpenter's direction to receive their parts for a little play, the 'most lamentable comedy, and most cruel death of Pyramus and Thisbe' to be presented at the Duke's wedding-feast. The dominating spirit is Bottom the weaver, who boisterously demands to play every part in turn as Quince lists and describes them, but is allotted that of the 'tragic' hero Pyramus.

Act II: We now meet the fourth group in the play, the fairy element. The mischievous Puck prepares us for the entry of Oberon the fairy king and Titania the queen, quarrelling over a little Indian changeling whom Titania has adopted and whom Oberon wants as his page. Oberon then despatches Puck to find a flower, 'love-in-idleness', the juice of which has the power, when applied to the eyelids of a sleeping human, of making that person fall in love with the first living creature seen on waking. He intends to use it on

Titania, to make her love 'lion, bear, or wolf, or bull, meddling monkey or busy ape', so that he can demand the Indian boy in return for freeing her from the charm. He then witnesses the anguished loving pursuit of Demetrius by Helena, his rejected love, and, sympathetic now, tells Puck to squeeze some of the juice in 'the disdainful youth's eyes' to make him love Helena, while he himself will do the same to Titania. This he does. The lovers Lysander and Hermia have eloped as planned and, weary, lie down separately to rest. Puck mistakenly applies the magic juice to Lysander's eyes, instead of those of Demetrius, who now re-enters, still pursued by Helena, and escapes from her. While she is lamenting, Lysander wakes, and under the influence of the charm instantly falls in love with her. Helena thinks he is making fun of her and departs, now lovingly pursued by Lysander, so that Hermia wakes up to find herself alone.

Act III: During a rehearsal of the play, Bottom goes off 'This green plot', their stage in the wood, and when he returns, Puck has slipped a donkey's head on him (of which he is unconscious). His companions flee in amazed terror, and, singing to keep up his spirits, he unknowingly wakes the sleeping Titania, who is immediately enamoured of him. Puck reports to Oberon ('My mistress with a monster is in love'), and they both draw aside when Hermia and Demetrius enter; she still rebuffs him, and Puck knows and Oberon realises that Puck has used the magic juice on the wrong Athenian lover. Demetrius having been left alone and lain down to sleep, Oberon squeezes juice on his eyelids and despatches Puck to find Helena and bring her here. Soon Helena comes, with Lysander who is now declaring his love to her, to her chagrin (because she loves Demetrius, and thinks Lysander is mocking her); their argument wakes Demetrius, whom the charm now makes enamoured of Helena – 'goddess, nymph, perfect, divine' – and this adoration she also thinks is mockery. Hermia now appears, to find Lysander, her lover, has become cold and distant. Helena is movingly distracted by the changes in all three; quarrelling breaks out and the two men, now rivals for Helena, go off to fight it out. Oberon, overhearing, instructs Puck to bring a fog and to lead both young men separately astray so that they shall not fight. When, wearied, they lie down to sleep unaware of each other's proximity, Puck squeezes an antidote to the charm on to Lysander's eyes. Both the girls, separately and unaware of each other's presence or of the sleeping young men, having wandered to the same place in the wood, also lie down to sleep.

Act IV: We see Bottom with the ass's head and Titania innocently and happily together, she completely enamoured, he enjoying all the attentions he is receiving. Oberon finds them asleep and tells Puck of meeting Titania shortly before and finding her mild and gentle, when she had immediately surrendered the changeling boy. So the fairy king and queen are reconciled, when the charm is undone, and the ass's head removed from the sleeping Bottom. He and the four lovers are still all sleeping when Theseus and Hippolyta find them, wake them, and discover that all has come right – Demetrius with Helena, Lysander with Hermia in concord. Bottom, remembering his encounter with Titania as a dream, rejoins his fellow 'handicraft men', to their relief; they had feared that without Bottom they would lose their chance of performing their play before the court.

Act V: After the marriages – for Theseus arranged for the two other pairs of lovers (Demetrius and Helena, and Lysander and Hermia) to be married when he married Hippolyta – all assemble for the entertainment, the 'tedious brief scene . . . very tragical mirth', ludicrously presented by Quince and his fellows. Although the grandees often interrupt it, jokingly commenting on its absurdities, at the end Theseus gracefully thanks the players – 'very notably discharged', and, midnight having come, leads all off to bed. The humans having departed, Puck, Oberon and Titania and the fairies take over the stage, and sing and dance. They then, at Oberon's bidding, disperse to bless 'each several chamber . . . / Through this palace with sweet peace', and the play ends with Puck, alone, asking the audience, if anything has offended them, to 'Think but this, . . . / That you have but slumber'd here / While these visions did appear.'

SOURCES   No single source; it has one of the few plots invented by Shakespeare. Something is owed to Chaucer's□ 'The Knight's Tale' (the marriage of Theseus and Hippolyta) and to his *Legend of Good Women* (Pyramus and Thisbe); something to the life of Theseus in North's□ translation (1579) of Plutarch's□ *Lives*; something to romance and to Italian comedy for the love-mistakes and confusions; something to Chaucer's 'Merchant's Tale' and to the romance *Huon of Bordeaux* (translated by Lord Berners in 1534) for the fairy king and queen; and something to Ovid's *Metamorphoses*,□ and Golding's□ translation (1567) of it.

TEXT   The First Quarto□ (1600), which seems to have been printed from Shakespeare's 'foul papers'□ (his autograph draft before the making of a 'fair copy'). The Second Quarto (1619, although falsely dated 1600) is based on it and probably on a prompt-book,□ and the First Folio□ (1623) derives from it.

Miracle plays. The name that used to be given to the large body of medieval drama that survives, now more generally known as the mystery cycles.□ These were plays portraying the lives and miracles of saints, of which some survive, and the name was given fairly indiscriminately to medieval religious plays in general.

Montaigne, Michel de (1533–92). A French landowner from near Bordeaux who retired to his chateau to study and write. His three volumes of *Essais* (which gave virtually a new *genre* and its name to English literature) of 1580 and 1588, humane, tolerant, sceptical and questioning, were translated into English by Florio□ and published in 1603. Shakespeare shows that he knew the work and Florio's□ translation.

Moors. Most Elizabethans, even in London, were even less likely to have seen a Moor than a Jew.□ Yet in *Titus Andronicus* Shakespeare presents a savage bloodthirsty Moor, Aaron, and in *Othello* has Iago using hatred, fear and contempt of black Moors to rouse feeling against Othello. There is a villainous Moor in George Peele's (1558–96) *The Battle of Alcazar* (about 1589) who can call up fiends from Hell. Marlowe's□ vile Ithamore in *The Jew of Malta* is in fact a Turk, but is the same type as Aaron and Muly Hamet in Peele's play, and all are of course Muhammadans. Some of the apparent latent feeling against Moors, which this implies, may have been colour fear or hatred, but principally it had a religious basis because they were pagan and anti-Christian. There seems to have been instinctive feeling about dark colour (and even in the dark races there is favour for the lighter, antipathy or contempt for the darker in colour). Medieval art provides evidence, for example from wall-paintings in churches, which Shakespeare could have seen, that demons, devils, the wicked consigned to Hell, and the persecutors, floggers and crucifiers of Christ, were often presented as dark or black. This no doubt contributed to the colour prejudice which the writers of these plays tacitly acknowledged. In Shakespeare's source for *Othello*, the Moor, named Christoforo Moro, is savage and brutal in his revenge, helping the Iago-figure to beat Disdemona, as she is named, to death with a stocking filled with sand. As with his portrayal of Shylock as a figure of considerable dignity and some pathos in *The Merchant of Venice*, Shakespeare most remarkably elevates his Moorish hero in *Othello*, a natural focus for audience animosity, into virtuous and dignified splendour and makes him a noble champion of the great Christian state and city of Venice.

Morality plays. Instructively moral plays dating apparently from the early fifteenth-century. The two most famous are *The Castle of Perseverance* (pronounced persévérance, meaning steadfastness, dutifulness) of about 1425, and *Everyman* of about 1500. Both are about the course of man's life and the continual fight for his soul between the virtues and the vices. It is typical of the *genre* that the characters are abstract virtues, vices and human traits, abstractions called by abstract names, rather than flesh-and-blood human characters. John Skelton's *Magnificence* (*c*.1515), although much longer, and the Scottish *A Satire of the Three Estates* (*c*.1540) by David Lindsay, which is immensely longer, although often called interludes□ (perhaps because they came late, after the morality plays had more or less been superseded by interludes), are built on the same subject and material, and although late, and satirical in a way that the original moralities are not, probably ought to be called morality plays.

Much Ado About Nothing. A high comedy, verging on 'problem comedy' (see Problem plays□) probably dating from middle or late 1598.

Act I: The Governor of Messina, Leonato, awaits the arrival of Don Pedro, Prince of Arragon, who has just defeated his rebellious brother, the bastard Don John, but reconciled himself to him. With them come Claudio and his friend Benedick who had both distinguished themselves in the fighting. Leonato's niece Beatrice and Benedick have long had a happy relationship, a 'merry war' of wit, but both are determined not to marry; 'they never meet but there's a skirmish of wit between them'. Claudio is in love with Leonato's niece, Beatrice's cousin Hero, and he asks Don Pedro to help him advance his suit by telling her father of it. The Prince proposes that he should go disguised as Claudio to the revelling called to celebrate the end of hostilities and woo her in his name. Before the banquet, Leonato is told by his brother Antonio that he has heard Don Pedro telling Claudio of his love for Hero and of his intention to reveal it to her that night. A follower of the bastard Don John, Borachio, has also overheard the conversation between Don Pedro and Claudio, and reports it to Don John. The latter, who hates Claudio ('that young start-up' who 'hath all the glory of my overthrow' in the recent rebellion), sees here a chance of doing him harm.

Act II: At the ball after the feast, when all the men are masked, Beatrice jokingly runs down Benedick – 'the Prince's jester, a very dull fool' – as they dance together. He later complains ruefully of her: 'She speaks poniards, and every word stabs', and asks for service at the world's end or in the Antipodes to get away from her. Don John maliciously informs Claudio that Don Pedro is wooing Hero for himself, which Claudio briefly believes. Soon, however, Don Pedro tells that he wooed her for Claudio, as arranged, and has got her father's approval, and the wedding is to be in a week's time. In the meantime, Don Pedro says he will set about the Herculean labour of bringing Beatrice and Benedick 'into a mountain of affection th'one with th'other'. Meanwhile Don John has plotted with his follower Borachio to forestall the marriage of Claudio and Hero: Borachio will arrange for his friend Margaret, Hero's waiting-woman, to appear at Hero's window the following night; Borachio will pay court to her as Hero, who will thus be seen to be unfaithful to Claudio. Borachio will also arrange for the real Hero to be absent, and Don John is to tell Don Pedro and Claudio that Hero really loves Borachio. A little plot to bring Beatrice and Benedick together is set on foot, as Don Pedro, Leonato and Claudio discuss in the orchard Beatrice's supposed secret love for Benedick, knowing that Benedick is concealed nearby in an arbour and will hear their talk.

Act III: Now there is another little plot in the orchard, arranged by Hero, who talks to her other gentlewoman, Ursula, of Benedick's secret love for Beatrice, which the latter, in the arbour, cannot avoid overhearing. Don Pedro, Leonato, and Claudio joke with Benedick about his being in love, and then Don John tells Claudio and Don Pedro that Hero is immoral, and if they will go the following night they will 'see her chamber-window entered, even the night before her wedding day'. On that night we meet the comic constables of the watch, whose word-muddling chief is Dogberry, going on duty. Two of them overhear Don John's two supporters Borachio and Conrade talking of the success of the plot, for Don Pedro and Claudio have witnessed Borachio's wooing of Margaret and thought it was Hero they had seen, welcoming a man to her bedchamber. The watch arrest Borachio and Conrade, and (after a short scene in which Hero dresses for her wedding while Beatrice talks about her love-sickness), Dogberry reports the arrest to Leonato. But Leonato is so busy with preparations for his daughter Hero's wedding that he tells them to examine the prisoners themselves.

Act IV: At the marriage ceremony Claudio bitterly denounces and rejects Hero: 'She knows the heat of a luxurious bed: / Her blush is guiltiness, not modesty.' Don Pedro and Don John report that they were witnesses to her offence, Hero swoons and Claudio and the two princes depart. Leonato in angry grief denounces his daughter, but Beatrice and Benedick are not convinced of her guilt and the Friar, sure of her innocence, proposes that Hero should 'awhile be secretly kept in' and reported to have died. Since 'what we have we prize not . . . but being lack'd and lost / . . . we find / The virtue that possession would not show us', he thinks Claudio will realise his grievous mistake and her 'wounded reputation' be restored. This plan is agreed, and Beatrice and Benedick are left alone in the church, she weeping for her cousin's humiliation, he asking what he can do to right the wrong. Suddenly he tells her he loves her, and she replies that she was about to declare her love for him. When he says

'Come, bid me do anything for thee' she replies 'Kill Claudio', and, after expressing reluctance, he decides he will challenge his friend. There is a sudden switch of mood as the scene changes to the ridiculous comedy of the examination of Borachio and Conrade by Dogberry, in the course of which the sexton reports the death of Hero and the sudden departure of Don John.

Act V: Leonato, simulating deep grief for Hero (though he knows she is not dead), angrily challenges Claudio to a duel for bringing about her death, and so does his old brother Antonio, who was not present at the marriage ceremony and is not privy to the plot. Benedick enters, looking for Claudio to challenge him, although Claudio and Don Pedro think at first that he is, as customarily, joking; he delivers the challenge, and departs, saying 'You have among you killed a sweet and innocent lady.' Then Dogberry and the watch enter with Borachio and Conrade whose plot is exposed and admitted readily by a repentant Borachio, who also asserts Margaret's innocence in the matter. A remorseful Claudio and a regretful Don Pedro ask forgiveness for their lack of trust in Hero, and Leonato accedes, telling Claudio then that he may marry, instead of the 'dead' Hero, his brother Antonio's daughter the following day. Beatrice and Benedick have their only real love scene, and that a short one, interrupted by news that all the villainy has been exposed and Don John 'the author of all, fled and gone'. But Claudio and Don Pedro do not yet know that Hero is in fact alive, and they are shown paying sad tribute at Leonato's family tomb. The following morning, Leonato stage-manages the dénouement, in which the ladies withdraw into another chamber and will appear masked after Don Pedro and Claudio have arrived. But before that Benedick asks Leonato if another marriage may be celebrated as well, his to Beatrice, which the Governor readily agrees to. When the ladies come, as the ceremony is about to begin, Hero takes off her mask, and to the amazed Don Pedro and Claudio, Leonato remarks 'She died my lord but whiles her slander liv'd.' Briefly Beatrice and Benedick battle in words again, pretending indifference to each other, until they stop their mouths with a kiss. The unions are to be delayed for a dance, which is about to start when word comes that Don John has been captured in flight, and the last words are Benedick's: 'think not on him till tomorrow; I'll devise thee / Brave punishments for him. Strike up, pipers!'

SOURCES The main story, of a lover deceived into thinking his beloved false, is ancient and common. While European literature can show a number of versions in the hundred years or so before Shakespeare wrote this play, notably Ariosto in his romantic epic *Orlando Furioso*, and Spenser□ in *The Faerie Queene*, both in fairly short narratives, it seems that the chief source was Matteo Bandello,□ the twenty-second tale in *La Prima Parte de le Novelle* (1554), a large collection of prose tales. This has the setting in Messina, some of the names, a similar courtship by a nobleman, the lover's rejection, the lady's fainting, her alleged death, and other elements. Bandello was translated into French by François de Belleforest□ (*Histoires Tragiques*, 1559–82), but Shakespeare is closer to the Italian than the French.

TEXT   The First Quarto□ (1600), from Shakespeare's 'foul papers'.□ The First Folio□ (1623) text was printed from this.

Music. Tudor and Elizabethan times formed one of England's few undeniably great musical eras. There are many references to music in Shakespeare and music imagery is common. The harmony of performed music was a natural symbol for order and degree□ in the world, and for the harmony, intended by God for his creation, which that implied. In addition, Shakespeare used music frequently, sometimes simply for entertainment and variety (for example, the hunting songs in *As You Like It*, drinking songs and songs by pages, fools or servants) but also to establish or change the atmosphere or emotion of a scene. He knew well the emotional power of music, whether to suggest romantic love in the Jessica-Lorenzo scene by moonlight in *The Merchant of Venice*, or drunken revelry as with Sir Toby Belch and his associates in *Twelfth Night* or the party on Pompey's galley in *Antony and Cleopatra*; to suggest contact with the gods or the supernatural world, as when Paulina prepares for Leontes to re-discover his wronged wife in *The Winter's Tale*, or Helena calls for divine help to heal the king in *All's Well That Ends Well*; or to heighten the pathos of madness (Ophelia) or the sad resignation and sense of impending death as Desdemona prepares to go to bed on what is to be her last night on earth; or to produce a sense of healing and calm after Lear's madness as he returns to consciousness and re-discovers his wronged daughter Cordelia.

Mystery cycles. (See also Miracle plays.□) The name derives from the late Latin *ministerium*, meaning trade, craft or profession, and records the fact that the plays were presented by members of the various trade 'guilds' – separate associations of members of parti-cular crafts or occupations. The mystery drama had grown from the increasingly acted liturgy of the early medieval church (not only in Britain) and from street processions and celebrations on holy days, originally, probably, with church encouragement and priestly help. They were almost certainly written by clerics, in verse which, in most cases – especially at York and Wakefield – is elaborately stanzaic and often full of variety. The individual plays were quite short, each one lasting twenty to thirty minutes in performance at the most, but the complete cycle would have taken up the whole of a very long day. The special day for performances of the cycle was commonly Corpus Christi (Body of Christ) Day, the Thursday after Trinity Sunday. The date can vary between 23 May and 24 June now, but was twelve days or so earlier in the Middle Ages (which used the Julian Calendar, replaced in Britain by the Gregorian in 1752). This is normally a reliably warm and sunny period in the English summer. (Chester, after 1447, seems to have changed to the Monday, Tuesday and Wednesday of Whit week, a week or so earlier.) The plays presented significant scenes from Biblical story, from the Creation of the World to the Resurrection of Christ and the Last Judgement. The most complete surviving cycle, York, has forty-eight plays; Wakefield (the Towneley plays) thirty-two; Chester twenty-four; and there is a collection of forty-two, once called the *Ludus Coventriae* (of Coventry) but now called the 'N-town' cycle because no one knows which town – Lincoln, Norwich and King's Lynn have all been claimed.

The cycles were performed in the open air on 'pageants' or 'stages'. These were carts large enough to contain a dozen or more actors and some simple scenery, and were probably moved round the town in sequence to a limited series of places (five or six only at Chester, for example), where the cart stopped and the individual play was presented. In some places, possibly at York, a number of pageant carts may have gathered in a rough circle with the audience standing in the middle and turning as the action moved from scene to scene, cart to cart; there is evidence that this happened also at 'N-town', Louth and Aberdeen. There are records of performances of mystery plays in nearly a hundred places between 1300 and 1600. At York they lasted until 1569, at Chester until 1575, but in the end the church authorities suppressed them, as they did in other Protestant countries. No doubt they would have died out anyway, and their death surely contributed directly and indirectly to the rise of the secular drama in England.

The nearest place to Stratford where a mystery cycle is known was Coventry, about eighteen miles away, where they are believed to have been last performed in 1580. It would be surprising if Shakespeare did not see the plays. He makes a number of incidental references to them. The presentation of the whole Christian cycle of God's loving creation of the world and of man, man's disobedience and sin, the aftermath of tragic dispute, anger and evil in the world, and the promise of ultimate forgiveness and reconciliation because of Christ's sacrifice, presented with force and vividness and a remarkable combination of poetry and rough realism, humour and gravity, must have had some impact on him. Furthermore, the effect of the widespread and long-continuing presentation of the plays to large popular audiences upon the later development of the drama in Elizabethan times was great.

N

North, Sir Thomas (?1535–1601). North translated the work of the Greek historian Plutarch,□ from the French version by Jacques Amyot, as *The Lives of the Noble Grecians and Romans* (1579). As great a source for Shakespeare as Holinshed□ was for English history, it gave much to all the Roman plays and also to *Timon of Athens*. That Shakespeare knew the translation well is shown by the many passages of North's excellent English prose which he put into blank verse often with little change, especially in *Julius Caesar* and *Antony and Cleopatra*.

O

Othello. A tragedy dating probably from 1604.

Act I: Night in Venice; the hearty, honest-seeming but in fact wicked ensign Iago has been pretending to help – for money – a young gentleman, Roderigo, in his hopeless endeavour to win the hand of Desdemona, before the play opens. Now he tells Roderigo that the Moorish general Othello, who serves the republic of Venice and in whose service he is, and whom he hates, has eloped with Desdemona. He bustles Roderigo along with him to her father's house and together they rouse the household. Iago tells her father Brabantio in foul animal terms of the elopement – 'an old black ram / Is tupping your white ewe'. Iago then hurries to Othello to tell him the alarm is up, and they are found by Cassio, Othello's newly-appointed lieutenant (whom Iago secretly hates, partly, he told Roderigo, because Cassio and not himself had received promotion). Cassio announces that the Duke of Venice requires Othello's presence immediately in connexion with the imminent despatch of forces under Othello's command to Cyprus. Before the Moor can go, Brabantio angrily appears with supporters and condemns Othello for 'enchanting' his daughter.

All adjourn to the Council Chamber where the Duke and Senators are making plans to deal with the imminent Turkish attack on Cyprus. This business is broken off as Brabantio accuses Othello to the Duke of stealing away his daughter (and 'by spells and medicines'). Gravely Othello speaks in his own defence, acknowledging his courtship and now his marriage; Brabantio had often invited him to his house and encouraged him to tell the story of his life and exotic travels and adventures, which had enthralled Desdemona. Desdemona has been sent for and now arrives; she confirms Othello's story and their mutual love, ('my heart's subdued / Even to the utmost pleasure of my lord') and asks for permission to accompany him on his mission to Cyprus. This is granted, despite the angry and anguished opposition of Brabantio, to whom the Duke says 'If virtue no delighted beauty lack, / Your son-in-law is far more fair than black.'

Iago reveals to Roderigo the base machinations of his mind, activated by hatred of Othello and Desdemona ('an erring barbarian, and a super-subtle Venetian') and of Cassio. He intends to go on fleecing Roderigo, promising him Desdemona and, left alone, plans the downfall of them all; he will 'abuse Othello's ear, / That [Cassio] is too familiar with his wife'.

Act II: The action moves to Cyprus, where the Governor, Montano, learns that severe storms have wrecked the Turkish fleet and scattered the Venetian ships. First Cassio's ship comes safely in, followed by that in which Desdemona, placed in Iago's care, had sailed. Othello's ship, which had left first, is the last to arrive. There is a scene of light flirtatious pleasantry between Desdemona, Iago and his wife Emilia and Cassio while they wait, strongly contrasted with the profoundly loving reunion of Desdemona and Othello. Iago now reveals his plans: enlisting Roderigo's help he implies that Desdemona – being already tired of Othello – is in love with Cassio and they will become lovers, so Roderigo is to help to discredit the lieutenant, which will help him to displant Cassio in Desdemona's affections. When Roderigo leaves him, Iago in a soliloquy adds another ingredient: he will 'put the Moor . . . into a jealousy so strong, / That judgement cannot cure'.

Celebrations of triumph at the dispersal of the Turkish fleet and of the marriage of the general, Othello, take place. Othello and Desdemona go early to bed on this their wedding night. Cassio is left responsible for the guard, but is persuaded to drink, against his wishes, for he has 'poor and unhappy brains for drinking', and quickly gets drunk. Roderigo, as arranged, picks a quarrel with the lieutenant, which develops into a brawl, involving also Montano. Othello comes, roused by the brawl, and demands to know what has happened. Iago, with every show of regret and reluctance, incriminates Cassio who is too ashamed to defend himself. He is dismissed from Othello's service. Iago, who is not at all suspected by Cassio, now reassures him that 'there are ways to recover the general again' – by approaching Desdemona and by means of their old friendship persuading her to intercede on his behalf with Othello. Left alone, Iago humorously asks who says he plays 'the villain,/ When this advice is free I give, and honest'; but he intends to make use of this development by insinuating to Othello that Desdemona only pleads for Cassio because she is lustfully involved with him.

Act III: Cassio, with the good services of Iago's wife Emilia, enlists Desdemona's help, and as he is leaving them Othello and Iago appear. The latter immediately says 'Ha, I like that not', and soon proceeds by a series of apparently casual questions – chiefly about how well Cassio had known Desdemona – and innocent comments to sow the seeds of suspicion (of Desdemona's moral integrity) in Othello's mind. Before long Othello is wretchedly disquieted, but when Iago warns him against 'jealousy . . . the green-ey'd monster', he stoutly declares that he won't harbour jealousy without testing it ('I'll see before I doubt, when I doubt, prove'). Yet when Iago immediately goes on to urge Othello 'Look to your wife, observe her well with Cassio', points out 'She did deceive her father, marrying you', and refers to Desdemona's choice of someone not 'of her own clime, complexion and degree' as perhaps a sign of 'a will most rank . . . thoughts unnatural', Othello is already deeply suspicious: 'O curse of marriage,/ That we can call these delicate creatures ours,/ And not their appetites!' In this bitter, anxious soliloquy he also declares that if she be proved false he will reject her utterly. Desdemona enters with Emilia at this point, thinks him not well, goes to bind his forehead which he has said pains him; but the handkerchief is too small and she inadvertently drops it. Emilia immediately picks it up, for Iago had apparently many times tried to persuade her to get hold of it; it was Othello's first gift to Desdemona. Iago comes in and, as Emilia is reluctant to give it to him, he snatches it, immediately deciding to use it to convince Othello of Desdemona's faithlessness by leaving it at Cassio's lodgings. Othello returns, already tormented but demanding proof, and Iago stokes the fires of his appalled doubt. Othello in this scene struggles to retain hold of his love and need for Desdemona, but again and again breaks into fierce denunciation. When Iago asks him about the handkerchief and says he has seen Cassio wipe his beard with it, Othello is convinced and dedicates himself to vengeance, abetted by Iago whom he now promotes to Lieutenant in Cassio's place.

When next Othello and Desdemona meet, he finds her moist hand a sign of 'fruitfulness, and liberal heart', says he has a cold and asks for the handkerchief (which she cannot produce); she presses on with her plea on Cassio's behalf, not realising that by doing so she is confirming his suspicion, and he storms out. Iago and Cassio enter and she tells them of his furious mood, which Emilia – rightly – reads as being caused by jealousy. In a short final scene Cassio meets his mistress Bianca who complains of his neglect, whereupon he gives her the handkerchief, which Iago had secretly left in his chamber.

Act IV: Iago continues to deceive Othello into deeper and fouler suspicions of Desdemona, and Othello falls to the ground in a sort of fit. Next, Iago has Othello conceal himself so as to observe but not overhear a ribald conversation between Cassio and Iago, which the Moor thinks is a slighting conversation about Desdemona; and then one between Cassio and Bianca, which confirms his suspicions because the handkerchief is returned by her. Othello's anguish is now at its height, for, his suspicions confirmed, he yet still loves and marvels at her, and his speeches move from 'O, the world has not a sweeter creature . . . O Iago, the pity of it Iago!' to savage cries like 'I will chop her into messes.' He tells Iago to get poison for him to give to Desdemona, but Iago tells him 'to strangle her in her bed, even the bed she hath contaminated', and Iago says he will also kill Cassio that night. When a Venetian, Lodovico, comes with Desdemona (his cousin) with messages from the Duke recalling Othello and naming Cassio to take his place, and Desdemona expresses pleasure, Othello strikes her and rushes distractedly off. Othello questions Emilia about Desdemona, but does not believe her avowal of her mistress's purity, and then in a terrible scene which leaves Desdemona dazed he accuses her of deceit and whoredom. Iago enters and pretends outraged sympathy. Roderigo comes to him complaining that his pursuit of Desdemona does not prosper, despite his gifts of money to Iago and jewels to Desdemona. Iago promises him reward, and enlists him in a plot to kill Cassio (on the grounds that if Cassio is killed Othello and Desdemona will have to stay in Cyprus and Roderigo may 'have' her). The act ends with a touching scene as Emilia helps Desdemona prepare for bed; Desdemona sings a sad song of a forsaken girl, 'Sing all a green willow', and wonders whether anywhere in the world 'there be women do abuse their husbands/ In such gross kind' as she is accused of.

Act V: Iago and Roderigo wait in the dark to attack Cassio. Roderigo is wounded; Iago who has been in hiding steps out and wounds Cassio and then departs. Othello, entering, hears Cassio's cry and thinks that 'honest and just' Iago has been true, and wildly declares he is going now to kill his 'strumpet' Desdemona. Others come and then Iago returns and kills Roderigo so that he cannot be exposed. When Bianca enters and weeps for Cassio's wound, Iago incriminates her.

Later, Othello comes to Desdemona's bedchamber where she is
asleep. He speaks of her beauty and appearance of purity yet has
come to kill her. He kisses her, wakes her and tells her to confess
herself to heaven, for 'I would not kill thy soul.' Shocked and
incredulous she speaks of her innocence and begs for mercy but,
angered by her protestation, he smothers her. Almost immediately
Emilia enters, to tell of Roderigo's death at the hands, she
mistakenly reports, of Cassio; she hears a sound from the bed and
discovers the dying Desdemona. She immediately condemns Othello,
refutes his charge of his wife's falseness, quickly suspects her
husband Iago's villainy and cries out for help. Montano and others
including Iago come. She calls on Iago to disprove Othello's
accusation of his part in the actions. Othello acknowledges the
murder to Gratiano, but says that 'she with Cassio hath the act of
shame/ A thousand times committed', citing the proof of the
handkerchief. At this Emilia realises the significance of the handkerchief, Iago goes to stab her and is prevented, and Othello realises
how he has been hideously misled and runs to attack Iago who
quickly stabs Emilia. Iago and Othello are disarmed and Montano
and Gratiano leave the room and go to guard the doors. Emilia dies,
singing a phrase from Desdemona's willow song as she does.
Othello is now in self-reproachful despair. When Montano re-enters
with Lodovico, the wounded Cassio carried in in a chair and Iago a
prisoner, Othello attacks and wounds Iago but is disarmed. Othello
despairingly admits the murder of Desdemona, though 'nought did
I in hate but all in honour', and having plotted with Iago the death
of Cassio, and he calls on Lodovico and Montano to 'demand that
demi-devil/ Why he has thus ensnar'd my soul and body'. Iago says
he will 'from this time forth . . . never speak word'; one by one all
his crimes and plots are revealed and he and Othello are ordered to
prison. But Othello makes a last speech, describing himself as 'one
that lov'd not wisely, but too well', in the course of which he
produces a dagger which his captors did not know of and
dramatically stabs himself. Crying 'I kiss'd thee ere I kill'd thee, no
way but this,/ Killing myself, to die upon a kiss', he falls on to the
bed where the dead Desdemona lies.

SOURCE   A novella in the *Hecatommithi* ('One Thousand Tales')
(1566) of Giovanni Battista Giraldi, known as Cinthio□ (1504–73).
Shakespeare greatly ennobled the Moor (Cristophoro Moro in
Cinthio) and complicated the plot to make it more than the
melodramatic sordid story of sexual intrigue, jealousy and brutality
of the original, in which the Moor and the Ensign Alfiero together
beat Disdemona to death with a sand-filled stocking and bring the
roof down on her.

TEXT   The First Quarto□ (1622), a good quarto, possibly set up from Shakespeare's manuscript, although this would have been written nearly twenty years earlier, or from a transcript of the prompt-book□. The First Folio (1623)□ text was based on a copy of Q1 apparently corrected from the prompt-book; it is about 160 lines longer, which supports the idea that Q1 was a cut version and probably a theatre text.

P

Painter, William (?1540–94). Best known as the compiler of *The Palace of Pleasure* (1560, sixty stories; second volume with thirty-four stories, in 1567), a collection of translations of tales, 'pleasant histories and excellent novels' from classical and Renaissance writers, especially from Boccaccio,□ Bandello□ and Cinthio.□ Shakespeare probably used Painter's translation as well as the originals for *All's Well That Ends Well*, and to some extent for *Romeo and Juliet* and *Timon of Athens*.

Palace of Pleasure, The. See Painter, William.□

Palladis Tamia. A collection of brief essays and entries on many topics, religious, philosophical and literary, by Francis Meres (1565–1647). It is important as giving a list of twelve of Shakespeare's plays known to him at the time of the publication of his book in September 1598. He sees the dramatist as 'among the English . . . the most excellent in both kinds for the stage: for Comedy witness his *Gentlemen of Verona*, his *Errors*, his *Love Labors lost*, his *Love labours wonne*, his *Midsummers night's dreame* and his *Merchant of Venice*: for Tragedy his *Richard the 2*, *Richard the 3*, *Henry the 4*, *King John*, *Titus Andronicus* and his *Romeo and Juliet*.' It omits the three parts of *Henry VI* and *The Taming of the Shrew* (but the puzzling title '*Love labours wonne*' may refer to the latter, and certainly accurately summarises the outcome of the play). But Meres does not claim to be giving a complete list; he gives what looks like a deliberately balancing list of six comedies and six 'tragedies'. It is interesting that he does not distinguish a category called History.

Pastoralism. In literature pastoralism is concerned with the days and ways, imagined or wished for, of idealised shepherds, an ideal world of innocence and generally of happiness, with life lived simply in natural surroundings. It expresses a deep-seated human desire for simplicity and innocence, and finds it in a long-ago world of Mediterranean, especially Greek and Sicilian, shepherd life. The shepherds of pastoral represent good men almost without exception. They also represent virtuous lovers, and almost always also stand for poets. Pastoral was a minor literary form in classical literature, but it had some valuable possibilities for poets, many of whom, from Virgil at least to the eighteenth century in England, have begun and learnt by writing pastorals. The great Elizabethan writers of romance, Sir Philip Sidney in prose (*Arcadia*,□ 1590) and Edmund Spenser□ in poetry (*The Faerie Queene*, 1590 and 1596), made great use of the pastoral ideal, seeing the pastoral world as a symbol of the natural order and harmony God intended for the world and which man forfeited by the Fall. Shakespeare followed them notably, although he questions the validity of aspects of pastoralism in *As You Like It*. In *The Winter's Tale* a quite Spenserian vision of simple virtue (Perdita is close kin to Pastorella in Book VI of *The Faerie Queene*) is presented, making a strong contrast between pastoral Bohemia and the royal court, invaded by jealousy, suspicion and death, of Leontes in Sicily. There are significant pastoral elements in *Cymbeline* – in the Welsh hills where the two lost sons of the king have been brought up in the simplicity of nature, and in *The Tempest*, as there had been, very early, in *Two Gentlemen of Verona*. In the histories, too, Shakespeare pauses in *Henry VI* and in *Richard II* to allow the king to long for pastoral simplicity and virtue far removed from the responsibilities, pressures and dangers of the court.

Performances. Performances of plays in the public theatres took place in the afternoon and lasted two hours or a little more. Shakespeare's company began at 2 o'clock. In the indoor theatres, where lighting was needed anyway, performances did not necessarily take place in the afternoon. At the open playhouses a flag was flown from the hut of the tiring-house□ to advertise that there would be a performance. If the the play was a tragedy, usually the tiring-house wall and perhaps the heavens□ would be hung with black curtaining. (See the opening of *Henry VI, Part 1* where Bedford cries: 'Hung be the heavens with black'.) 'Gatherers' collected the entry money at the main entrance, and others the extra charges at the entrances to the seats in the galleries. The beginning of the performance was signalled by three trumpet calls from the hut of the tiring-house.

Pericles, Prince of Tyre. The first of the late romances, dating from late 1607–early 1608. The rambling story is clarified a little by having the Chorus□ or presenter – Gower□ – introduce each act and summarise or recapitulate events, or, as he expresses it, 'stand i' th' gaps to teach you / The stages of our story'.

Act I: Gower tells us of King Antiochus's incestuous relationship with his daughter, who is so beautiful that many princes come to woo her. To keep her to himself, Antiochus requires all suitors to answer a riddle or lose their lives. So far none has succeeded. Now Pericles Prince of Tyre comes. He quickly realises that the riddle he is set reveals the incestuous affair. Antiochus perceives this, urges him to stay, and orders a lord, Thaliard, to kill him. But Pericles senses danger and quickly departs, returning to Tyre. He is welcomed joyfully, but reveals his fear of Antiochus's hatred to Lord Helicanus, who urges him to travel for a while. He leaves Helicanus as his deputy and sets sail. He arrives at Tarsus, which is famine-stricken, bringing shiploads of corn, and is gratefully welcomed by the govenor Cleon and his wife Dionyza.

Act II: Pericles hears that Thaliard, Antiochus's agent, is still pursuing him in order to assassinate him. He sets sail again, is wrecked in a storm and cast up at Pentapolis. As he emerges from the sea three kindly comic fishermen help him. His armour, already rusted, is then found in the fishermen's nets. He learns that good Simonides the king has arranged a tournament in honour of his daughter Thaisa, and resolves to take part, wearing the rusty armour. We witness the procession of princely suitors, sixth and last of whom comes Pericles in his rusty armour which provokes some comment, but about which King Simonides remarks 'Opinion's but a fool, that makes us scan / The outward habit by the inward man.' Shouts proclaim the victory of Pericles, and this is celebrated at a banquet. In Tyre, Helicanus reports the death, by lightning sent from heaven, of Antiochus and his daughter. Pericles's continued absence troubles the lords, who wish to proclaim Helicanus king; this he forbids, telling them that he will accept in a twelvemonth if Pericles does not return, but that they are to search the world for him meanwhile. In Pentapolis, Simonides hastens the departure of the other suitors but then pretends to be displeased and accuses Pericles of bewitching Thaisa. The prince's spirited protestations and Thaisa's evident love of him lead to the king's ready approval of their marrying.

Act III: A brief dumbshow 'presented' by Gower is followed by his explanation: that Helicanus has sent messages from Tyre imploring the prince's return within twelve months; the discovery of Pericles's royalty delights Simonides; Thaisa, now with child, and accompanied by a nurse, Lychorida, departs with Pericles by sea. During a storm on board ship Pericles is brought the newborn child by Lychorida, who reports Thaisa's death in childbirth. The superstitious sailors demand her burial at sea, and this is done, and the ship makes for Tarsus. At Ephesus a lord, Cerimon, who has great medical skills, is brought the chest containing the body of Thaisa which has been washed ashore. She has been dead some five hours, but by his art he is able to bring her back to life. Pericles, after a sojourn at Tarsus, must return to Tyre. Thanking Cleon the Governor for his hospitality he asks him and his wife Dionyza to look after and bring up the baby, which he has named Marina. Meanwhile Thaisa has completely recovered, but thinking Pericles to have been drowned she has entered the temple of Diana to lead the life of a vestal virgin.

Act IV: Gower introduces us to a much later time; while Pericles has remained in Tyre and Thaisa in Ephesus, each thinking the other dead, Marina has grown up in Tarsus. She is so beautiful and accomplished that Dionyza, whose own daughter is outshone by her, plots to murder her. Dionyza tells her servant Leonine to walk with Marina on the shore and kill her. He is about to do so when some pirates appear and seize her from him. They take her to Mytilene where they sell her to a brothel-keeper. When Cleon hears from Dionyza that she has had Marina killed – and Leonine poisoned – he is appalled and amazed at her monstrous deed. Gower tells us that Pericles has sailed from Tyre to see his daughter, accompanied by old Helicanus, and presents another dumbshow, of Pericles being shown Marina's tomb and of his passionate grief. Meanwhile Marina has not only remained inviolate in the brothel but has persuaded clients to give up brothel-going and live virtuously; and now we see her speaking 'holy words to the Lord Lysimachus', another customer, although Governor of Mytilene, who is moved by her beauty and innocence. He rebukes Boult, the pander's comic servant, as he leaves. The pander and the bawd order Boult to 'crack the glass of her virginity' but she manages to charm even him, persuading him to arrange for her to enter a family where she can live by teaching singing, dance and needlework.

Act V: Gower tells us that this was arranged and 'She sings like one immortal, and . . . dances/ As goddess-like'. Pericles, unkempt and self-neglectful since he heard of Marina's supposed death, arrives in Mytilene. He has not spoken for three months, nor cut his beard or hair for fourteen years since the apparent death of his wife in childbirth, old Helicanus tells the Governor, Lysimachus, when he comes aboard to welcome Pericles. One of Lysimachus's lords suggests that Marina should be brought to the ship, and Lysimachus, agreeing that she 'with her sweet harmony' would be able, if anyone were, to break through Pericles's grief and silence, asks for her to be brought. She comes, sings to him, and then tells him of her own woeful history, and he gradually realises that she is his own long-lost daughter. Overcome with joy, he is disposed to sleep by strange music, which he calls 'the music of the spheres'; and as he sleeps the goddess Diana appears to him and tells him to go to her temple and tell his story to the 'maiden-priests'. He goes to the temple with Marina and Lysimachus, (who, Gower tells us, has declared his love for Marina) and on telling his story the high priestess (who is Thaisa) faints. Cerimon, the physician-lord who had restored the drowned Thaisa to life fourteen years before, tells Pericles that this must be his wife, and there is a joyful reunion of husband and wife, mother and daughter. Marina and Lysimachus are betrothed and are to rule in Tyre while Pericles and Thaisa will live in Pentapolis, Thaisa's father Simonides having died.

SOURCE   The tale of 'Apollonius of Tyre', which was retold by John Gower,☐ Chaucer's contemporary, in his collection of tales *Confessio Amantis* (1385–93) ('Confession of a Lover').

TEXT   The Quarto☐ of 1609, a corrupt text; that is, it is based on report or memory of a stage-text inadequately recalled and badly printed. In addition, the play is not entirely Shakespeare's, though most of the last three acts is attributed to him, and passages in the first two sound genuinely Shakespearian. He *may* have hastily or incompletely revised someone else's play; some think the play was a collaboration. It did not appear in the First Folio☐ (1623). (It eventually appeared in the 3rd edition of the Folio in 1664.)

Plague. Like all densely populated cities London suffered from occasional serious outbreaks of plague, usually bubonic plague, carried by fleas on rats. In time of plague the theatres were often closed, to reduce the risk of spreading the disease through large numbers of people assembling in confined spaces. There was severe plague in the years 1592–4 and again in 1603–4. The theatres seem to have been closed virtually from autumn 1592 to May 1594, and from April 1603 to April 1604. When the theatres closed in London the players often toured in the provinces, where they had to compete with local companies. Shakespeare seems to have written his two narrative poems *Venus and Adonis* and *The Rape of Lucrece* during the plague years 1592–4.

Plautus, Titus Maccius (*c.*250–184BC). A Roman writer of stage comedy, derived in part from the fourth-century Greek writer Menander, in part from rough Roman farce. His plays had plots based on intrigue, secret love affairs, mistaken identity, families separated and later to be re-united, played out among a selection of stock characters: braggart soldier, crafty servant(s), miser, pedant, young lovers. As Plautus was studied in English grammar schools Shakespeare almost certainly first read his works at school, and there are a number of references to Plautus as well as many variations and developments of his farcical plots and stock characters, especially in the early comedies. *The Comedy of Errors* is based chiefly on *Menaechmi* (the name of the twin brothers long separated) with an episode (the husband locked out of his own house) from *Amphitruo*. Episodes such as Jessica's elopement in *The Merchant of Venice* may owe something to the elopement of the miser's daughter in *Aulularia* (The Crock of Gold). Berowne in *Love's Labour's Lost* lists the comic characters in the action – 'the pedant, the braggart, the hedge-priest, the fool and the boy' – which come from the Roman comedy such as that of Plautus, possibly with extra ideas from the Italian *commedia dell'arte*□ which itself had its distant ancestry in the classical comedy. Plautus's woman disguised as a man in *Casina* may have been the ultimate origin of the girls in male disguise so loved by Shakespeare – Julia, Portia, Rosalind, Viola, Imogen.

Playhouses. The first building specially built for a theatre, and probably designed roughly on the model of the inn-yards with galleries where plays had hitherto been performed, was The Theatre, built in 1576. Because of the hostility of the Corporation of London to the drama, believing it attracted crime and lawlessness as well as crowds and the possibility of spreading disease, both it and the Fortune, built in the following year, were well outside the City's walled boundary. They were in the north-eastern suburbs, in Shoreditch. No public theatres were built within the City, the Blackfriars□ being an adaptation of an existing building. The Globe□ was built across the river to the south, and so outside the City, in the Bankside district of Southwark, in 1599, and so were the Rose (1587), the Hope (1614) and the Swan□ (1595).

The early theatres seem to have been virtually round or polygonal, like the bear-baiting houses, and were built of lath-and-plaster infilling on a timber structure. Three galleries (it is thought) surrounded the yard into which the stage or platform extended some 40 feet (12.2 m). At the back of the stage was the tiring-house□ where the actors changed into costume□ and waited; the wall which separated it from the stage had two or more doors to the stage, and was partly covered in curtaining. At the level of the first gallery was a stage-gallery, sometimes called the tarras, which could be used for some scenes, with steps leading to it. Above that, and projecting forward, supported on two great decorated wooden pillars, was the roof and the heavens□ which gave some shelter from rain to much of the stage area and from which when needed things could be lowered on to the stage. The underside of the canopy was richly painted with sun, moon, stars, etc. Above the roof was a hut or huts, with a small platform from which the flag to advertise a performance was hung, and from which the trumpeter sounded to begin the performance; from the hut(s) stage-hands could operate machinery and make the sound of thunder by rolling large iron balls along a wooden trough, etc. The stage had often a large trap-door near the front.

The builder's contract for the Fortune, built in 1600 for Henslowe,□ survives. It was unusual, being square, 80 ft (24.4 m)

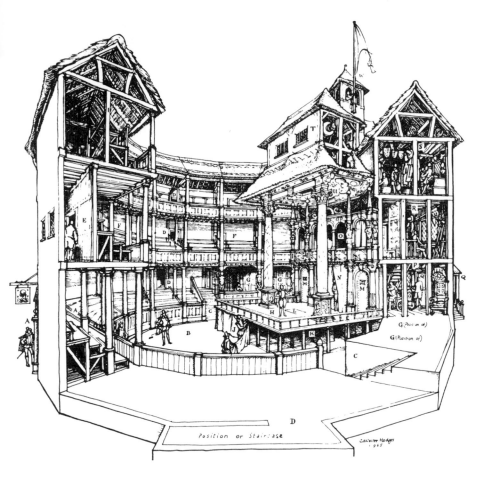

AA Main entrance
 B The Yard
CC Entrances to lowest gallery
 D Entrance to staircase and upper galleries
 E Corridor serving the different sections of the
   middle gallery
 F Middle gallery ('Twopenny Rooms')
 G 'Gentlemen's Rooms' or 'Lords' Rooms'
 H The stage
 J The hanging being put up round the stage
 K The 'Hell' under the stage
 L The stage trap, leading down to the Hell
MM Stage doors

N Curtained 'place behind the stage'
O Gallery above the stage, used as required
   sometimes by musicians, sometimes by
   spectators, and often as part of the play
P Back-stage area (the tiring-house)
Q Tiring-house door
R Dressing-rooms
S Wardrobe and storage
T The hut housing the machine for lowering
   enthroned gods, etc., to the stage
U The 'Heavens'
W Hoisting the playhouse flag

PLATE 3: A conjectural reconstruction of the interior of the Globe, by C. W. Hodges.

square on the outside, 55 ft (16.8 m) inside. The gallery roofs were tiled; we learn that the ground floor gallery was 12 ft (3.7 m) high, the one above that 11 ft (3.3 m) and the topmost one 9 ft (2.8 m). The stage was 43 ft (13.3 m) wide, and projected 27½ ft (8.4 m) into the yard (that is, half way into it). We do not know much more than this, because the contract stipulated that in other details for the stage, for gentleman's rooms (private boxes), for the tiring-house and backstage areas, it was to be built 'like unto . . . the playhouse called The Globe' which had been built the year before by the same builder, Peter Streete. From the evidence of Shakespeare's plays, it seems that The Globe had a covered inner-stage area, for example, for the 'discovery' (revealing) of Ferdinand and Miranda playing chess in Prospero's cave, perhaps between the doors in the tiring-house wall, and probably supported by smaller pillars behind the two great pillars supporting the heavens; and that a gallery above this served as an additional acting area. In fact more than half the plays (by all authors) staged at the Globe between 1599 and 1609 seem to require an upper acting area, for walls, windows, Juliet's balcony, Cleopatra's monument, battlements in *Richard II*; and thirteen scenes in Shakespeare require players to descend or ascend from or to it.

We know little about the private theatres in the City, though a little more about James Burbage's Blackfriars, an adaptation of the upper frater (dormitory) of the old priory. Here almost certainly the stage area was at the far end, not along one of the (longest) side walls. This would have been very like the great halls in the Inns of Court (or in great houses); there was probably a rear gallery, and there might have been side galleries too. Although smaller and shallower than in the public theatres, the stage was probably roughly similar in what it offered in the way of exits, entrances and supplementary acting areas, for after 1608 the King's Men, Shakespeare's company, used both Blackfriars and the Globe, the former during the colder months of the year. The public theatres seem to have been able to hold the amazing number of over three thousand people, the private theatres probably not many more than five or six hundred, though the Blackfriars was reported to be a place where 'a thousand men in judgement sit'.

Plot. In the Elizabethan theatre, a scene-by-scene abstract or condensation of the action of a play. It was prepared, usually by the book-keeper,□ from the prompt-book□ of the play. It showed the characters who appear in each scene and where they appear (by which entrance), together with properties (objects the characters need, like a sword, a basket for Falstaff's escape in *Merry Wives*, a letter, a bed for Lear) and showing also where sounds – bells, thunder, 'alarum', horns – are needed. It was pasted on thin board and hung on a peg, presumably in the tiring-house,□ for actors and stage-hands to see, as a reminder.

Plutarch (*c*.AD45–130). A Greek writer and teacher, who lived for a time in Rome under Trajan, who made him consul and governor of Illyricum. He retired to Greece and wrote his *Parallel Lives*, a collection of fifty biographies of famous Greeks and Romans, forty-six of which are arranged in pairs linked by comparisons. A valuable historical source-book, it was translated into French by Jacques Amyot (1513–93), a version which Sir Thomas North□ translated into English (1579) as *The Lives of the Noble Grecians and Romans*. This was the chief source for *Julius Caesar, Antony and Cleopatra*, and *Coriolanus*, and it contributed also to *Timon of Athens*.

Problem plays. A late Victorian scholar first used the phrase about *Hamlet, All's Well That Ends Well, Troilus and Cressida* and *Measure for Measure*, because he thought the point of view in the plays was ambiguous and made for problems of interpretation. Some writers associate the 'problem' comedies with what Ben Jonson□ invented and called 'comical satire' when he introduced his *Every Man Out of his Humour* (1599) which combined satire with traditional comic features. Even leaving *Hamlet* out of the reckoning, the other plays are not much like Jonson's 'comical satire' but have some Jonsonian features: criticism of society, satirical portrayal of some characters (Parolles, Lucio and Thersites who are the producers or receivers of comic slander and abuse); exposure of folly and vice. But Jonson never went in for the repentance and reconciliation we find in *All's Well That Ends Well* or *Measure for Measure*. These two plays pose and discuss serious and important moral problems, and solve them surprisingly in the way of romantic comedy. *Troilus and Cressida* remains unique – not a comedy, not a tragedy, not a history, full of satirical and reductive comment, seeing the classic great tale of love and war as amorousness and immorality on the one hand and wasteful unnecessary conflict for base or foolish motives on the other.

Prompt-book, prompt-copy. The copy or 'book' of the play prepared from the author's manuscript or a transcript of it and kept by the book-keeper.□ It was the recognised text, and probably had more detailed stage-directions, lists of characters, processions, etc. than the original. It had to be licensed by the Master of the Revels.□ Some of the printed 'good' Quartos□ and the previously unpublished versions in the First Folio□ were set up from the prompt-books.

Q

Quarto. A printer's term for a book size, named 'quarto' because the pages of quarto size are one-fourth the size of the sheet of paper on which they are printed. Each sheet is folded twice (to make four leaves). The size varies a little, depending on the size of the sheet, but an average and common size is 9 inches deep by 7 inches wide (22.8 cm by 17.7 cm). The Shakespeare Quartos were printings in quarto book form of nineteen of his plays before the publication of the First Folio collected edition in 1623, but some of them were 'bad' quartos.□

quarto, bad. See Bad quarto.

Queen Elizabeth. See Elizabeth, Queen.

R

Reconstruction, memorial. See Memorial reconstruction.

Revels, Master of the. See Master of the Revels.

Richard II. A history play dealing with the last years of the King's reign; he was deposed by Bolingbroke in 1399 and died in 1400. For date see below.

Act I: At Windsor, before the King, Bolingbroke, son of the King's uncle John of Gaunt, accuses Mowbray, Duke of Norfolk, of misusing royal funds and plotting the death of another uncle (Gloucester), both of which charges Mowbray denies. Resisting all attempts at pacification, they are ordered by the King to meet in single combat. The widow of Gloucester goes to Gaunt, her brother-in-law, to urge him to avenge the murder; but in vain, for he will not 'lift an angry arm against [God's] minister', the King, whom he believes to have been responsible. The single combat at Coventry is ceremonially started, but before the fight begins the King stops it, having decided to banish his cousin Bolingbroke for ten years (soon reduced to six) and Norfolk for life. King Richard talks with another cousin, Aumerle, of Bolingbroke's 'courtship to the common people' and his popularity with them as he went into exile. The King is about to go to Ireland to deal with a rebellion, but remarks on a shortage of money; when news comes to him of his uncle Gaunt's grievous illness, he hopes for his quick death so that he may seize his wealth.

Act II: John of Gaunt on his deathbed talks with his brother York about the King's selfish extravagance and his surrounding himself with flatterers. He makes the celebrated speech lamenting the present sad state of 'this scept'red isle,/ This earth of majesty, this seat of Mars,/ This other Eden, demi-paradise' under the selfish, irresponsible king. The King comes to see him and coldly and cruelly berates him for attempting to reprove and advise him. The dying Gaunt is carried out, and when his death is reported a few moments later, the young king immediately orders the confiscation of his 'plate, coin, revenues and moveables'. York remonstrates, reminding his nephew the King of exiled Bolingbroke's rights in his father's estate, but to no avail. The King's actions are angrily discussed by Northumberland, Ross and Willoughby, and Northumberland confides to them that Bolingbroke with an army of three thousand men has set sail for England. The Queen, Isabel, sad and anxious over Richard's departure for Ireland feels 'some unborn sorrow ripe in Fortune's womb' coming towards her, and receives news that Bolingbroke has landed at Ravensburgh on the Yorkshire coast, and that Northumberland and his son Harry Percy and Worcester have joined him.

The old Duke of York, regent during the king's absence, is horrified and bewildered by the turn of events; both Richard and Bolingbroke are his kinsmen. He goes to Berkeley in Gloucestershire, calling on Bushy, Bagot and Greene, favoured courtiers, to meet him there. He meets and challenges Bolingbroke, who is accompanied by Northumberland, Harry Percy and others. Bolingbroke assures him he has broken his exile only to claim his inheritance, now that he has succeeded his dead father as Duke of Lancaster. York, to some extent sympathetic to Bolingbroke's cause, tells him that he will remain neutral.

Act III: Bolingbroke orders the death of the two favourites Bushy and Greene whom he had captured at Bristol and sends York with kindly messages to the Queen. Meanwhile King Richard has returned from Ireland, confident in his kingly authority – 'Not all the water in the rough rude sea/Can wash the balm off from an anointed king;/The breath of worldly men cannot depose/The deputy elected by the Lord.' He is soon, however, in despair, as news comes first that twelve thousand Welsh troops have joined Bolingbroke, then that many – 'white-beards . . . boys with women's voices . . . beadsmen' (old men pensioned to pray for the benefactor) – have risen against the King: 'Yea, distaff-women manage rusty bills [weapons]/Against thy seat: both young and old rebel.' The final blow is the news that even York has joined the rebels.

Richard flees to Flint Castle, whither Bolingbroke, Northumberland and the sad and troubled York repair, and are joined by Harry Percy. Bolingbroke sends a message to the King, declaring his allegiance provided his banishment is repealed, but threatening civil war if it is not. The King appears on the walls; Northumberland brings Bolingbroke's message; Richard accepts the demand, but instantly regrets it and reviles himself, wishing he were 'as great as is my grief'. He knows that Bolingbroke is powerful and determined, and assumes that his abdication is inevitable, but his rebel cousin again declares 'I come but for mine own.' The Queen in the garden of York's house with two of her ladies, watches and overhears the gardener and two of his men, who moralise on England as a neglected garden, which is being pruned, trimmed and dressed by Bolingbroke, and she learns that Richard has been brought to London by the rebel.

Act IV: Begins with charges laid against Aumerle of responsibility for Gloucester's death and of hostility to Bolingbroke. This takes us back to the opening scene of the play, when Mowbray was similarly charged, and we now hear of his death in exile. York enters with a message from Richard, who is prepared to abdicate. Bolingbroke immediately declares he will ascend the throne, the Bishop of Carlisle protests and is arrested, and the King is sent for 'that in common view/ He may surrender'. Grief-stricken and self-pitying, Richard yields up the crown, recalling the betrayal of Christ by Judas and by Pilate, and wishing he 'were a mockery king of snow,/ Standing before the sun of Bolingbroke,/ To melt myself away in water-drops'. He asks leave to go, and brutally Bolingbroke orders him to the Tower of London. Aumerle, the Bishop of Carlisle and the Abbot of Westminster (who had been ordered to hold the bishop prisoner earlier in the scene) remain briefly and agree to plot against Bolingbroke.

Act V: The Queen watches for Richard as he is taken a prisoner to the Tower, sadly greets him, and gently reproaches him for his meekness. They part sorrowfully, the more miserably as Northumberland brings orders for Richard to be imprisoned at Pomfret in Yorkshire, not in London, and word of the Queen's imminent despatch to France. We learn from a conversation between York and his wife of the people's welcome to Bolingbroke. They are joined by their son Aumerle – deprived of his dukedom because of his loyal support of Richard – and discover by accident that he is implicated in a plot to kill the new king. York angrily accuses him of treason, and despite his wife's entreaties, hastens to report him to the King. The Duchess urges her son to get to the King and confess first, and herself also hastens to Windsor, where Bolingbroke, now King Henry IV, pardons him; but he will not pardon the other conspirators. In Pomfret Castle, Richard laments his state and philosophises, and is moved by a brief visit from a loyal groom. He is suddenly murdered by Sir Pierce of Exton, who thought Bolingbroke had hinted he should rid him 'of this living fear'. In the final scene Bolingbroke pardons the Bishop of Carlisle, and, when Exton brings him the coffined corpse of Richard, expresses his horror ('Though I did wish him dead,/ I hate the murtherer, love him murthered') and resolves to go in penance on a voyage 'to the Holy Land,/ To wash the blood off from my guilty hand'.

SOURCES   Chiefly Holinshed's□ *Chronicles of England, Scotland and Ireland*□ (2nd edition 1587). Shakespeare greatly ameliorated the character of John of Gaunt – possibly because he remembered Froissart's (1333–?1400) *Chronicles* translated (1523–5) by Lord Berners (1467–1533), possibly from the contemporary play, *Woodstock*, which dealt with the immediately preceding years of Richard II's reign. But there is dispute about whether *Richard II* is indebted to *Woodstock* or vice versa; and the same doubt exists about possible debts to Samuel Daniel's□ (1562–1619) historical epic poem, *The Civile Warres*□ (first four books 1595).

DATE   If Shakespeare was indebted to Daniel, *Richard II* was completed after the beginning of 1595; if vice versa, it could have been 1594. It was not entered for publication until 29 August 1597.

TEXT   The First Quarto□ (1597), likely to be from Shakespeare's own manuscript, that is, his 'foul papers'.□ There were four other quartos (1598 (two), 1608, 1615) before the First Folio□ of 1623; each quarto reprints its predecessor. The Folio was printed probably from Q3 and Q5, except for the abdication scene (IV.1.154–318) which was not printed in Elizabeth's lifetime (not until Q4, 1608), presumably because of fear about political repercussions.

Richard III: A history play which concludes the *Henry VI* sequence, although complete on its own; it is entitled '*The tragedie of Kinge Richard the Third*' in the quarto title-pages and in the heading of the play in the First Folio,□ but appears in the First Folio among the Histories, and is so listed there in the 'Catalogue' or Table of Contents, although its actual title in the 'Catalogue' is '*The Life and Death of Richard the Third*'. It was probably written straight after the three *Henry VI* plays and so in 1591–2.

Act I: The act begins with Richard, Duke of Gloucester's soliloquy in which he states that he is 'determined to prove a villain', shows his older brother Clarence – whom he has secretly defamed to their brother King Edward IV – being taken to the Tower, a prisoner, and further reveals Richard's gleeful deviousness, wickedness and ambition for the throne. Richard impudently woos the Lady Anne as she accompanies the coffin of her father-in-law King Henry VI, insolently attacks the new queen, Elizabeth, and her family who have been much advanced by the marriage, and is cursed by the old Queen Margaret. A troubled Clarence tells the Keeper of the Tower of his dream in which he had drowned, 'struck overboard' by Gloucester, and then in Hell had been visited by those he had wronged, betrayed and murdered 'that now give evidence against my soul'; he is then killed by two murderers, employed by Gloucester.

Act II: The King, who is seriously ill, tries to ensure all-round amity at court before he dies, especially to achieve reconciliation between Hastings and Queen Elizabeth and her kinsmen, and then between them and Gloucester, who pretends cordiality. When Clarence's name is mentioned, Gloucester immediately reports that he is dead, holding the dying king responsible for ordering his execution. Edward is grief-stricken and repentant, and Gloucester does not ignore the opportunity of blaming the Queen's kindred for having urged it on the King. Edward IV's death follows soon, and the lamentations of his mother the old Duchess of York and of Queen Elizabeth. The young prince Edward is to be brought privately to London, but word comes that Gloucester and his cousin Buckingham have seized Rivers and Grey, the Queen's brother and son, who had been despatched to bring the young prince.

Act III: The young prince comes to London. The Queen has gone with his younger brother, Duke of York, into sanctuary on hearing of Gloucester's action. Buckingham sends Hastings to fetch the boy, and Gloucester arranges for them to be lodged at the Tower, in a scene of menace behind much word-play and joking. Buckingham is in the plot to place Gloucester on the throne, and sends his colleague Catesby to sound out Hastings in the matter. Hastings, despite his hostility to the Queen and her family, robustly refuses to support the enthronement of Gloucester, even though news comes that the kindred of the Queen are to be murdered that day at Pomfret. His optimistic steadfastness is soon punished, when it is clear at a council that Gloucester means the crown for himself, and Hastings is arrested and executed. Gloucester orders the Lord Mayor of London to speak to the people of Edward IV's immorality, his probable illegitimacy and the illegitimacy of his children. This attempt indirectly to promote his own claims produces little response from the citizens, and later he arranges a hypocritical charade, himself with two bishops 'divinely bent to meditation'. His henchman Buckingham then persuades an apparently humble and reluctant Gloucester to be not only Protector but King.

Act IV: Queen Elizabeth, the old Duchess of York and Anne, now Gloucester's enforced wife, go to the Tower to visit the two young princes, but on 'the King's' orders are refused admittance, to their horror and terror. Elizabeth's son Dorset is sent for safety to the Earl of Richmond in voluntary exile in Brittany, who, since the murders of Henry VI and his little son, is head of the House of Lancaster. Gloucester is crowned as Richard III; he asks Buckingham to kill the two princes, but 'high-reaching Buckingham grows circumspect'. Richard arranges for their murder with Sir James Tyrrel, and disposes of his wife Anne. Buckingham departs and begins to raise forces. Three mourning women come. Old Queen Margaret is vindictive still and 'hungry for revenge' and curses the House of York. With the old Duchess of York and the Queen she rehearses the terrible catalogue of murder and vengeance they have all been associated with. When Richard enters, his mother the Duchess of York deeply curses him; the Queen reviles him for his murders and cruelty, but when he talks of her daughter Elizabeth (his own niece) and makes a proposal of marriage to her, after shocked refusal she succumbs to his arguments and agrees to forward the suggestion. The act ends with a succession of messengers reporting the advance of Richmond, who has landed in West Wales, the gathering of other forces to attack the King, and the capture of Buckingham.

Act V: Buckingham is executed. At Bosworth in Leicestershire Richard's and Richmond's armies meet. Richmond, in his tent, is shown to be calm, virtuous, purposeful. Richard, in his, sleeps ill, and in his dreams is visited by the ghosts of those he has slain, bidding him 'despair, and die'. Each ghostly visitant also speaks words of cheer, support and admiration for Richmond. In the battle, Richard is killed in single combat with Richmond, whose armies are completely successful, and the play ends with his hope of reconciling 'divided York and Lancaster' and that England may enjoy 'smiling plenty, and fair prosperous days'.

SOURCE   The second edition (1587) of Holinshed's□ *Chronicles of England, Scotland and Ireland*□ which made great use of Hall's□ chronicle *The Union of the Two Noble and Illustre Famelies of Lancastre and York* (1548). Hall himself was influenced by Sir Thomas More's *Life of Richard III* (1513), from which the chief aspects of Richard's character and the ironic tone of the writer's attitude to him were probably derived.

TEXT   There are quarto□ printings of (1) 1597, (2) 1598, (3) 1602, (4) 1605, (5) 1612, (6) 1622, before it appeared in the First Folio□ (1623), where the text seems to be based on Q3. Q1 seems to have been a memorial reconstruction□ and lacks about 200 lines found in the later versions.

Romance. The word derives from the name given to the languages –
French, Italian, Spanish and Portuguese – which descend from the
'Roman' language, Latin. In the middle ages it came to be applied to
and is still used of the then dominant literary form: stories of
adventure, combat, quest, journeying and love. These varied greatly
in style, scope, form, and in different countries and different
centuries. Within the definition of 'romance' can be found descendants of the epic `chansons de geste`, the great Arthurian romances,
and the early Renaissance epic romances or romantic epics, especially
of Boiardo, Ariosto and Tasso, as well as a world of smaller,
shorter, lighter, more comic and sometimes bawdy tales, whether in
verse or prose. What is chiefly to be found in romances is a
delightful mixture of adventure, endless journeying, chivalrous
combat and 'romance' in the modern sense of amatory feeling. The
modern word 'romance' of course derives from the medieval and
early Renaissance 'romances', in which love, problems in love,
difficulties placed in the way of love, are the staple. Magic and a
sense of wonder are also to be found, associated too with a sense of
idealism, or at least an awareness of high moral values, especially of
the code of chivalry. Male friendship and loyalty, valour in battle,
courtesy, dutiful service to the lord or king, as well as devotion to
the beloved, are also vital. The world of romance tends to be
timeless, untied to a particular place, period, or country, and so can
readily become generally metaphorical or symbolic of life itself. The
romance proved to be a natural vehicle for the conveying of moral
teaching – in the Arthurian stories early on, and most notably in
Tasso's *Gerusalemme Liberata* and in Spenser's□ *The Faerie Queene*
in the sixteenth century – because of its concern for virtuous
behaviour directed towards the ideal. It continued to be the most
popular literary form throughout the sixteenth century in England,
Spenser's great poem and Sir Philip Sidney's *Arcadia*□ marking its
highest points, dozens of ballads its more popular appeal.

  Dramatists also turned to romance. Philip Henslowe□ bought or
drew revenue from dramas founded on old romances, among them
Huon of Bordeaux, Uther Pendragon, Tristram of Lyones. It flourished
in the prose romances of Greene□ and Lodge,□ in the prose and
plays of John Lyly,□ in the plays of Greene and Peele, and most
notably in the early comedies, and, in a form closest to Spenser, in the
late romances of Shakespeare. Shakespeare used romance sources
(for example Greene's *Pandosto*, Lodge's *Rosalynde*) and overcame
the difficulties in adapting the long, wandering narrative form to
brief dramatic action. His early comedies, especially *Two Gentlemen
of Verona* and *Love's Labour's Lost*, and his middle comedies,
especially *As You Like It* and *Twelfth Night*, are imbued with the

spirit of romance, and use romance *motifs* and concerns: disguise, journeying, love-obstacles established and removed, faith, friendship. His late plays, *Pericles, Cymbeline* and *The Winter's Tale* especially, with their long time-span, journeying, generalised place and settings, disguise and mistaken identity, conflict resolved and wickedness defeated, and their steady impulse towards the success of virtue, are indebted to romance, and are rightly called his 'late romances'. There is a strain in sixteenth-century romance which derives ultimately from the late Greek prose romances of the second and third centuries AD, the best-known and most influential being Longus's *Daphnis and Chloe*, Heliodorus's *Aethiopica* or *Theagenes and Chariclea* and Achilles Tatius's *Cleitophon and Leucippe*. These are characteristic of the genre in weaving elaborate adventures, combats and dangers, journeys and strange and sometimes magic happenings round a central love story. Sidney and Greene, and to a lesser extent Spenser, Lyly and Lodge, are indebted to Greek romance, and Shakespeare indirectly through them. The romance moved towards and grew into the novel, and the French word for the novel, *le roman*, makes the connection clear.

Romeo and Juliet. An early tragedy, written between 1594 and 1596.

Act I: In Verona there is a fresh outbreak of the long feud between the Montagues and the Capulets when two servants of each family fight each other, and Benvolio of the Montagues and Tybalt of the Capulets get involved. The Prince quells the brawl and decrees death to the participants in any future outbreak. Lady Montague, although relieved her son Romeo was not involved, is worried about his melancholy, which his cousin Benvolio finds is caused by hapless love for Rosaline, who has 'forsworn to love'. He urges Romeo to forget her, and to come that evening to a feast at Capulet's house (despite the danger of so doing) where he may compare Rosaline with other ladies. We learn that the young Count Paris seeks the hand of Capulet's daughter Juliet, and then meet Juliet herself, who is not yet fourteen, with her mother and her affectionate, doting, garrulous Nurse; she is told of Paris's request, but says marriage 'is an honour that I dream not of'. Romeo with Benvolio and another friend Mercutio go masked to the feast, only delaying on the way for Mercutio's fantastical speech about Queen Mab, the 'fairies' midwife' who 'delivers' men of their dreams – and Romeo has had a moment of foreboding ("tis not wit to go' . . . 'I dreamt a dream tonight'.) At the feast Romeo is spotted by Juliet's cousin, the fiery Tybalt, who is restrained from attacking him for being a Montague by old Capulet; and Romeo and Juliet meet, fall in love, kiss and, parting, discover to their grief and fear that each belongs to the enemy family.

Act II: In the celebrated 'balcony scene' Romeo comes at night to the Capulets' orchard, and overhears Juliet on her balcony lamenting that her new-found beloved is a Montague. They exchange passionate declarations of love for each other and agree to marry as soon as they can, whatever the obstacles and difficulties. Romeo then goes to Friar Laurence, his 'ghostly [spiritual] father', who soon agrees to marry them 'For this alliance may so happy prove / To turn your households' rancour to pure love'. Benvolio tells Mercutio that Tybalt has sent a challenge to Romeo. Romeo and his two friends jest together and briefly make fun of the Nurse when she appears. She has come in search of Romeo on Juliet's behalf to find out what arrangements Romeo has made. Romeo goes to Friar Laurence at his cell, swiftly joined by Juliet, for him to marry them.

Act III: An hour or so after the secret wedding, Tybalt provokes a fight with Mercutio. Romeo tries to keep the peace, and then to separate them, but Mercutio is killed in the scuffle, whereupon Romeo challenges and kills Tybalt, and escapes, crying 'O, I am fortune's fool.' Juliet, impatiently awaiting her lover, learns to her grief and despair from the grieving Nurse that Tybalt has been slain by Romeo and Romeo sentenced to banishment. Romeo, hiding at the cell, learns from Friar Laurence of his banishment, becomes desperate and is only saved from killing himself by the Friar, who reproaches him severely and then gives him hope, telling him to go to Juliet and comfort her and then to journey to exile in Mantua and wait for better days. Capulet agrees to Paris's renewed offer for his daughter. Romeo and Juliet spend their first (and last) night together, and when Romeo leaves at daybreak, Juliet's distress is increased by her parents' insistence that she shall marry Paris on Thursday. Even the Nurse urges this.

Act IV: Paris comes to Friar Laurence to insist on his wedding to Juliet taking place on Thursday. Juliet, coming for help to the Friar, is 'past hope, past cure, past help!' The Friar has a plan: she is to agree to marry Paris; on the wedding-eve she is to take a potion the Friar will give her which will make her as if dead; her body will be taken to the Capulets' vault where the Friar will watch her coming round from the effects of the drug, and Romeo, informed of the plan, will bear her off to Mantua. On the wedding-eve, Juliet fearfully but resolutely takes the potion, and seems, to the dismay of the Capulet household, to have died.

Act V: Romeo's servant Balthasar comes to Mantua to tell his master of Juliet's death. Romeo immediately decides to join her in death and goes to an apothecary for a suicide-draught. The Friar's plan has misfired, for Friar John, his messenger to Romeo, had been prevented from getting to Mantua. But Romeo has hastened back to

Verona, and gone to the vault, where he surprises Paris who had been to strew flowers on Juliet's bier. Paris, thinking of Romeo as a Montague and an enemy attacks him and is killed. Romeo movingly says farewell to his bride, takes the potion and dies. Friar Laurence, coming in haste, finds the corpses of Paris and of Romeo just as Juliet revives from her drug. When she realises that Romeo is dead, she kills herself with a dagger. Word of the deaths quickly spreads, and the Capulets, the Montagues and the Prince gather at the vault. The Friar unfolds the tragic tale, and the grief-stricken enemy families make peace, Montague resolving to raise a statue to Capulet's daughter and Capulet one to Romeo.

SOURCE *The Tragicall Historye of Romeus and Juliet* (1562) by Arthur Brooke,□ a poem of 3020 lines in couplets and poulters', or poulterers', measure (lines alternating between twelve and fourteen syllables), based on a French translation (by Boiastuau) of one of the *novelle* (long, romantic short-stories or tales) of Bandello.□ It is a clumsy poem, but Shakespeare kept closely to its plot although he greatly compressed the action and removed all trace of its Protestant moralising. There are late classical analogues, and several Renaissance versions, with a plot depending on enforced separation, sleeping-potion and the activity of a Friar, in some cases presented as true accounts. There were opposed families of Montecchi (in Verona) and Capelletti (in Cremona) in the thirteenth century, and Dante in *Purgatorio*, VI, mentions them as examples of civil discord.

TEXT The First Quarto□ (1597), is a 'bad' quarto, pirated and dependent on actors' memories of a stage text. This was followed by the Second Quarto in 1599, 'newly corrected, augmented and amended', which is nearly half as long again as Q1. Later Quartos (3) 1609 and (4) 1622 each derived from the preceding one. The First Folio□ text (1623) depended chiefly on Q3.

Roses, Wars of the. See Wars of the Roses.

S

Seneca, Lucius Annaeus (?4BC–AD56). A Roman tragic writer (he was also a philosopher and tutor to the young Nero) whose influence on Renaissance drama in Europe was great. Greek tragedy, which was little known directly, became known through Seneca's taking up its form and many of its stories and plots. His tragedies, of which the *Hercules Furens* (mad), *Thyestes, Phaedra, Oedipus* and *Agamemnon* are the best known, are divided into five acts, use a Chorus,□ observe the unities of time, place and action (one action in one place covering not more than twenty-four hours), tell terrible stories of blood, family crime, adultery and incest, vengeance and retribution, but do not show violent action on the stage. Some think they were not intended for theatrical performance, but for declaiming, but this seems improbable. Other strong motifs are revenge and ghostly visitation.

Seneca was studied in grammar schools and Shakespeare almost certainly read and perhaps also took part in declamations of his work. There was an English translation of the *Tenne Tragedies* of Seneca in 1581. *Gorboduc*□ was one of the first English plays influenced by Seneca. Shakespeare shows signs of Senecan influence in *Titus Andronicus* (the bloody revenge and the 'horrid banquet') and in the early history plays up to and including *Richard III*, again in revenge themes, retribution and ghostly visiting, but Shakespeare was prepared to show violent action on stage. *Hamlet* sensitively and profoundly transmutes a basically Senecan revenge-plot, complete with ghost; and *Macbeth* is again an ennobling of typically Senecan ingredients – murder, ghost, vengeance, retribution. But Shakespeare did not consciously or deliberately imitate or follow Seneca, and there is such naturalness of life, humour and humanity in Shakespeare that it seems odd even to write as much as this about connections between them, except in relation to some of Shakespeare's earliest work.

Shakespeare, William. Shakespeare was born at Stratford-upon-Avon in Warwickshire, very near the centre of England, in 1564. He was baptised on 26 April, and 23 April has been accepted traditionally as his birthday. April 23 is the feast-day of St George, and it was on 23 April in 1616 that Shakespeare died. It seems appropriate to celebrate on the same day England's greatest writer as well as her patron saint. His father, John Shakespeare, was a glover but also had extensive dealings in wool and was a prominent citizen who owned a fair amount of property in Stratford. He became an alderman and a Justice of the Peace. His mother, Mary Arden,□ was the daughter of a substantial farmer from Wilmcote near Stratford. Almost certainly Shakespeare went to the grammar school at Stratford (the Grammar School of King Edward VI) (see Education,□ Shakespeare's, and Stratford-upon-Avon□) although there is no documentary proof of this. The original school buildings, as well as Shakespeare's birthplace and a number of other houses and buildings with which he was connected, may still be seen at Stratford. It is not known how long Shakespeare stayed at school, but some think that he left before completing the full curriculum. His father seems to have fallen on difficult days financially when Shakespeare was aged about thirteen or fourteen, and Shakespeare might well have been apprenticed then in the town. (John Shakespeare stopped attending council meetings after 1576; in 1578 he mortgaged a house and land belonging to his wife; in 1586, not having attended council meetings 'for a long time' his name was struck out.) There is no evidence about the rumour that Shakespeare was apprenticed to a butcher. More probably, he helped in his father's apparently dwindling business at this time.

At the age of eighteen Shakespeare married Anne Hathaway, the daughter of a well-to-do farmer of Shottery, about two miles from Stratford. Anne seems to have been nearly eight years older than William; the marriage was, exceptionally, by special licence, and their first child was born six months later. This is all we know about Shakespeare's wife, except that she bore him three children, Susannah in 1583 and the twins Hamnet and Judith. From the time of the birth of the twins in 1585 we know nothing about where he was or what he was doing until 1592.

There have been many conjectures about this period. One is that he was for a time a country schoolmaster, but certainly at some stage he became associated with an acting company. By 1592, as we know from an allusion to him by Robert Greene,□ a writer of romances and plays, in *A Groatsworth of Wit*, he was both an actor and a playwright, and clearly, although Greene calls him 'an upstart Crow', a well-known man of the theatre. By 1594 he is a member of the company known as the Lord Chamberlain's Men,□ and is not only a leading actor but a 'sharer'□ in that company, meaning that he was a part-owner of the company, receiving a portion of the profits. He later became a 'housekeeper'□ too, meaning that he had a share in the ownership of the theatre. It was a very successful as well as distinguished company, which in 1598 set about constructing its own playhouse, the Globe□ theatre. It was an unusual venture in ownership, as London theatres were usually leased from businessmen or owners not necessarily connected with the theatre. In 1603, when Queen Elizabeth died, the Lord Chamberlain's Men came under the patronage of the new monarch, King James I, and became known as the King's Men. The company in 1608 also leased a second theatre, the Blackfriars.□ It was a covered private theatre, and a more intimate theatre than the Globe, and this may have influenced to some extent the writing of Shakespeare's plays after that date. Here the company played in the colder months.

Shakespeare seems to have been a regular actor, and tradition has it that he played, among other parts, Adam in *As You Like It*, the Ghost in *Hamlet*, the Duke in *The Merchant of Venice* and in *Othello*, and Escalus in *Romeo and Juliet*. He seems not to have been a star actor and, if this tradition is true, he tended to play elderly or authoritative parts. But of course his chief activity was as a playwright and poet, who in the course of his career wrote thirty-seven plays and two long poems, *Venus and Adonis* and *The Rape of Lucrece*, as well as the sequence of one hundred and fifty sonnets. But he was also an effective administrator and man of business who was extremely successful in the theatre world, and was enabled to retire to his home town of Stratford to a substantial property, New Place, which he had bought at a comparatively early age. He had retired to Stratford by the spring of 1612, when he was about forty-eight. He died in 1616.

Although it is not possible to be definite about the order of writing (see Chronology□) or of first presentations of the plays, it is reasonable to see some pattern. Shakespeare seems to have begun by writing chronicle or history plays, the *Henry VI* plays and perhaps the crudely tragic *Titus Andronicus*, and then to have turned to writing light comedies, sometimes with complicated plots, showing the triumph of young love over difficulties, deceits or obstructions. Possibly the first of these was *The Comedy of Errors*, closely followed by *Two Gentlemen of Verona*. By the late 1590s he was not only writing more mature comedies, such as *As You Like It*, *Much Ado About Nothing* and *Twelfth Night*, with more developed characters, and even more humanity and humour, but also history plays at once more profound and more comic (the two parts of *Henry IV*) than the earliest history plays, and was beginning to turn towards tragic writing.

The first few years of the seventeenth century saw the writing of the great tragedies: *Hamlet*, *Othello*, *King Lear*, *Macbeth*, and *Antony and Cleopatra*. Towards the end of his writing career, and possibly influenced by the availability to his company of the Blackfriars theatre, he turned to a new kind of writing, which it would not be quite fair to call tragi-comic but which has many of the elements of both his comedies and his tragedies. These plays, *Pericles*, *Cymbeline*, *The Winter's Tale* and *The Tempest*, which are also more poetic and symbolic than any of his earlier writing, instead show a movement through tragic scenes or scenes of potential tragedy to end, after wrongs have been righted and sins repented, in the triumphant happiness of a younger generation unsoiled by the errors or crimes of the older generation.

Although there are periods of Shakespeare's life about which we know nothing or next to nothing, we still know more about him, his work and his business transactions than of most other writers of his time, indeed than of most Elizabethans. We do not know what he looked like, although there are several portraits supposedly of him,

as well as the poor bust in Stratford-upon-Avon church, which has
been described as being a portrayal of a 'self-satisfied pork butcher'.
The likeness there differs markedly from the other representations
of him, including the best-known portrait, the engraving by the
Flemish engraver Martin Droeshout which appeared on the title
page of the First Folio□ in 1623 (see Plate 1 on p. 6). Contemporaries
referred to him as 'sweet Shakespeare', 'friendly Shakespeare',
'gentle Shakespeare' and the like, and all accounts agree in
affectionate admiration of Shakespeare the man. He seems to have
been good-humoured and sweet-natured, and evidently remarkable
in life for the understanding, tolerance and human sympathy which
are so clearly seen in his plays.

Sharer. A permanent member of an actors' company who was a part-
owner of their assets, paid for a share of the expenses and received a
share of the profits. Shakespeare was one of the sharers in the Lord
Chamberlain's Men,□ later the King's Men. A 'sharer' had a share
in the acting company, as distinct from a 'housekeeper'□ who had a
share in the ownership of the theatre itself. It was of course possible
to be both, and Shakespeare was. There were eight 'sharers' in the
Lord Chamberlain's Men by 1596, and twelve from 1603, when they
became the King's Men.

Songs. There are songs, mostly Shakespeare's own, in *Two Gentlemen
of Verona*, *Love's Labour's Lost*, *A Midsummer Night's Dream*, *The
Merchant of Venice*, *Much Ado About Nothing*, *As You Like It*,
Twelfth Night, *Measure for Measure*, *Cymbeline*, *The Winter's Tale*,
The Tempest and *Henry VIII*. The songs in the tragedies, Ophelia's,
the Fool's in *King Lear*, Desdemona's Willow Song, were popular
songs of the day; they are used for more significant dramatic
purpose, and are also more powerful in evoking atmosphere and
emotion, as it happens, than the songs elsewhere, though Feste's in
Twelfth Night and the song to Mariana in *Measure for Measure* are
also moving. Music survives for some of the songs, by Thomas
Morley, Robert Johnson, Robert Jones, Thomas Ford, John Hilton
and John Wilson; whether it was written for the songs, or the songs
written to fit known tunes, is unresolved.

Sources. Shakespeare rarely invented a whole plot. Many of the plays
can be shown to be related to, perhaps descended from, existing
writings; but they are not thefts or the sign of an empty or
uninventive mind. Virtually everything he uses he transmutes. It is
noteworthy that his sources are sometimes trivial, feeble or even
base; in his hands even these are irradiated. His chief indebtedness
was to Holinshed□ or Hall□ for English history, to North's□
Plutarch□ for Roman history, to Cinthio,□ Boccaccio□ and
Plautus.□ But he never simply takes over a plot: he always changes,

subtilises, compresses, adds character and themes, interweaves with sub-plots from elsewhere.

Spenser, Edmund (1552–97). The greatest non-dramatic poet of the Elizabethan age. He set about to create a poetic language fit for great poetry and for a great heroic poem in English, and introduced and by his versatility and poetic skill made native many of the poetic forms of European literature which the country lacked. He greatly extended the possibilities of pastoral in *The Faerie Queene* and in 'Colin Clouts Come Home Againe'. *The Faerie Queene*, the greatest English poem between Chaucer and Milton, was the last to combine two great traditions, epic and romance.□ It deals with lasting human concerns, preoccupations, pressures, hopes and fears, although set in a romance and epic imaginative world. It has some vivid presentation of human types, even of character, and some excellent dramatic dialogue.

Shakespeare often shows in phrases his knowledge of Spenser, especially in the early plays. He and Spenser shared a humane and compassionate vision of life, however different the forms in which they presented it. In the late romances, Shakespeare comes closest to the spirit and mood of Spenser. *The Winter's Tale* especially is related to Book VI of *The Faerie Queene*, but the other romances, *Pericles* and *Cymbeline*, also are concerned with virtue steadfast through long assault by evil, and show its power especially in the radiant innocence of the young, who often restore the virtuous harmony their elders have lost or destroyed. The simplified almost symbolic figures of the late romances, even their names (Perdita = that which was lost, Miranda = to be wondered at, Florizel suggests flowers (like Spenser's Lady Florimell), Marina suggests the sea which lost and restored her, Ariel the airy spirit and Caliban the cannibal-like savage), make one think of Spenser; and the loose rambling 'romance' structures are like the Spenserian structures of *The Faerie Queene*, where time and the passage of time are more important than place, geography or vivid characterisation. If Spenser had written plays they would have been like this. Of course Spenser and Shakespeare had similar educational (Elizabethan grammar school) backgrounds (see Education,□ Shakespeare's), and Ovid and Virgil and Roman comedy and Renaissance Italy seem to have been as well known and loved by the one as by the other. Spenser was more learned and concerned to instruct, Shakespeare more popular and concerned to entertain. There seem also to be small actual debts, for example, in the sub-plot of *Much Ado About Nothing* and *Twelfth Night* (but they both knew the earlier versions both in Italian and translated), in *King Lear* and *Cymbeline*. Does Shylock, torn between ducats and daughter owe something to

Malbecco in Book III, Ancient Pistol and Bardolph to Braggadocchio? Spenser seems to allude to Shakespeare in 'Colin Clouts Come Home Againe' (dated 1591, published 1595) in a list of a company of shepherds (meaning poets) as 'last not least/ A gentler shepheard may no where be found,/ Whose Muse full of high thoughts invention/ Doth like himselfe Heroically sound'; no other poet of the time had a name as 'heroic' as Shake-speare.

Stationers' Company. The association of stationers of London, which dates from the first decade of the fifteenth century, was incorporated by Royal Charter in 1557. It had a monopoly of printing for the whole of England, with the exception of books printed by the University presses of Oxford and Cambridge. All the London booksellers (which at that time meant publishers) and most of the printers were freemen of the Company.

Stationers' Register. All books had to be licensed before printing. The Stationers' Company□ kept a register of books in which members intending to print a book had to record it. In theory this assured the copyright – that that member alone had the right to print it (or have it printed). 'Pirated' editions, not registered, were intended to avoid this. Although not a complete record, the Register has been one of the most useful sources of information about Shakespeare's plays.

Stratford-upon-Avon. In Shakespeare's day Stratford was a prosperous small market town of about two thousand inhabitants. (It is still quite a small town by modern standards, and still has quite a lot of buildings which were there in Shakespeare's time, including his birthplace and his wife's home, not to mention Holy Trinity Church, the School and the Guild Hall.) It is on the River Avon, and not far away in Shakespeare's time began the beautiful woodlands of the Forest of Arden.□ The large Midlands city of Birmingham was then only a very small village, and the Midlands, now heavily industrialised, were still rural and pastoral. The town was organised and administered by a corporation of a Bailiff and fourteen aldermen, the Bailiff and one alderman acting as justices. (Shakespeare's father was Bailiff for the year in 1568–9.) The grammar school had replaced the ancient Guild School when the Guild of the Holy Cross (which had endowed and run the school as well as a 'college' for priests, the almshouse and other charities) was dissolved in 1547. Its headmaster was paid well and the school was one of the best in England. Warwick and Kenilworth were within ten miles of Stratford, and Coventry (where the mystery plays continued to be performed) within twenty. Kenilworth Castle belonged to the Earl of Leicester, a favourite of the Queen whom he entertained lavishly and with spectacular entertainment in 1575

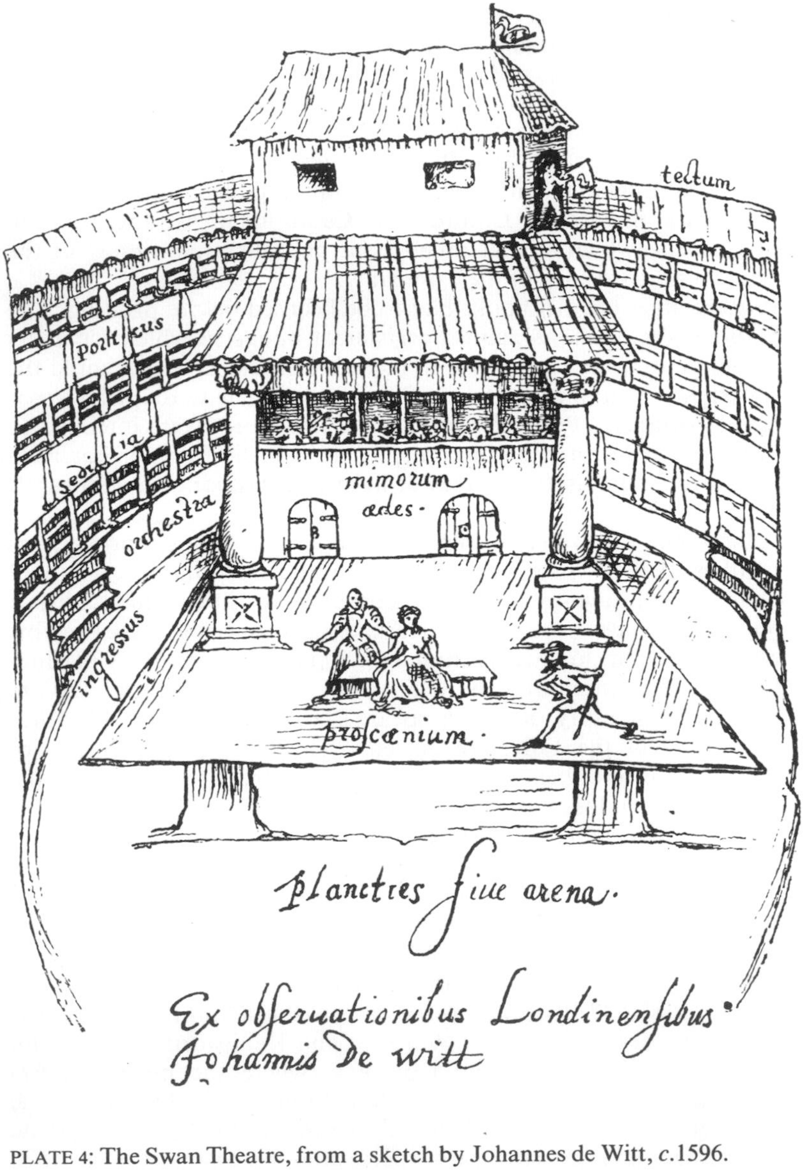

PLATE 4: The Swan Theatre, from a sketch by Johannes de Witt, *c*.1596.

when she was on a 'progress' or tour. Visiting companies of actors came to Stratford on tour several times during Shakespeare's youth, performing officially in the Guild Hall and also in inn-yards.

In 1769 the eighteenth-century actor David Garrick organised a Shakespeare Jubilee celebration in Stratford. The first Shakespeare Festival took place in 1864, the third centenary of the dramatist's birth, when six plays were performed in a temporary theatre. Ten years later the Memorial Theatre opened on Shakespeare's birthday, 23 April 1879 (the first production being of *Much Ado About Nothing*) and from then on there were regular summer seasons until the theatre was burned down in 1926. The new (and present) theatre opened on 23 April 1932. The festival has become a long season, and the Royal Shakespeare Company also performs in London at the Barbican Centre.

Swan Theatre. The Swan is the theatre best known to students of Shakespeare because of the famous drawing by the Dutch student – Johannes de Witt – of which a copy by someone else survives – the only known view of an Elizabethan theatre from inside (see Plate 4; also Playhouses□). The Swan was south of the river on the Bankside in Southwark, and was built in about 1595 near to where the Globe was built four years later. The drawing looks like a drawing or rough sketch from memory, and while it gives a good idea of the round or polygonal shape of a typical Elizabethan playhouse, shows the three galleries for spectators, the raised stage projecting half-way into the yard, the 'heavens'□ and the hut above it complete with flag and trumpeter, and two entries at the back of the stage, it cannot be completely reliable evidence – though it is the best we have – of what the Globe was like.

T

Taming of the Shrew, The. An early comedy, the Arden editor in 1981 claiming it as the earliest and proposing 1589. Internal evidence of assured skilful writing perhaps rebuts that claim. It probably dates from between 1592 and 1594. It has an *Induction*, the only example in Shakespeare, though common in other dramatists. A drunken tinker, Christopher Sly, is found and removed by a lord to his great house, where for the amusement of the lord, he is dressed in fine clothes and made to believe he is a great gentleman. Members of a travelling theatrical company which arrives are involved, a boy actor impersonating the supposed wife of the drunkard, who is persuaded that he has slept for fifteen years. The play of the taming of the shrew is a play presented before Sly, who briefly interrupts at the end of Scene 1 but then is heard – and in most productions seen – no more.

Act I: A young gentleman, Lucentio, has come to Padua with his servant Tranio to study. He quickly falls in love at first sight with Baptista's younger daughter Bianca. Her elder sister, Katherina, is such a shrew that Baptista has decided that the younger daughter must be kept at home and must not marry until her sister is disposed of in marriage. Bianca's suitors, Hortensio and the 'pantaloon' Gremio, forget their rivalry and decide to join in finding a husband for Katherina. Baptista asks for suggestions about tutors for Bianca, and Lucentio plans to disguise himself – changing clothes with his servant Tranio – and present himself as a tutor. There now arrives in Padua a friend of Hortensio's, Petruchio, who is looking for a wife – a rich one. Hortensio immediately tells him of Katherina, but also warns him of her shrewishness; Petruchio, however, is not deterred. Hortensio and Gremio agree to help to pay the costs of Petruchio's wooing.

Act II: Petruchio asks Baptista for Katherina's hand, declaring he is 'as peremptory as she proud-minded'. He presents Hortensio in disguise as a music-tutor for Bianca, Gremio likewise presenting Lucentio, disguised as 'Cambio'. Things are further complicated when Tranio, disguised as Lucentio, presents himself as a suitor for Bianca. When Hortensio returns and tells that the shrew has broken the lute over his head, Petruchio admires her spirit the more, and when she enters, he woos her with wit and rough humour, affecting to find her mild and sweet as well as 'pleasant, gamesome', and declares they must be married, and on the coming Sunday, entirely ignoring her angry refusal. Gremio and Tranio-Lucentio then compete for Bianca's hand, declaring what riches they can assure her; Baptista finds Tranio-Lucentio has more to offer, and will accept him provided he can bring guarantees from his father.

Act III: Lucentio and Hortensio, both in disguise, vie with each other in 'teaching' Bianca; the former declares his identity and love secretly while pretending to translate Ovid, the other in a musical deceit, and Bianca gives Lucentio some encouragement. On the Sunday, Petruchio arrives deliberately late for his wedding, and grotesquely mounted and clad. He refuses to change, forces the wedding on, at which, we are told, he behaves with wild impropriety, and whirls the protesting Katherina away without waiting for the marriage feast.

Act IV: Petruchio brings Katherina to his house, tired and dirty after a disastrous ride, where he finds fault with everything, including the food, and hales her off to bed unfed, returning to tell the audience of his further plans to 'curb her mad and headstrong humour'. In

Padua, two of the disguised suitors, Hortensio and Tranio/Lucentio, accept that Bianca loves the disguised Lucentio and 'vow/ Never to woo her more'. Lucentio's other servant, Biondello, having been instructed to find an old man to impersonate Lucentio's father Vincentio and to 'guarantee' the fortune offered for Bianca, brings in a Pedant who agrees to help in the tricking. Petruchio continues his 'taming' of Katherina, denying her sleep and taunting her with promises of food and new clothes which he then withdraws. In Padua, old Baptista is successfully deceived into thinking the Pedant is Vincentio, and so into agreeing to Bianca's marriage to Lucentio. Meanwhile the persecution of Katherina as she and Petruchio journey back to Padua has come to an end when Katherina suddenly stops being obstinate and contradictory ('And be it moon, or sun, or what you please/ And if you please to call it a rush-candle,/ Henceforth I vow it shall be so for me.'). On the way they encounter the true Vincentio, Lucentio's father, also journeying to Padua to see his son; Petruchio greets him warmly, saying they are now related for Lucentio has married Katherina's sister.
Act V: Lucentio and Bianca slip off to the priest to be married, as arranged by Biondello. Petruchio, Katherina and Vincentio arrive and go to Baptista's house where the true and the false Vincentio – the Pedant – confront each other. Lucentio's servant Tranio, still in his master's clothes, appears, to add to the confusions, which are cleared up by the entry of Lucentio, now safely married to Bianca. The last scene is devoted to a banquet, celebrating the marriage of the two sisters, and of Hortensio to his widow. A discussion of wifely obedience leads to a wager, which Katherina the tamed shrew wins for Petruchio by her meekness; then, at Petruchio's bidding, she tells 'these headstrong women/ What duty they do owe their lords', in a noble speech presenting the Elizabethan and Renaissance view: 'Such duty as the subject owes the prince/ Even such a woman oweth to her husband.'

SOURCES   A play called *The Taming of a Shrew* (published 1594) was long thought to be the source but is now recognised as a 'bad' quarto.□ The main plot of the taming is common in folk-tales – its main elements the successful younger daughter, the taming of the shrew, the test of bridal obedience and the accompanying wager – and it is neither necessary nor practicable to expect a direct source. The sub-plot of the disguised secret wooing and the other attendant intrigues come from *Supposes* (1566) by George Gascoigne (1542–77), itself derived from *I Suppositi* by Ariosto (1474–1533), but of course with Shakespeare's usual increments of comic complication.

TEXT   The First Folio□ (1623), the text probably being set up from a transcript of Shakespeare's own but with some annotation by the theatre's book-keeper or prompter, without its actually being the prompt-book.□

Tempest, The. A late romance of late 1610 or 1611.

Act I: A vessel carrying Alonso, King of Naples, his son Ferdinand, his brother Sebastian, old Gonzalo and Antonio the usurping Duke of Milan and others is caught in a tremendous storm near an island; they abandon ship. In the second scene we learn that the storm has been summoned by magic art by Prospero, one-time Duke of Milan, in order to wreck close by the shore of the island he now inhabits his wicked brother Antonio the usurper and his confederate Alonso, King of Naples. Prospero in front of his cave, dressed in his magic-making robes, tells his daughter Miranda how twelve years ago, when she was only three, he and she had been set adrift in a boat after his brother Antonio had seized the dukedom; the noble old Gonzalo, forced to superintend this action, had secretly provided them with food and water, clothes and other necessaries and some of the magical books Prospero had devoted himself to (to the neglect of his ducal responsibilities). Prospero now charms his daughter asleep and summons Ariel his 'airy spirit', who reports how he has 'perform'd . . . the tempest' on Prospero's orders; he reassures him that all are safe and the ship itself with its mariners hidden 'safely in harbour', and reports also that he has dispersed the wrecked voyagers in different parts of the island. Ariel, whom Prospero when he first arrived had freed from a cloven pine, in which he had been set by the Circe-like witch Sycorax, now dead, the previous occupant of the isle, now asks for his freedom, but Prospero requires other services of him: he is to make himself 'like a nymph o' th' sea' and bring Ferdinand, Prince of Naples, to him. Meanwhile, Prospero wakes Miranda and they visit Caliban, son of the witch Sycorax, 'a savage and deformed slave', who curses them but also strangely speaks some poetic imaginative lines about 'his' island, on which he thinks Prospero a usurper as well as tyrant. Ariel, invisible, leads Ferdinand by song ('Come unto these yellow sands'). Amazed to be alive after the storm, he is further amazed at the sight of Miranda, with whom he falls in love, as she with him; Prospero intends and hopes for this, but fears 'lest too light winning/ Make the prize light' and seems to disapprove, and to treat the young prince harshly.

Act II: In another part of the island, Alonso, his brother Sebastian, Antonio (Prospero's wicked usurping brother), old Gonzalo and several courtiers discuss their escape from drowning. Alonso bewails the supposed loss of his son Ferdinand; Sebastian and

Antonio mock Gonzalo. Ariel comes, invisible, and with 'solemn music' lulls all asleep except Sebastian and Antonio. The latter proposes that Sebastian should take advantage of this opportunity and kill his brother in order to get the throne of Naples, as he himself had gained the dukedom of Milan by planning the drowning of Prospero twelve years before. Antonio is to kill the sleeping Alonso, Sebastian the faithful Gonzalo; the other lords will, they think, prove acquiescent. As they draw their swords Ariel re-enters, invisible, and wakens Gonzalo, and the others wake; the plotters explain that they had heard the sound of wild beasts.

Bringing wood for Prospero, Caliban encounters another survivor from the ship, Trinculo, a jester. Frightened, Caliban lies on the ground; Trinculo, seeking shelter from an approaching storm, finds him, thinks him a poor monster of the island and crawls under his cloak. Another survivor, Stephano, a butler who has escaped on a butt of sherry and is drunk, turns up, finds the two-voiced, four-legged 'monster' is made up of his friend Trinculo and the strange Caliban, gives them both drink, and Caliban quickly worships him as master and god and drunkenly swears to serve Prospero no longer.

Act III: Ferdinand, put to carrying and piling logs, declares his love to Miranda, and she hers for him. Prospero looks on, quietly 'rejoicing'. Caliban, Stephano and Trinculo, all drunk, are watched by Ariel, invisible, as they develop a plot to kill Prospero; then Stephano will marry Miranda and rule with the monster and jester as his viceroys. They are bewildered by Ariel's invisible interventions, but go off to seek Prospero, whom Ariel of course will warn of the plot. In another part of the island the other plotters Antonio and Sebastian are still resolved, when opportunity shall offer, to carry out their plan to kill Alonso and Gonzalo. Prospero appears above, and 'several strange shapes, bringing in a banquet' salute them and dance before them, inviting them to eat. When they go to do so, in a sudden burst of thunder and lightning Ariel appears 'like a Harpy' (a mythological avenging beast with eagle body and woman's face), causes the banquet to vanish and denounces Alonso, Antonio and Sebastian as 'three men of sin' brought to the island by Destiny. He charges them with the crime against Prospero, tells Alonso of the loss of Ferdinand and calls on them to repent. The watching Prospero commends Ariel's performing of this task. Alonso is stricken by guilt and grief, and rushes off to drown himself, followed by Sebastian and Antonio, and then by Gonzalo who calls on the others to pursue all three and 'hinder them from what this ecstasy [madness] / May now provoke them to'.

Act IV: Prospero expresses his gratification at the mutual love of

Miranda and Ferdinand, and acknowledges his stern treatment of the latter, but repeats his warning that they must not anticipate the wedding night. He calls Ariel to bring the lesser spirits, who then appear before him and the lovers in a masque celebrating marriage – as Ceres, Juno, Iris, nymphs and harvesters. Prospero interrupts the final dance as he remembers 'that foul conspiracy/Of the beast Caliban and his confederates'. Ariel comes to report that he has led Caliban and the other two, drunk, into a filthy pond, and then brings out on Prospero's orders a lot of gaudy clothes which he hangs on a line in front of Prospero's cave. The conspirators come, and despite Caliban's dignified pleadings, the other two squabble over the garments which they mean to steal, and are driven out by more spirits in the 'shape of dogs and hounds, hunting them about'. Prospero, now that all his enemies lie at his mercy, tells Ariel that he shall soon have his freedom.

Act V: Prospero in his magic robes awaits the conclusion of his 'project'. Ariel tells him that he has the distracted King and his followers prisoners in the lime grove near the cell. Their misery and grief are such that Ariel thinks if Prospero saw it his 'affections/ Would become tender'; he says 'Mine would, sir, were I human.' Prospero tells Ariel that now the malefactors are penitent, he has achieved his purpose and 'the rarer action is/ In virtue than in vengeance'. Left alone while Ariel releases them he passes in his mind over the magical powers he has enjoyed and then abjures 'this rough magic', saying that he intends to destroy his magical staff and book. To music Ariel leads the King and his followers into the magic ring Prospero has made outside his cell. He affectionately greets 'Holy Gonzalo, honourable man,' his 'true preserver' twelve years ago, rebukes Alonso and Sebastian and his own brother Antonio for their cruel act against him – and forgives them. He is dressed then by Ariel in his costume as Duke of Milan, and sends Ariel to bring the Master and boatswain of the ship. Alonso, having begged for and been granted pardon, still grieves over the loss of his son, until Prospero reveals to view Ferdinand and Miranda playing chess. The happy reunion that takes place is interrupted first by the entry of the ship's master, amazed and reporting that the battered ship is miraculously restored (the final magic work of Ariel), and then by Stephano, Trinculo and Caliban driven in by Ariel, Caliban fearful of punishment and chiding himself for his folly in mistaking them for gods and conspiring against his master. Prospero invites the royal party for the night before they set sail for Italy, and finally releases Ariel.

SOURCES   There is no positive source, and a German play, performed before 1605 but not published until 1618, *Die Schöne Sidea* by Jacob

Ayrer, containing a magician, his daughter who falls in love with a captive prince and a happy ending, is no longer thought of as connected with *The Tempest*, which has many ingredients found in pastoral tragicomedy of the *commedia dell'arte*:□ magician, distant island, spirits, a cave, storms, and so on. It is still not known how much *commedia dell'arte* drama could actually have been seen in England; yet the relationship of *The Tempest* to such scenarios seems clear. Some pamphlets dealing with the wreck of the ship 'The Sea-Venture' on the coast of Bermuda, and Montaigne's□ (1533–92) *Essays*, translated by Giovanni Florio□ (?1553–1625) and published in 1603 seem to have been well known by Shakespeare.

TEXT   First Folio□ (1623) – the first play in the volume, carefully printed, with unusually detailed stage-directions, from a good manuscript.

Terence. Publius Terentius Afer (?195–159BC) was born in Carthage, brought to Rome as a slave but educated and freed by an enlightened master. Like Plautus, who died at about the same time as or shortly after Terence was born, his theatrical origins were in Greek comedy, especially Menander. His plays (six are known, of which *Phormio*, *Andria*, *Eunuchus* and *Adelphi* are the most famous) use similar stock comic situations of intrigue, deceit, mistaken identity, and employ stock characters, wily servants, braggart soldiers, and young lovers. Terence was studied and performed in grammar schools, and Shakespeare must first have encountered his work at school. The plays of Terence were often acted in the universities and at Court early in the sixteenth century and influenced the developing native comedy. The type or kind of comedy, plot and character influenced Shakespeare, who did not really use Terence as a direct source.

Tetralogy, the First (tetralogy, from Greek, meaning 'four writings'). The four plays *Henry VI* (in three separate parts) and *Richard III* dealing with the Wars of the Roses,□ 1454–85. The first tetralogy, written between 1589 and 1592, deals with later events than the second tetralogy (see below); it deals with the events – the civil wars of rival but related families and their followers – of the second half of the fifteenth century.

Tetralogy, the Second. The four plays *Richard II*, *Henry IV* (in two separate parts) and *Henry V*, dealing with the usurpation of Richard II's throne by Bolingbroke (Henry IV), and the Welsh, Scottish and other rebellions and the troubled reign that followed, concluding with Henry V's triumphant military successes in recapturing large areas of France which had been lost. The second tetralogy, written between 1596 and 1599, deals with earlier events than the first tetralogy (see above), with happenings from about 1390 to 1420.

Timon of Athens. A tragedy probably of about 1607 for it recalls *King Lear* and may have come between it and the Roman plays, though some would place it earlier, near to *Troilus and Cressida* (1601–2) because of its bitter and cynical view of humanity, and some would put it later, thinking that the style resembles the freer verse and more complex and metaphorical poetry of the late romances (1609–11).

Act I: A poet, a painter, and a jeweller meet outside the house of Timon, a rich and generous Athenian, each bringing an offering: book, picture, jewel. Senators of Athens come, and enter Timon's house while the others discuss the quality of the presents they are carrying and the generosity of Timon. Timon emerges, and receives requests which he readily accedes to, sending money to pay off a debt for Ventidius and giving money to help a young man to marry. A discordant note is struck by Apemantus, a churlish railing philosopher, who condemns flattery and stands for 'plain-dealing', but he is evidently on close terms with Timon who genially responds to his trenchant, mordant jokes. Alcibiades, an Athenian captain, arrives and is invited to join the great feast Timon is giving. At the feast – during which there is a short masque of ladies as Amazons presented by Cupid – Timon generously declines to take back the sum given to Ventidius, whose father's sudden death has made wealthy, and continues to dispense lavish gifts and to receive some insincere ones. Apemantus continues his mocking criticism and warnings, and his own anxious steward Flavius in asides lets us know that Timon's fortune is almost totally spent.

Act II: Senators, 'friends' and usurers begin to press Timon for repayment of sums borrowed. When he refers them to his steward he is amazed to learn from him not only of his debts but that if all his assets were disposed of the return would not add up to half the amount he owes. However, he is sure that those to whom he has been so generous will tide him over, and he asks his steward to go to the Senators who had courted him and sends servants to Lucius, Lucullus and Sempronius. But the steward has already approached the Senators and been denied. Timon tells him to go to Ventidius (whose debt he had paid in the first scene, and who had told him, in the second scene, that his father's sudden death had made him wealthy).

Act III: Lucullus, Lucius and Sempronius each refuse help to Timon, giving his messengers different reasons: one, that he had always warned Timon of the folly of his lavish generosity, and now is 'no time to lend money'; another that unluckily he has just invested his money and cannot help; the third that he is angry at being the third to be sent to, and only after others had been approached. Then servants of many rich men are sent to Timon's house to seek repayment; they see the steward leaving, muffled in a cloak; ('I have no more to reckon, he to spend'). Timon in a rage appears, drives off the suppliant servants, and bids the steward go to his one-time friends and beneficiaries and 'invite them all, let in the tide / Of knaves once more, to one more feast'.

In the Senate, Alcibiades pleads for mercy for a friend, a valiant and loyal soldier, who is under sentence of death for killing a man in an angry quarrel. The Senators ignore his pleas – that 'pity is the virtue of the law' and the man has 'done fair service, / And slain in fight many of your enemies' – and angered by Alcibiades's persistence, they banish him. Senators and other friends and beneficiaries come to Timon's house, with protestations of friendship and sorrowful apologies for having been temporarily unable to help him when he was in need. Timon presents a noble-looking table of silver covered dishes, recites a bitterly ironic 'grace' and reveals that the dishes contain only warm water which he dashes in the faces of these 'Courteous destroyers, affable wolves, meek bears', driving them out in scornful fury.

Act IV: Timon leaves Athens, cursing it as he goes. His faithful steward and several other servants of Timon lament his ruin and departure, and the steward resolves to seek for him to serve him. Living wild in the woods, Timon, while digging for roots for food, turns up gold, and is disturbed by the sound of a drum. Alcibiades enters, on his way to assault Athens. Now completely misanthropic (and so naming himself to the soldier), Timon rebuffs Alcibiades's friendship, calls on him to destroy Athens completely and gives him some of the newly found gold; and give some also, mockingly, to the soldier's two mistresses, who flatter and beg for it though they had begun by reviling him. Now to Timon comes Apemantus who urges him not to be an Apemantus but to be 'a flatterer now, and seek to thrive / By that which has undone thee'. In a long conversation, Apemantus shows his honesty and clearsightedness beneath his railing tone; as earlier he had chided Timon for being so trusting and gullible, so now he points to the extravagance of Timon's reaction in misanthropy: 'The middle of humanity thou never knewest, but the extremity of both ends.' Timon has indeed become an Apemantus, even exceeding him in bitter abuse and scorn, and drives the philosopher away.

Some thieves, having heard rumour of Timon's hoard, come to beg or to steal some of it. Timon gives them some gold, urging them to continue in their thieving ways since everything in nature steals from something else – sun from the sea, moon from the sun, and so on – and mankind is rotten ('All that you meet are thieves'). Now Timon's faithful steward comes. He wonders 'Is yond despis'd and ruinous man my lord?/ Full of decay and failing?' Timon does not recognise him at first, but when he does, acknowledges that there is at least one honest man in the world – 'So true, so just and now so comfortable [comforting]'. He gives him gold but tells him to 'Hate all, curse all, show charity to none', and drives him away not to earn his curses.

Act V: Others have heard of Timon's gold. Poet and painter, thinking he is wealthy again, come to ingratiate themselves, and flee from his blows. Then come two senators as emissaries to entreat him to return to Athens, and indeed to be their captain against Alcibiades's threat. He plays with them, finally saying that the people of Athens may 'stop affliction' by hanging themselves. He tells them to report to Athens that 'Timon hath made his everlasting mansion/Upon the beached verge of the salt flood' (prepared his own grave on the sea shore), and ends 'Sun, hide thy beams, Timon hath done his reign.'

Alcibiades appears with his army before Athens. Senators appear on the walls; with flattery and entreaties they attempt to excuse themselves and invite Alcibiades to enter and to take one life in ten if it is revenge he wants, but only to kill those who have offended him. The soldier is magnanimous and agrees to this, when word is brought of Timon's death, and of his epitaph, a final curse. Alcibiades pauses to refer to 'noble Timon, of whose memory/ Hereafter more' and declares he will 'use the olive with my sword,/ Make war breed peace'.

SOURCE In Sir Thomas North's□ (?1535–1601) translation (1579) of Amyot's French translation of Plutarch's□ *Lives*, in the 'Life of Marcus Antonius' there is a digression on 'the life and example of *Timon Misanthropos* the Athenian' from which Shakespeare took a number of details, especially the solitary life, Apemantus, the adjuration to Athenians to hang themselves, the sea-shore grave and the epitaph. Probably from the 'Life of Alcibiades' he got the disgracing of Alcibiades and his return to attack the city. But he seems to have made most use of the dialogue *Timon Misanthropus* of Lucian (*c*.AD125–90), the Greek satirist, probably in a Latin or French translation. The Timon story was well known in Elizabethan times, there being many literary allusions to it.

TEXT The First Folio□ (1623), probably printed partly from Shakespeare's 'foul papers'□ and partly from a transcript of them. Some think the play unfinished; certainly it is fairly short and it finishes abruptly with Timon's vague death and Alcibiades's return to Athens, but by that time the satirical and moral point has been clearly established.

Tiring-house. The room or rooms in the Elizabethan playhouse where the actors 'tired' (attired, costumed) themselves, and waited until their call to go on stage. It was pretty certainly behind the wall at the back of the stage, there being access to it through two or more doors from the stage, and also direct access, at the back of the theatre, to the street. The prompter probably stationed himself in the tiring-house, and here the 'plot'□ was hung up.

Titus Andronicus. An early tragedy of 1588 or 1589.

Act I: The play opens with the two sons of the late Roman Emperor, Saturninus and Bassianus, in contention about which shall succeed to the throne. The tribune Marcus Andronicus advances the claims of his great brother Titus, hero of the ten years' war against the Goths which has just ended. Titus enters with his four sons (and the coffin of a fifth) and his prisoners, Tamora, Queen of the Goths and her two sons and Aaron her Moorish favourite. One of Titus's sons asks for the killing of Tamora's oldest son as a sacrifice, and this is acceded to, despite her tearful pleas. Titus declines to be a candidate for the throne and offers his support of Saturninus, who declares his wish to make Lavinia, daughter of Titus, his queen; but she is claimed by Saturninus's brother Bassianus who promptly abducts her, helped by her brothers, one of whom is slain by Titus in the consequent scuffle. Saturninus, now emperor, declares his intention of marrying Tamora. The brother and sons of Titus plead with him (Titus) for honourable burial of the son he has slain; reluctant to accord this honour to one 'basely slain in brawls', Titus gives in with bad grace. Saturninus, bent on revenge against both Titus and Bassianus, is persuaded to dissemble by his newly-wed wife Tamora, and the act ends in seeming amity.

Act II: Two of Tamora's sons, Chiron and Demetrius, quarrel over Lavinia (now married to Bassianus), whom both lust after. Aaron suggests they may both have her, and that they should lie in wait during the forthcoming royal hunt. On the day of the hunt Tamora waits amorously for Aaron, but the Moor is not thus inclined, as he brings word that Bassianus is to be killed that day and his wife Lavinia raped. Bassianus and Lavinia appear, and contemptuously revile Tamora over her 'black' lover. When her two sons arrive on their foul mission, Tamora tells them that she has been enticed thither by Bassianus and Lavinia, who intend to torture and kill her, whereupon they instantly stab Bassianus, dumping his corpse in a deep hole in the wood, and hale Lavinia away to rape her. Aaron returns, with two of the sons of Titus Andronicus. One falls into the hole, and the other, helping him out, also falls. Aaron disappears to fetch the Emperor, who assumes, as Aaron intended, that the two brothers have killed his brother Bassianus, and orders their arrest

and trial. Lavinia, raped, her hands cut off and her tongue cut out, is
found by Marcus Andronicus.

Act III: Old Titus pleads for his sons' reprieve to the judges as they
proceed to the place of execution, but in vain. An older son, Lucius,
comes to him; he is now banished for attempting to rescue the two.
To them come Titus's brother Marcus and daughter, the mutilated
Lavinia, and a moving scene of grief and love takes place, until
Aaron enters with word from the Emperor, that if one of them will
cut off his hand and send it to Saturninus, the two sons will be freed
and returned to their father. Lucius and Marcus both offer to
sacrifice a hand, but while they go off to fetch an axe, Titus gets
Aaron to cut off his right hand and sends it to the emperor. Very
shortly the hand is returned to him together with the heads of both
the sons. Two scenes of pain, grief and despair follow, in which
Titus despatches his son Lucius to the Goths to 'raise a pow'r,/ To
be reveng'd on Rome and Saturnine'.

Act IV: Lavinia contrives to turn the pages of a copy of Ovid's
Metamorphoses□ and to scratch names in the sand to tell Titus and
Marcus exactly what befell her and to name the two wicked sons of
Tamora. Titus vows revenge. Young Lucius, son of Lucius and
grandson of Titus, has been with his grandfather for several scenes,
since his father set off to ally with the Goths. Now he is sent with
fine weapons as presents for Chiron and Demetrius with a Latin
quotation which they fail to understand but which Aaron realises
points to their guilt (and incriminates him). Trumpets sound to
announce the birth of a child to Tamora, and a nurse hastens in with
the baby, looking for Aaron, for it is a blackamoor child, fathered
by him. Chiron and Demetrius are outraged and go to kill it but are
quelled by the Moor, who swiftly kills the nurse and dominates
them; he resolves to exchange the child for one born yesterday to the
wife of a Moor known to him, yet a fair-haired child, taking the
blackamoor baby away. Titus seems to have gone mad, spending his
time sending arrows into the air which bear written messages – the
goddess of justice has left earth, and the great gods are solicited 'To
send down Justice for to wreak our wrongs'. A clown comes and
Titus sends him with a written message to the Emperor. The latter,
alarmed by Titus's mad behaviour, receives the message and
immediately news is brought that Lucius, now general of the Goths,
is marching on Rome with a large army. Saturninus's alarm is
allayed by Tamora who says she 'will enchant the old Andronicus'
and 'temper him with all the art I have/ To pluck good Lucius from
the warlike Goths'.

Act V: Lucius at the head of an army of Goths approaches Rome.
To him comes a Goth, leading Aaron who is carrying his blackamoor

child in his arms. At first Lucius orders 'the incarnate devil' and the child to be hanged, but is persuaded by Aaron to spare the child and give him a chance of life by letting him tell of the terrible things that had happened – much of which would never be known if Aaron were killed. Aaron then tells his tale, 'of murthers, rapes and massacres, / Acts of black night, abominable deeds, / Complots of mischief, treason, villainies'. An emissary comes from the Emperor, craving a parley at the house of Titus Andronicus, to which Lucius agrees.

Tamora, disguised as Revenge, with her sons as Murder and Rape, comes to Titus. She thinks to dominate him in his 'madness', and having done so, to use him to remove the threat posed by the arrival of his son Lucius and the Goths. Titus, though, is not mad, and secretly recognises Tamora and her sons, but he agrees to her suggestion that Lucius should be asked to a solemn feast at his house, to which the Emperor and the Empress and her sons will also be invited. He already has a plan to 'o'erreach them in their own devices'. Titus has Tamora's two sons bound, and cuts their throats. He has brought Lavinia in, and she holds a basin between her stumps to catch the blood of her two ravishers. At the feast which follows, Titus appears as the cook. He brings himself to kill his own daughter, the ill-used Lavinia, and so ends her misery and dishonour. He then calls on the Emperor Saturninus and Tamora to eat the pie, revealing that its meat is the flesh of her two sons, stabs Tamora, is immediately killed by Saturninus, who is then killed by Lucius. Titus's brother Marcus and Lucius tell the people of Rome of the terrible happenings. Lucius is hailed as Emperor. Aaron is condemned to death by starvation, set 'breast-deep in earth'; the other dead are given burial but Tamora's body is to be thrown 'forth to beasts and birds to prey'.

SOURCES No definite source is known. An eighteenth-century chap-book, only discovered in 1936, *The History of Titus Andronicus*, must have derived from the same source as Shakespeare's lost one. The play is much more concentrated and powerful, the characters of Saturninus and Aaron especially are much strengthened and the actions of Lucius invented. The tragic violation of Lavinia, as Shakespeare makes clear, owes much to the story of Philomela, Procne and Tereus in Ovid's *Metamorphoses*□ VI; the serving of the dreadful feast may have come from Seneca's□ *Thyestes*.

TEXT The play was first published in quarto,□ known as the First Quarto, in 1594; this is considered the best text, though it lacks the moving second scene of Act III which only appeared in the First Folio□ (1623). Some (including Dr Johnson) did not like to think this savage play to have been written by Shakespeare. Others think there was a collaborator, either Peele or Kyd. I detect some touches of Marlowe.□ But crude though it often is, it is a powerful, moving and imaginative play, however flawed and brutal.

Troilus and Cressida. What is it? A comedy, a tragedy or a problem play?□ The title-page of the first Quarto (1609) calls it a 'Historie', but an epistle to the reader places it among the 'wittie' comedies. In the First Folio□ (1623) it is not included in the list of plays but is printed as the first of the Tragedies. It was probably written in late 1602.

Act I: The Trojan war, fought because Prince Paris of Troy had carried off Helen, wife of Menelaus King of Sparta, has now been going on for seven years. We first see some Trojans: another son of Priam king of Troy, Troilus, is deeply in love with Cressida and hopes her uncle Pandarus will help his suit. (Her father Calchas, a Trojan priest, has gone over to the Greek side.) In a soliloquy she reveals her love for Troilus, and her determination still 'to hold off', for 'Men prize the thing ungain'd more than it is.'

In the Greek camp, the leader Agamemnon comments on the disappointing progress of the war and seeks remedies. Ulysses in a famous speech refers to factions and disputes among them. The proper order or 'degree' is not maintained: 'Take but degree away, / untune that string,/ And hark what discord follows'; he declares 'Troy in our weakness stands, not in her strength'. He points chiefly to great Achilles's arrogant subversive non-co-operation, and Nestor also refers to Ajax, 'grown self-will'd'. Aeneas comes from Troy, bearing a challenge to single combat from Hector. The challenge is meant for Achilles, but Nestor falls in with the subtle Aeneas's proposal that Achilles should not be honoured by appearing as the Greeks' champion but that a rigged lottery shall 'let blockish Ajax draw/ The sort to fight with Hector', which will teach Achilles a lesson.

Act II: We meet more Greeks: first the 'dull brainless Ajax' with Thersites, a deformed, scurrilous and disgusting 'jester', evil-tongued, cynical and abusive, but acutely diagnosing follies and pretensions; and then Achilles with his intimate friend young Patroclus. In Troy, King Priam reports on an offer from the Greeks, brought by Nestor, of immediate peace if Helen is returned to them. Hector urges acceptance, for they have lost many more men than the cause warrants: 'she is not worth what she doth cost/ The keeping'. Troilus thinks honour demands rejection, reminding the assembly that all had 'thought meet/ Paris should do some vengeance on the Greeks'. Their visionary sister Cassandra enters prophesying woe, that Troy will burn unless the war is ended and

Helen yielded up. Paris asserts the glory of Helen and urges that they should in honour fight for her, and Troilus speaks of her as 'a theme of honour and renown,/ A spur to valiant and magnanimous deeds'. Hector, although still thinking it would be morally right to return Helen, allows himself to be persuaded, and then tells the court of his challenge to the Greeks. Agamemnon and other leaders come to Achilles's tent, but the warrior, 'lion-sick – sick of proud heart', refuses to see them. Ulysses is sent in to him and rebuffed. Agamemnon then proposes that Ajax try; but Ulysses, abetted by Nestor, by fulsome praise persuades Ajax that he would demean himself by so doing.

Act III: Paris and Helen dally while most of 'the gallantry of Troy' are engaged in action. Pandarus now effects the love-meeting at last of Troilus and Cressida, he nervous and breathless with love, she much more assured; he is, as he says, 'as true as truth's simplicity,/ And simpler than the infancy of truth'. They pledge themselves each to the other. He envisages a future time when 'As true as Troilus' will be proverbial, she calls on the future to say of false maids 'As false as Cressid' if she should ever be false, and Pandarus, sealing the bargain between them (as he calls it) wants the name pander to be used of all 'brokers-between' if they should prove false. Cressida's father Calchas in the Greek camp asks for her to be exchanged for Antenor, a high-ranking Trojan captured the day before. Agememnon agrees, sending Diomedes to the Trojans to request the exchange. Achilles is deliberately snubbed, at Ulysses's suggestion, by Agamemnon, Nestor and Ajax. Ulysses explains to him that he is now outdone by Ajax, and urges Achilles, indirectly, to rouse himself. Thersites is sent by Achilles to Ajax to ask him to invite the Trojan lords, after the single combat, to visit him.

Act IV: The Greek Diomedes, come to Troy to negotiate the exchange of Cressida for Antenor, converses with Paris, bluntly damning Helen – for her dishonour and because 'For every false drop in her bawdy veins/ A Grecian's life hath sunk' – and the Trojans equally. Troilus and Cressida on the morning of their first night together are visited by a suggestively joking Pandarus, but very soon they learn the shocking news that Cressida is to be exchanged and sent to the Greek lines. The lovers part in grief, exchanging oaths of constancy. Troilus gives her a sleeve and she him a glove to wear, and he, while warning her of the 'Grecian youths', says he will often bribe the Greek sentries in order to visit her at night. Diomedes, come to escort her away, openly praises her beauty and is rebuked by Troilus. But immediately we see her arriving in the Greek camp, and being kissed in turn by most of the Greek leaders. She receives their salutations gamesomely and coquettishly jokes with them, to the disgust of Ulysses. Great Hector arrives for the single combat, which only lasts one inconclusive bout, for Hector, declaring that Ajax is related to Priam, is unwilling to shed a kinsman's blood. In an atmosphere of temporary amity, only Achilles remains hostile, and boasts that he will next day destroy Hector. At the end of the scene Troilus discovers from Ulysses where Cressida is in the Greek lines, and also that Diomedes 'gives all gaze and bent of amorous view' on her.

Act V: Achilles receives the Greek leaders at his tent at night. Diomedes slips away, followed by Ulysses (who knows he is going to Calchas's tent) and Troilus. Thersites gives his usual base reductive view of what is going on ('Diomed's a false-hearted knave . . . They say he keeps a Trojan drab, and uses the traitor Calchas' tent . . . Nothing but lechery') and follows. Then all three witness Diomedes's expert lascivious courtship of Cressida and her wanton and willing response to it. She even gives him as a token the sleeve Troilus had given her. An appalled Troilus, hardly able to believe it is his Cressida, at last curses her and vows to kill Diomedes, and again a scene ends with scornful comment from Thersites: 'Lechery, lechery, still wars and lechery!' In Troy, Hector's wife Andromache and then his sister the prophetess Cassandra try to persuade him not to go to battle that day, and are joined in this by King Priam; all have had ominous dreams or forebodings, which Hector ignores, although he tries to dissuade his younger brother Troilus from going. Pandarus brings Troilus a letter from Cressida, which he reads and then tears up, muttering 'Words, words, mere words, no matter from the heart'. He goes to battle, meets Diomedes, and they fight their way offstage. In a series of short scenes we observe Agamemnon lamenting the loss of many Greeks, including Patroclus slain by Hector; Achilles, angered at this loss and fiercely arming to avenge him; Achilles attacking Hector; Menelaus and Paris fighting; and Thersites from time to time appearing to rail and curse and scorn – often comically. After a strange encounter with a sumptuously armoured Greek whom he slays, Hector takes off his own armour and is caught by Achilles and a pack of his followers, the Myrmidons, who murder him. The news of Hector's death suggests victory to Agamemnon, but to Troilus and the Trojans great grief; but also in Troilus a renewal of desperate 'hope of revenge' to 'hide our inward woe'. At the last he scornfully rejects Pandarus, who is left on the stage, old, alone and ill, as he tells us, with venereal disease.

SOURCES   Shakespeare seems to have known a number of versions of stories of the Trojan War, especially Chaucer's□ *Troilus and Criseyde* (c.1382), John Lydgate's (c.1370–1451) *Troy Book* (1412–?20), William Caxton's (1421–91) *Recuyell of the Histories of Troy* (1475), and Robert Henryson's□ (?1425–1500) *Testament of Cresseid* (which was printed in Thynne's *Chaucer* (1532) as being by Chaucer), as well as George Chapman's (*c*.1560–1634) translations of Homer, of which seven books (I, II, VII–XI) of the *Iliad* appeared in 1598. Shakespeare is most indebted to Chaucer for the love-story, to Caxton and Chapman chiefly for the Trojan War material.

TEXT   The Quarto□ (1609), very probably a transcript of Shakespeare's 'foul papers'.□ The First Folio□ (1623) text is printed from the quarto and also from some other manuscript, and, containing more and fuller stage-directions, shows revision for stage use.

Twelfth Night, or *What You Will*, a mature comedy, thought by some to have been written for performance at Court on Twelfth Night (6 January) 1601, by others for the hall of the Middle Temple on 6 January 1602.

Act I: The Duke of Illyria, Orsino, is in love with the lady Olivia, who has in the last year been bereaved by the death of her father and then of her loved brother; she maintains deep mourning and 'hath abjured the sight/ And company of men'. This information is quickly learned by Viola, who has been shipwrecked and separated from her twin brother, who, it is thought, may have been drowned. Viola decides to disguise herself and seek service as a page to Duke Orsino. Olivia has a disreputable drunken relative, Sir Toby Belch, living in her house. Her waiting-gentlewoman Maria warns him that Olivia deplores his rioting. Maria also mentions Olivia's displeasure at Belch's introduction to the house of Sir Andrew Aguecheek, who then enters; he is a rich and foolish gentleman-idler, whom Sir Toby has persuaded to woo Olivia. Within two or three days, Viola, now Cesario, has won the confidence and intimacy of Orsino, who sends 'him' to woo Olivia on his behalf; in an aside she reveals her disinclination to do so, for she has fallen in love with Orsino. Olivia, with her little 'court', Maria, Feste the clown and Malvolio her self-important and conceited steward, receives Viola, who pays court on Orsino's behalf with wit and nonchalance. Olivia is charmed by the 'page', although she still rejects Orsino's suit: ('Let him send no more/ Unless, perchance, you come to me again'); and when Viola departs she sends Malvolio after 'him' with a ring, pretending Viola had left it behind.

Act II: (Viola's twin, Sebastian, has also survived the shipwreck and has resolved to set out for Orsino's court.) When Malvolio brings Viola the ring, she realises the love complication which has formed: Orsino loves Olivia who loves Viola who loves Orsino. A drunken carousal – Belch, Aguecheek and Feste – is interrupted by Maria warning them that Olivia, sleepless, is sending the steward Malvolio to restrain them. After his intervention, drunkenly made fun of – 'Dost thou think, because thou art virtuous, there shall be no more cakes and ale?' – Maria hits on a plan to expose Malvolio's self-love, ambition and pride: she will write him a letter, as if from his mistress, which will make him think she is in love with him, and they shall be in hiding to watch his reaction. Orsino is again seen indulging his love-melancholy to the sound of music – Feste's famous song 'Come away, come away death' – and discussing love with Viola. In answer to his question Viola/Cesario admits that 'he' has been in love, with someone of about the age and colouring of Orsino, and says that 'his' father 'had a daughter loved a man' but 'she never told her love'. Maria's plot works perfectly: Sir Toby, Sir Andrew and a minor character of the household, Fabian, watch and overhear Malvolio dreaming of grandeur if only he could marry Olivia, finding the letter, and in absurd anticipation resolving to obey the injunctions in the letter and be 'strange, stout, in yellow stockings and cross-gartered'.

Act III: Viola goes again to Olivia's house, meeting Sir Toby, Sir Andrew and Maria at the gates. Olivia cannot prevent herself telling Viola/Cesario that she loves 'him'. Aguecheek, annoyed that Cesario has been admitted to Olivia's presence and he denied, is persuaded by Belch to challenge the 'youth'. Viola's brother Sebastian has been lovingly followed by Antonio and both come to Illyria; Antonio gives his friend his purse and goes to look at the town. Malvolio, grotesquely smiling, preens himself before Olivia, quoting passages from 'her' letter; she thinks he has gone mad and orders him to be looked after; Sir Toby decides to have him put in a dark room and bound. And Sir Toby advances his other little plot, emphasising the valour and sword-skill of Aguecheek to Viola and *vice versa*. The adversaries are equally reluctant, but are forced into a bout, which is interrupted by the entry of Antonio, who tries to prevent it, thinking Viola is his friend, her brother Sebastian. Antonio is arrested. Asking Viola for his money he is hurt by her mystified reply that she does not know him.

Act IV: There are further confusions as Feste addresses Sebastian as Cesario, and Sir Andrew, entering, strikes Sebastian thinking him Viola/Cesario. As the dispute grows more serious, to Sebastian's bewilderment Olivia enters and angrily dismisses the two knights, and urges Sebastian to come to her house, which to her surprise and pleasure he gladly agrees to do. Now the tricking of Malvolio develops: Feste as a curate, Sir Topas, baits him in his dark cell with Maria and Belch joining in. But soon Belch decides things have gone too far; he will be in disgrace with Olivia and he tells Feste to end the fooling. Sebastian, still bemused by the confused happenings and the loving solicitude of Olivia, agrees to go with her and a priest to his chantry and be betrothed to Olivia.

Act V: Orsino accompanied by Viola/Cesario waits at Olivia's gate hoping to see her. Antonio under arrest passes by. Orsino recognises him as a one-time enemy sea-captain, while Antonio 'recognises' Viola/Cesario as his ungrateful friend Sebastian and reviles 'him', to her perplexity. When Olivia comes, she also thinks Viola/Cesario is Sebastian to whom she has become betrothed, and when the betrothal is attested to by the priest, it is Orsino's turn to be angry with Viola/Cesario as a 'dissembling cub'. In this state of all-round confusion over mistaken identity – Viola/Cesario mistaken for Sebastian – Sir Andrew soon followed by Sir Toby rushes in calling for a surgeon; they have been wounded by 'Cesario' (that is, Sebastian). When the knights go off to have their wounds attended to, Sebastian himself appears, apologising for hurting them when they challenged him. Soon the confusions are made clear, now that brother and sister, Viola and Sebastian are both on the stage together, and are restored to each other. Orsino immediately says to Viola that as a boy 'thou hast said to me . . . Thou never shouldst love woman like to me' and Viola reasserts her love for him. Olivia is reminded of Malvolio and has him sent for, while a letter of complaint he had asked Feste (as Sir Topas) to give to her is read out. When Malvolio, bitterly indignant and hurt, is brought on, Fabian confesses that he, Maria and Sir Toby were responsible for the baiting of the steward; he also reports that Belch has married Maria. Malvolio departs angrily vowing revenge, but Orsino sends after him 'to entreat him to a peace'. Orsino then calls Viola 'Cesario' for the last time but also 'Orsino's mistress, and his fancy's queen'.

SOURCES   Barnaby Rich (?1504–1617), in his collection of eight stories *Farewell to Militarie Profession* (1581), told the story of *Apollonius and Silla* from which the main plot of Orsino-Olivia-Viola/Cesario-Sebastian comes. He had the story from Bandello□ via Belleforest's□ French translation, but it derives from an anonymous play *Gli' Ingannati* (The Deceived) acted in Siena in 1531, though the mood and tone are quite different. The festive sub-plot of the rioting Sir Toby and the baiting of the conceited steward are entirely Shakespeare's invention.

TEXT   The First Folio□ (1623), from the theatre prompt-book□ or a copy of it.

Two Gentlemen of Verona, The. An early comedy, possibly from 1592, but there seem to have been several phases, not to say versions, which show clearly in mistakes and inconsistencies in the play as we have it, and which may derive from an earlier attempt than 1592.

Act I: Valentine takes leave of Proteus, mocking his friend for being love-lorn. He is on his way to Milan. Proteus loves Julia, who is unaware of his adoration. He sends her a letter by Valentine's witty servant, Speed. Julia discusses her suitors with her maid Lucetta who praises Proteus and gives her his letter, which Julia, declaring her indifference to him, first returns and then tears up. However, left alone she pieces the letter together, and is pleased at Proteus's declaration of love. In Scene 3 Proteus is told by his father, to his dismay, that he must follow his friend Valentine to Milan.

Act II: Valentine in Milan has fallen in love with the Duke's daughter Silvia; at her behest he has written a love-letter 'to one she loves'. She wishes it had been 'writ more movingly', thus declaring her love for him, which his quick-witted servant had already realised. In Verona, Proteus's servant Launce describes the weeping of his whole family at his impending departure, and comically points out that his unfeeling dog Crab – with him on the stage – has not wept at all. Proteus arrives at Milan, meeting Valentine, Silvia and Sir Thurio, a wealthy suitor of Silvia favoured by her father. Valentine tells him he is in love, indeed betrothed to Silvia, and that they have planned to elope; he is to go with a rope ladder to her window to effect this. Left alone, Proteus reveals that he himself has suddenly fallen in love with Silvia. He quickly plots to tell the Duke of the elopement plan, so that Valentine will be banished. In Verona, Julia, longing for Proteus, decides with Lucetta to follow him to Milan, disguising herself as a page to 'prevent/ The loose encounters of lascivious men'.

Act III: Proteus, while protesting that he does it out of love for the Duke not hatred of Valentine, tells the former of his friend's plot to elope. The Duke traps Valentine and discovers the rope ladder and a letter to Silvia under his cloak, whereupon he banishes him. He does not reveal Proteus's treachery. Thurio does not prosper in his passion for Silvia, despite the removal of Valentine. The Duke, greatly wanting the match, persuades Proteus, who still falsely protests his love for his friend, to slander Valentine and praise Thurio to her, and Proteus also tutors Thurio in how to win her by flattery and poetry.

Act IV: The banished Valentine, with Speed, is ambushed in a forest by some outlaws; they are in fact gentlemen who have been banished for youthful crimes. They invite Valentine to live with them and be their chief, to which he agrees. In Milan, Proteus has been unsuccessfully wooing Silvia for himself, while pretending to be advancing Thurio's suit. Julia in boy's clothes now arrives, and secretly and to her horror observes Proteus wooing Silvia at her window after a serenade with Thurio, during which the famous song

'Who is Silvia?' is sung. Silvia angrily rejects Proteus, chiding him for his falseness to Valentine and to his own beloved Julia. Silvia resolves to flee to join Valentine, and calls on the help of Sir Eglamour, a paragon of a knight, who willingly agrees to go with her to protect her. Launce with his dog has a brief comic soliloquy about Crab's bad behaviour, interrupted by Proteus, who has unknowingly engaged Julia as his page Sebastian. Proteus sends Sebastian/Julia to Silvia with a ring, which is in fact one Julia had given him; the ring is to be in exchange for a promised portrait of Silvia. Grieving, though still doting on him ('Because I love him, I must pity him'), she goes to Silvia, who gives the picture but rejects the ring, which she knows Proteus had been given by Julia.

Act V: Silvia flees with Sir Eglamour. The Duke urges Proteus and Thurio to join him in pursuing them. Silvia is captured by Valentine's outlaws, and, before they can take her to their 'captain', is rescued by Proteus who begs his desired reward, and is about to enforce it ('I'll force thee yield to my desire') when Valentine, who has witnessed the scene, steps forward and reveals himself. His angry reproaches immediately elicit a confession of 'shame and guilt' from Proteus, who is as instantly forgiven by his friend Valentine. When Valentine, more generous still, says 'All that was mine in Silvia I give thee', Julia/Sebastian, who has been present throughout as Proteus's page, briefly falls in a swoon. She tries to cover up by saying she had neglected to give Silvia a ring from Proteus, gives him the wrong one (that which had been given her by Proteus when as lovers they had sadly parted in Verona), then produces the other ring and reveals herself. Proteus is again immediately contrite, and finds Julia even more attractive than Silvia after all. Suddenly the outlaws bring in as prisoners the Duke and Thurio: the latter immediately claims Silvia but is intimidated by Valentine and swiftly and basely relinquishes his claim. All ends in concord: Valentine gladly accepted by the Duke as Silvia's future husband, Proteus happily reunited with Julia and the outlaws pardoned at Valentine's request.

SOURCES The play is related to the 'friendship literature' or 'friendship cult' of late medieval and Renaissance literature, in which male friendship is celebrated, often as a nobler or more worthy human relationship than man-woman love. Shakespeare knew Chaucer's□ *Knight's Tale* of Palamon and Arcite (and had a part in a dramatisation of it, *The Two Noble Kinsmen*, late in his career), and probably knew the story of Titus and Gisippus 'whereby is fully declared the figure of perfect amitie' in Sir Thomas Elyot's *The Boke named the Governour* (1531), itself derived from Boccaccio's□ *Decameron*. But a chief source, though not directly, is

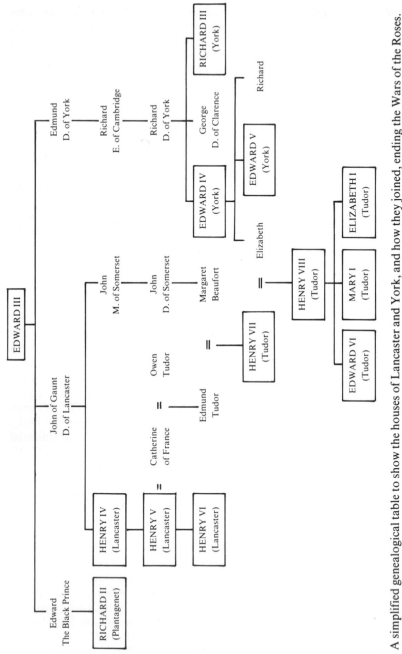

A simplified genealogical table to show the houses of Lancaster and York, and how they joined, ending the Wars of the Roses. (Reigning monarchs are shown in capital letters and boxes; D=Duke, M=Marquis, E=Earl.)

the Spanish romance *Diana Enamorada* by the Portuguese Jorge de Montemayor (*c*. 1559) in which that part of the tale concerned with Don Felix and his love Felismena has many details with counterparts in Shakespeare, notably the page-disguise, the maid, the parting and the giving of the ring, a father opposed to the match, a serenade and Julia's swoon.

TEXT   The only text is the First Folio□ (1623). It is a short play, of less than 2400 lines, and the Folio shows clear signs of abridgement, and of having been put together originally from the company's prompt-book,□ itself deriving from Shakespeare's 'foul papers'□ which almost certainly bore many signs of change and revision.

V

Vice, the. The chief comic character always in interludes.□ As a character he seems to have developed from vices in morality plays,□ in which gradually – no doubt because of audience demand for laughter and actors' desire to raise it – some vices became comic. In late moralities and interludes, with names like Ill Report and Iniquity, scorning man's folly and his efforts to be good, he sets about stirring up trouble and causing or hoping to cause tragic outcomes. He seems early to have been associated with the jesters, and often wore particoloured clothes and carried a fool's bauble and sometimes wore a fool's hat with bells, as well as carrying the, wooden dagger he had had as the devil's companion. The comic 'Vice' first appears with a name in Heywood's *Love* (No-lover-nor-loved) and *Weather* (Merry Report) each of whom is referred to as the Vice. Here he is mischief-making rather than wicked. In the later *Cambyses*, he is Ambidexter, double-dealer. In Shakespeare, traces of the Vice convention may be found in the presentation of Richard III, Iago, perhaps even Edmund and Oswald, and, in quite different ways, of Falstaff, the great comic leader-astray and liar, who is called 'reverend Vice' and 'grey iniquity' by Prince Hal.

W

Wars of the Roses. A pretty name for a long and ugly series of conflicts between rival and related noble families for the English crown in the second half of the fifteenth century, which Shakespeare made the subject of his first tetralogy□ (*Henry VI* in three parts and *Richard III*). (See genealogical table on p. 164.)
   The struggles began during the weak reign (1422–61) of King

Henry VI, who had a son born to him a month after he became insane. If he had not had an heir, the able and effective Richard, Duke of York, would have come to the throne. Henry VI was the great-grandson of John of Gaunt, York the grandson of Gaunt's younger brother, Edmund of York, both being descended from Edward III. John of Gaunt and his descendants, Henry IV, Henry V and Henry VI, were members of the Lancaster branch of the descendants of Edward III. The Yorkists were the junior branch. Richard of York had been Regent during a period of Henry VI's insanity. When dismissed from this office of power he took up arms at the end of 1454 and won the small battle of St Albans in May 1455, defeating and killing John of Somerset, another cousin. (In *Henry VI, Part 1*, Act II, Scene 4, Shakespeare invented a scene in a garden in which Richard of York quarrels with Somerset and plucks a white rose, calling on those who support him to do the same. Somerset similarly picks a red rose.) York was killed at the Battle of Wakefield in 1460 by the royal party led by Henry VI's queen, Margaret, who was herself defeated the next year at Towton near York. Henry VI was deposed, and York's son Edward became king as Edward IV. Edward was deposed in 1469 and Henry VI briefly restored, but Edward IV with his brothers Clarence and Gloucester (later Richard III) defeated the royal troops at Barnet and at Tewkesbury in 1471. (Shakespeare deals with these events in *Henry VI, Part 3*).

Edward IV then ruled until his death in 1483, when his brother Richard of Gloucester seized the throne as Richard III. Shakespeare follows Tudor historians in presenting Richard III as a devilish monster and justifies thereby the campaign in which Henry Tudor, another descendant of John of Gaunt, raised a successful rebellion in 1485. He defeated and killed Richard III at Bosworth Field in Leicestershire, and came to the throne as Henry VII. He was a Lancastrian (red rose) and was married to a Yorkist (white rose), a daughter of Edward IV; the uniting of the two houses in this marriage and reign brought the Wars of the Roses to an end. From the union of the two roses came the Tudor line (Henry VII, Henry VIII, Edward VI, Mary Tudor, culminating in Queen Elizabeth).

Shakespeare's handling of this period, roughly 1454–85, in the first tetralogy,□ from *Henry VI Part 1* to *Richard III*, is of course influenced by his historical sources, especially the chronicles of Hall□ and Holinshed.□ They naturally perpetuate the 'Tudor myth' in which the successful family, the royal family of the time, is presented favourably and its opponents often vilified, especially Henry VI's queen, Margaret, and Richard III.

In the second tetralogy,□ *Richard II* to *Henry V,* which deals with an earlier period, roughly 1390 to 1420, but was written later, the ultimate origins of the Wars of the Roses are to be found in the deposing of the gifted but wastrel king Richard II by his cousin Bolingbroke, who became Henry IV.

Winter's Tale, The. A late romance written early in 1611.

Act I: Leontes, King of Sicily, has been host for nine months to his schooldays friend Polixenes, King of Bohemia, and tries to persuade him to stay longer. But Polixenes must return. Leontes urges his wife Hermione to add her persuasions to his, which she does with such success that Polixenes agrees. Leontes, watching them together, is suddenly convinced that they are lovers, and that Polixenes is the father of the unborn child she is carrying. Leontes speaks of this to the Lord Camillo and tells him to administer poison to Polixenes. Camillo asserts his belief in Hermione's virtue, but says that he will do it provided Leontes takes his wife fully back into favour. In fact, however, Camillo has no intention of doing the evil deed, and instantly tells Polixenes who has been perplexed by the change in Leontes's attitude to him. Polixenes decides to leave Sicily immediately, taking Camillo with him.

Act II: Leontes is confirmed in his own mind in his mad jealousy when he learns of the flight of Polixenes and Camillo. It increases his new angry hatred of Hermione; he deprives her of their young son Mamillius and has her imprisoned, and sends to the oracle at Delphi for confirmation of the truth. In prison Hermione gives birth to a daughter, whom the loyal and loving Paulina, wife of Lord Antigonus, takes to show to Leontes, hoping 'he may soften at the sight o' th' child'. Paulina forces her way with the baby into Leontes's presence, loudly protesting Hermione's virtue and the legitimacy of the child. At first, after ejecting Paulina, Leontes intends to have the child burned alive but yields to Antigonus's pleading and requires him to take the baby to 'some remote and desert place' and leave it 'Where chance may nurse or end it'.

Act III: Hermione is brought to trial, wrongly charged with adultery with Polixenes and with plotting with Camillo to murder Leontes. Proudly denying the charges, she speaks of her loyal love to Leontes and of the honourableness of Polixenes and honesty of Camillo. The message from the oracle is read out: it affirms their innocence, names Leontes a 'jealous tyrant' and declares 'The King shall live without an heir, if that which is lost be not found.' As Leontes is denying the truth of the oracle, a servant rushes in with news of Mamillius's death, at which Hermione falls to the ground in a dead faint, and is borne away. Immediately Leontes acknowledges his false suspicion and injustice, and declares his intention to be reconciled to Polixenes and 'new woo my Queen'. But it is too late, for Paulina enters, grief-stricken, with news of Hermione's death. Leontes vows lifetime repentance, and daily visitation to the graves of wife and son. Antigonus lands on the coast of Bohemia as a storm is brewing and reluctantly leaves the baby, which on the instructions of Hermione, who had appeared to him in a dream, he named Perdita. He departs 'pursued by a bear'. An old shepherd finds the baby as the storm increases, and his son enters, reports the death of Antigonus and the sinking of the ship which brought him; his father exclaims 'Thou met'st with things dying, I with things new-born.'

Act IV: As 'TIME, the Chorus'□ tells us, sixteen years pass; the babe, Perdita, has been brought up by the old shepherd as his daughter. Polixenes, King of Bohemia, persuades Camillo, who is longing for Sicily after this long time away, to stay a little longer and help him to find out why his son Prince Florizel is so often absent, and at 'the house of a most homely shepherd'; they are to go thither in disguise.

Autolycus, a humorous thieving pedlar, encounters the old shepherd's clown-son on his way to buy groceries for the sheep-shearing feast and picks his pocket. Before the feast Florizel tells Perdita – both in festive garb – that she looks not like a shepherdess but a goddess – Flora; she is worried by the difference in rank between them, and fears the King's anger when he discovers they love each other. The old shepherd her 'father' bids her to welcome the two strangers (Polixenes and Camillo in disguise). Autolycus comes and adds to the entertainment with his songs, and there is a dance of farm-labourers disguised as satyrs. Polixenes closely watches his son and Perdita and while appreciating her beauty and grace he notes with disfavour his son's adoration. When Florizel and Perdita are about to plight their troth, he asks whether the young man's father knows, and receiving a negative answer and a refusal to inform his father, in anger reveals who he is and forbids the match, threatening to disinherit Florizel and execute Perdita. The feast is broken up in confusion, but Camillo stays and learning that Florizel means to sail away from Bohemia with Perdita, decides he can help them and achieve his own desire of returning to Sicily by proposing that they should go thither. He is sure Leontes will welcome them. He intends then to tell his master and friend Polixenes, in the hope that he will follow them, taking Camillo with him. Autolycus, who has had a good day at the feast, both in selling all his goods and in picking pockets, is persuaded by Camillo to change clothes with Florizel to help the escape. Autolycus then overhears the old shepherd and his son, both fearful of punishment, decide to go to the King, reveal the facts about Perdita's discovery as a baby and give him the fine cloth and the gold that had been found beside her. In Florizel's grander feast-clothes, Autolycus convinces them he is a courtier, and telling them the King has taken ship hurries them along, for gold, to join the ship.

Act V: In Sicily, Leontes continues in remorse and penitence. Two of his lords tell him he has 'done enough, and have performed / A saint-like sorrow'; they want him to re-marry to ensure an heir, but Paulina commandingly opposes, and her hold over Leontes, who greatly respects her now, is so great, that she is able to make him promise not to marry again 'unless another, / As like Hermione as is her picture'. Florizel arrives unexpectedly with Perdita, saying that he brings warm greetings from his father, and is warmly welcomed by Leontes, even though they reinforce his grief that, through his own wicked folly, he had 'lost a couple, that 'twixt heaven and earth / Might thus have stood, begetting wonder'. Florizel introduces Perdita as a Libyan lady, but news comes that Polixenes has arrived in the city pursuing his runaway son, and has met and is threatening her 'father' and 'brother' with death. Florizel asks Leontes to be his advocate with his father. We hear in a conversation between three gentlemen of the happy meeting of Leontes and Polixenes, and the reunion of Leontes with his lost daughter, his ready acceptance of Florizel, his gratitude to the old shepherd. We also hear of a life-like statue of Hermione which Paulina takes Perdita to see.

In the final scene all the re-united forgather at Paulina's house to see the statue, Leontes amazed at its lifelikeness, though he notes the face is a little more wrinkled than Hermione had been. He goes forward to kiss it but is stopped by Paulina, who then says she can 'make the statue move indeed; descend, / And take you by the hand', which she proceeds to do to the sound of music. Of course it is Hermione herself, who had not died but been kept in secrecy by Paulina for the sixteen years of Leontes's penitence. So the oracle is fulfilled, the forgiven King has his Queen again, the Queen her husband, daughter and son-in-law, and Paulina is rewarded with the hand of the faithful Camillo.

SOURCE *Pandosto, or the Triumph of Time* (1588), a *novella* by Robert Greene□ (1558–92) but Sicily and Bohemia are changed about, the wronged Queen dies after the trial and the King eventually commits suicide, after imprisoning the Florizel character and lusting after the Perdita character (his own daughter). There is of course no statue coming to life, which was entirely Shakespeare's invention. That may have come from Ovid's *Metamorphoses*,□ the story of Pygmalion and Galatea.

TEXT The First Folio□ (1623), from either Shakespeare's 'foul papers'□ or a good transcript. The play appears at the end of the 'Comedies' section.

Select bibliography

Shakespeare, his life and his plays

ALEXANDER, P. (ED.): *Studies in Shakespeare*, Oxford University Press, London, 1964.

BRADLEY, A. C.: *Shakespearian Tragedy*, Macmillan, London, 1904, reprinted.

BROWN, J. R.: *Shakespeare's Plays in Performance*, Edward Arnold, London, 1966.

CHAMBERS, E. K.: *William Shakespeare*, 2 vols, Clarendon Press, Oxford, 1930.

CLEMEN, W. H.: *The Development of Shakespeare's Imagery*, Methuen, London, 1951, 2nd edn. 1977.

GRANVILLE-BARKER, H.: *Prefaces to Shakespeare*, 5 vols, Sidgwick & Jackson, London, 1927–47.

REESE, M. M.: *Shakespeare: His World and His Work*, Edward Arnold, London, 1953, rev. edn. 1980.

SCHOENBAUM, S.: *William Shakespeare: A Documentary Life*, Oxford University Press, London, 1975 (Compact edition 1977).

STYAN, J. L.: *Shakespeare's Stagecraft*, Cambridge University Press, Cambridge, 1967.

The Elizabethan background

Shakespeare's England, Clarendon Press, Oxford, 1916.

TILLYARD, E. M. W.: *The Elizabethan World Picture*, Chatto & Windus, London, 1943, reprinted.

The theatre and the drama

GURR, A.: *The Shakespearean Stage, 1574–1642*, Cambridge University Press, Cambridge, 1980.

HARBAGE, A.: *Shakespeare's Audience*, Columbia University Press, New York, 1941.

ORRELL, J.: *The Quest for Shakespeare's Globe*, Cambridge University Press, Cambridge, 1983.

Select bibliography · 171

ROSSITER, A. P.: *English Drama from Early Times to the Elizabethans*, Hutchinson, London, 1950.

THOMSON, P.: *Shakespeare's Theatre*, Routledge & Kegan Paul, London, 1983.

TYDEMAN, W. M.: *The Theatre in the Middle Ages*, Cambridge University Press, Cambridge, 1978.

WILSON, F. P.: *The English Drama 1485–1585*, edited by G. K. Hunter, Clarendon Press, Oxford, 1969.

Editions

Complete works:

ALEXANDER, P. (ED.): *William Shakespeare: The Complete Works*, Collins, London, 1951. In one volume, glossary, no notes.

BARNET, S. (ED.): *The Complete Signet Classic Shakespeare*, Harcourt Brace Jovanovich, New York, 1972. Useful introductory material, comments on the individual plays, extensive annotation and bibliography. Each play available separately in paperback.

BLAKEMORE EVANS, G. (ED.): *The Riverside Shakespeare*, Houghton, Mifflin, Boston, 1974. Useful introductory material, footnotes, etc., and a list of the chief textual variants.

Separate plays:

The Arden Shakespeare (Methuen, London) and the new Oxford and Cambridge editions, now in the process of publication, are the best editions of individual plays. The Arden Shakespeare has fuller introductions and annotation, the Oxford and Cambridge editions are more economical on the whole and, of course, are more up to date. The volumes of the New Penguin Shakespeare (Penguin Books, Harmondsworth) are slighter and cheaper, but they have good texts with sensible comment and notes and are admirable student editions.

Sources

BULLOUGH, G.: *Narrative and Dramatic Sources of Shakespeare*, 8 vols, Routledge & Kegan Paul, London 1957–75. A complete collection, in translation where necessary.

MUIR, K.: *The Sources of Shakespeare's Plays*, Methuen, London, 1977. A survey rather than a collection.

Miscellaneous

CAMPBELL, O. J. and QUINN, E. G. (EDS.): *A Shakespeare Encyclopaedia*, Methuen, London, 1967. (Published in the U.S.A. as *A Reader's*

Encyclopaedia of Shakespeare, T. Y. Crowell, New York, 1966.) Invaluable on most aspects of Shakespeare and his age.

ONIONS, C. T.: *A Shakespeare Glossary*, Clarendon Press, Oxford, 1911, rev. edn. 1953. A useful short dictionary of Shakespearian usage.

WELLS, S.: *Shakespeare* (Select Bibliographical Guides), Clarendon Press, Oxford, 1973. A useful guide to a wide range of scholarly and critical writings on Shakespeare.

The York Notes Series, Longman/York Press, London, various dates, includes volumes on most of the plays.

The earlier critics should be referred to:

JOHNSON, SAMUEL: *Johnson on Shakespeare*, edited by A. Sherbo, 2 vols. (vols. VII and VIII of The Yale Edition of Johnson), Yale University Press, New Haven, 1968.

JOHNSON, SAMUEL: *Johnson on Shakespeare*, ed. Sir Walter Raleigh, Clarendon Press, Oxford, 1908, often reprinted.

COLERIDGE, S. T.: *Shakespearean Criticism*, ed. T. M. Raysor, 2 vols., Everyman Series, Dent, London, 1960.

COLERIDGE, S. T.: *Coleridge on Shakespeare* (The 1811–12 Shakespeare Lectures), ed. R. A. Foakes, Routledge & Kegan Paul, London, 1971.

HAZLITT, W.: *The Characters of Shakespear's Plays* (London, 1817), Everyman Series, Dent, London, 1936.

DOWDEN, EDWARD: *Shakespere*, Routledge & Kegan Paul, London, 1875; 26th impression 1967.

The annual *Shakespeare Survey* (Cambridge University Press, Cambridge) and the *Stratford-upon-Avon Studies*, vols. 1, 3, 5, 8, 9 and 14 (Edward Arnold, London, various dates) should also be consulted.

Index

Page numbers in **bold** indicate where the subject is treated at length as a main entry in the book.

The author of this Handbook

P. C. BAYLEY is a graduate of University College, Oxford, and was afterwards for twenty-five years Fellow and Praelector in English of the college, and a University lecturer. He was Master of Collingwood College, University of Durham and a member of the English Department of Durham University from 1971 to 1978, when he became Berry Professor and Head of the Department of English at the University of St Andrews in Scotland. He is now Professor Emeritus of St Andrews.

He has written *Edmund Spenser, Prince of Poets*, Hutchinson, London, 1971, and has edited Book I (1966) and Book II (1965) of Edmund Spenser's *The Faerie Queene*, Oxford University Press; the Macmillan *Casebook on The Faerie Queene*, London, 1977; and *Loves and Deaths*, Oxford University Press, 1972, a selection of short stories by the great nineteenth-century English novelists. He prepared the York Notes volume *Selected Poems of Milton*, 1982. He has produced *British Council Recorded Seminars* on *Macbeth* and *Antony and Cleopatra*.